The Haitian Revolution

A Documentary History

The Haitian Revolution

A Documentary History

Edited and Translated, with an Introduction, by
DAVID GEGGUS

Hackett Publishing Company, Inc.
Indianapolis/Cambridge

17 16 15 14   1 2 3 4 5 6 7

For further information, please address
    Hackett Publishing Company, Inc.
    P.O. Box 44937
    Indianapolis, Indiana 46244-0937

    www.hackettpublishing.com

Interior design by Elizabeth L. Wilson
Composition by Aptara, Inc.

Library of Congress Cataloging-in-Publication Data

Geggus, David Patrick.
  The Haitian Revolution : a documentary history / edited and translated, with an introduction, by David Geggus.
      pages cm
  Includes bibliographical references and index.
  ISBN 978-0-87220-865-0 (pbk.) — ISBN 978-0-87220-866-7 (cloth)
  1. Haiti—History—Revolution, 1791–1804. 2. Haiti—History—To 1791.
3. Slavery—Haiti—History—18th century. 4. Slavery—Santo Domingo—Early works to 1800. 5. Haiti—History—Revolution, 1791–1804—Sources. I. Title.
  F1923.G338 2014
  972.94'03—dc23   2014006053

The paper used in this publication meets the minimum requirements of American National Standard for Information Sciences—Permanence of Paper for Printed Library Materials, ANSI Z39.48–1984.

∞

Contents

Introduction

The slave uprising that, between 1791 and 1803, transformed the French colony of Saint Domingue into the independent black state of Haiti was by far the largest to occur in the Americas and one of very few to succeed. Saint Domingue became the first major slave-owning society to abolish slavery and the first to outlaw racial discrimination. Haiti was the first modern state in the tropics and the first after the United States to throw off European rule. Of all American struggles for colonial independence, the Haitian Revolution involved the greatest degree of mass mobilization and brought about the greatest social and economic change. In twelve years of desolating warfare one of the most productive colonies of the day was destroyed, its economy ruined, and its ruling class entirely eliminated.

The Haitian Revolution is an event of global significance because of its uniqueness, its precedence in the narratives of antislavery and decolonization, and also because of the importance of the colony where it took place. Although Saint Domingue was no bigger than Maryland or Vermont, it was a powerhouse of the Atlantic economy whose exports exceeded those of the United States and were worth more than those of Brazil and Mexico combined. The revolution reshaped world commodity markets and great power politics while swallowing up armies sent from France, Spain, and Britain. It inspired slave resistance and planter paranoia across the Americas, as well as poetry and novels in several languages. It created a widespread refugee diaspora and powerfully affected arguments about race and the future of slavery.

Saint Domingue on the Eve of Revolution

In the late eighteenth century, Saint Domingue had the Americas' strongest export economy. It produced more sugar and coffee than anywhere else, as well as cotton, cacao, and indigo. These were not the cheap bulk commodities they later became but valuable staples, the lifeblood of Atlantic commerce. Saint Domingue was not "the wealthiest colony in the world," as sometimes is said; its taxable population and towns were small compared to those of Mexico or Bengal, or Britain's North American colonies. Yet it represented the apogee of the European colonizing process begun three centuries earlier, for the purpose of colonies was to export what Europe could not produce. Saint Domingue's exports kept an entire navy in business. The French government received substantial revenue from taxing its trade, and the colony also had the best naval base in the Caribbean. It was important to France not just for economic reasons but fiscal and strategic ones as well.

By the late 1780s Saint Domingue had become the single main destination of the Atlantic slave trade. Its enslaved population was almost as large as that of the United States south of the Potomac, with the important difference that more than half had been born in Africa. When the French Revolution broke out, Saint Domingue was home to about 30,000 white colonists, a roughly equal number of free people of color, and almost a half million slaves. European visitors found it materialistic, profane, and fast-living, a place where sexual license and the pursuit of profit ruled, and religion, family, and tradition counted for little (doc. 1). Large landowners, merchants, and judges formed the colony's social elite, but the white community also included numerous plantation employees and urban workers who had crossed the Atlantic hoping to make their fortune. They resented the disdain showed them by their richer neighbors and were envious of their wealth (doc. 2).

The enslaved population was very heterogeneous. Split up between 7,000 plantations, working sunup to sundown six days per week, it was divided not only by location but by differences of culture and class. About one in three adults was born locally and grew up in slavery speaking the local Creole language. From their ranks were chosen most of the domestic servants, artisan craftsmen, and slave drivers who made up the slave elite. Field hands were generally Africans, who had been sold and branded after crossing the Atlantic beneath the deck of a slave ship (doc. 3). On a typical sugar plantation of 200 workers, there might be speakers of a dozen or more different languages, all at different stages of assimilation into colonial society. Long accustomed to growing their own food and marketing the surplus, the creoles tended to be wealthier than the Africans, and more likely to live in families and to have some familiarity with Christianity.

Working conditions varied considerably between different types of plantations. They were at their worst on the lowland sugar estates, where slaves worked all day and part of the night during the grueling harvest season. These estates often belonged to absentee owners and were run by managers whose incentive was to maximize output at whatever cost (doc. 4). One-third of Saint Domingue's enslaved inhabitants lived on sugar plantations. A slightly smaller proportion lived on the mountain coffee plantations, where overwork, underfeeding, and infectious disease were less prevalent, although heinous acts of cruelty were no rarer and as likely to go unpunished (doc 5). With forty to fifty slaves on average, coffee and indigo plantations were considerably smaller than sugar estates, but—much larger than most U.S. cotton farms—they still formed mini-communities, where elements of African cultures could be preserved or blended.

Free people of color made up the middle tier of Saint Domingue society. They covered a broad social range from recently freed Africans to rich landowners and tradesmen who were almost indistinguishable from their white counterparts in appearance and culture. They were more numerous than in most Caribbean colonies and notably more wealthy. Most of the men were probably artisan craftsmen or rural smallholders, and most of the women were market traders or white men's mistresses. Saint Domingue was unusual, however, in that a substantial proportion of free people of color were prosperous planters, some of whom were educated in France. Most white colonists were bachelors and many endowed with property the children they had with enslaved women. Such mixed-race offspring also profited from their local knowledge to build up fortunes in the coffee and indigo sectors, which required less initial investment than did sugar.

About two-thirds of the free people of color were of mixed racial descent; some had both whites and slaves for relatives. Many were slave owners or members of the militia or rural police force who hunted down fugitive slaves. Their position in colonial society was thus highly ambiguous. Although some were far wealthier than most whites, all were subject to the discriminatory legal restrictions then typical of American colonies (doc. 6). Race relations had been fairly fluid in earlier times, but discrimination became more widespread after 1760. Not only unequal before the law, free coloreds also suffered extra-legal harassment and sometimes brutal victimization (doc. 7).

Historians disagree whether Saint Domingue would have undergone revolution without being destabilized by the French Revolution of 1789. The desire for self-government and free trade among its self-confident but indebted planter class perhaps increased after its North American counterparts achieved independence in 1783. Yet the insecurity of island colonies with large slave majorities made them peculiarly dependent on European protection. The American Revolutionary War also boosted the ambitions of the fast-growing free colored population; having contributed two battalions of soldiers to overseas expeditions, its leaders began to lobby the government for more equal treatment, albeit very discreetly (doc. 7). Most astonishing perhaps was the rapid expansion of the slave population in the late 1780s. Although not quite unique, it was among the fastest growing, largest, and most unbalanced between black and white in the Americas.

Slave Resistance

Assessments of the likelihood of revolution partly turn on interpreting the evidence of how enslaved people had previously resisted the colonial regime. Historians group under the rubric "slave resistance" a wide spectrum of individual and collective acts, ranging from satire and mockery (doc. 8) to violent rebellion. In the 1780s, some colonists feared that urban life in Saint Domingue's small port towns was undermining social control by making slaves disturbingly assertive (doc. 9). Urban slave revolts, however, were always extremely rare in the

Americas, and the Haitian Revolution would be no exception. Fears of poisoning swept Saint Domingue in the middle decades of the eighteenth century (doc. 10), but some thought white paranoia was chiefly responsible for this anxiety, and in the 1780s such fears considerably subsided.

The slaves' clandestine religious ceremonies that colonists called *Vaudou* were felt by some to be harmless, but others saw them as extremely dangerous because of the influence religious leaders had over their followers (docs. 11, 12). Particularly alarming was the emergence of the new and violent "Don Pedro" cult, which we can link to the growing number of Africans from the Congo region in the slave population (doc. 13). Scholars generally argue that Vodou (the preferred modern spelling) helped launch the Haitian Revolution by uniting different ethnic groups in a shared, syncretic religion. No one has proved, however, that the pan-African, "umbrella" structure of modern Vodou evolved before the revolution. Some evidence suggests that ethnic and religious differences were divisive until after independence, and that Vodou's inclusive structure was less a cause than a result of fighting a common war of liberation.

Enslaved workers, like their free counterparts, sometimes withdrew their labor to bargain for better conditions or to get a hated supervisor dismissed (doc. 14). Such strikes usually took the form of a temporary collective escape. Short-term absenteeism by individual slaves who ran off to visit friends and family on other plantations was endemic in Saint Domingue, as was theft from plantation stores by underfed workers (doc. 15). Some fugitives sought to pass for free and start a new life in the colony's towns; others formed armed bands in the mountains and forests that attacked travelers or isolated plantations. All sorts of slaves became maroons (runaways), but the great majority were young males, especially Africans. A few future leaders of the slave revolution can be found among their ranks (doc. 16).

Historians have disagreed about the frequency and political significance of maroonage (slave absenteeism) and of slave resistance in general. Did they foster a "culture of resistance" out of which the Haitian Revolution emerged? Or did they function as a "safety valve" that helped preserve the slave regime? Unlike neighboring Jamaica, Saint Domingue experienced few rebellions and conspiracies. Perhaps this was because maroonage siphoned off the impulse to change the system. However, by the 1780s, as new settlements spread into the frontier regions and the colony's forests were felled, maroon bands were becoming a thing of the past. It may be, therefore, that by the 1780s slave dissidents were coming to see revolt as a more viable alternative.

Saint Domingue and the French Revolution

Scholars vary in their assessment of these internal stresses within Saint Domingue society and in their interpretation of how they were affected by the French

Revolution of 1789–1804 and the world war to which it gave rise in 1793. While giving different weight to external and internal factors, some emphasize the French Revolution's ideological impact—its novel focus on freedom and equality—and others, the way it undermined power in more material ways, by dividing the white population, weakening the garrison, and causing foreign invasions.

Colonial policy obviously tracked the movement of politics in France: increasingly radical until 1794; gradually more conservative thereafter. But it was generally made in response to events in the Caribbean. Interaction between the two revolutions thus complicates the question. From the meeting of the States-General in 1789, which opened up vistas of sweeping change in France, to the crowning of Napoleon Bonaparte as emperor in 1804, the metropolitan revolution created new possibilities and conflicts for people in the colonies. In both revolutions, participants were continually reacting to news from the other side of the Atlantic that was several months out of date.

The key to understanding the Haitian Revolution's complicated narrative is to think of it as the pursuit of three political goals (freedom, equality, independence), by three social groups (slaves, free coloreds, whites), in a colony whose North, West, and South provinces produced three regional variants of the revolution. Its chronology also might be fitted into a tripartite structure. The first two years (1789–1791), before the slaves became involved, and the last two years (1802–1803), the War of Independence, form distinct units separated by a long middle section. This middle period (1791–1801) can be similarly subdivided, with the abolition of slavery (1793) and the expulsion of foreign invaders (1798) serving as major turning points.

The Haitian Revolution is rightly seen as a slave revolution, but it began as a bid for self-government and free trade by white colonists, and it could not have succeeded without the separate pursuit of equality and independence by the free colored population. Like the French Revolution, it was several revolutions in one. Sharing the social and political complexity of its French counterpart, Haiti's revolution went further than the other colonial revolutions of the Americas in involving all sectors of society as active participants and in transforming economy, society, and politics.

The Race and Slavery Questions in the French National Assembly

Slavery is one of the oldest human institutions. Accepted as part of the human condition, like warfare or gender inequality, it was rarely singled out as evil in any culture until the mid-eighteenth century. *Philosophes* of the French Enlightenment, such as Montesquieu and Voltaire, were key figures in creating the modern critique of slavery, but their interests were intellectual and tinged with a biological racism that was becoming increasingly explicit. They displayed no practical concern with the institution that burgeoned in the eighteenth-century Caribbean (doc. 17). The antislavery movement that began in England in the 1780s was only weakly echoed in France; the Amis des Noirs (Friends of the Blacks) society, founded in 1788, attracted some famous names but had no popular following (doc. 18). When the French monarchy went bankrupt that year and called the States-General (that soon became the National Assembly) to recommend far-reaching reforms, few expected colonies thousands of miles away to participate in the national "regeneration."

The French monarchy was absolute, not constitutional, as in England, so neither France nor its colonies had much experience of representative government. It was an exhilarating step into the unknown. Ignoring royal officials, Saint Domingue's planter elite organized secret elections and, in July 1789, cajoled their way into the National Assembly. This was the first time any colony was allowed elected representation in a metropolitan government. Early in 1790, white colonists elected their own local assemblies in Saint Domingue, which the revolutionary government in Paris then recognized. White activists thus quickly gained most of what they wanted from the revolution. But they got much more than they bargained for. Colonists in Paris were shocked to find slavery and racial discrimination, the pillars of their colonial world, suddenly under attack (doc. 19). The Declaration of the Rights of Man and the Citizen, voted in August 1789, proclaimed all men free and equal in rights. It was unclear if it would apply to the colonies, but colonists had reason to be fearful, as they watched the revolution in France rapidly dismantle centuries-old privileges of the monarchy, aristocracy, and church in an atmosphere of reforming zeal.

Yet, throughout its two-year history, the National Assembly was to avoid even discussing slavery or the slave trade. Thrown on the defensive, the colonial lobby found many allies among deputies who were afraid of jeopardizing colonial commerce, the only vibrant sector of the French economy. And property, like liberty, was one of the Rights of Man. Rumors of reform, moreover, might provoke slave rebellion. Actual reform could push planters to cast off French rule.

The colonists made the same arguments in defense of racial discrimination, which they insisted was an essential bulwark of the slave regime. The civil rights of tax-paying free men of color, however, were not so easily ignored. Unlike slavery, they involved no conflict between liberty and property rights, and they were defended in Paris both by the Amis des Noirs and by a small pressure group of free men of color, the Society of American Colonists. They called for representation in the National Assembly and equal rights in the colonies (docs. 20, 21). With the legal position of nonwhites in France—and of many Jews—unsettled until September 1791, it was the first test of the racial boundaries of the French Revolution.

White colonists depicted the free men of color as unpropertied, loose-living individuals of illegitimate birth, who included many domestic servants, although in France the colonists avoided the racist language more freely used in the Caribbean. Some who felt that free colored support was essential in maintaining slavery were willing to make minor concessions, but the revolution had greatly raised the stakes. The new egalitarian ideology made it harder to co-opt only a wealthy few free coloreds, and because of voting rights, racial equality now meant potential political power, not just the right to become a lawyer or doctor. The abolitionist threat to slavery also greatly heightened fears of making concessions in the area of race relations.

Free coloreds' attitudes to slavery are controversial, yet they have been little studied. A few historians have claimed them as closet abolitionists, but most emphasize that antiracism did not mean antislavery. Although almost all free coloreds were descendants of slaves, many were slaveowners and, at first, none were overtly abolitionist. Free colored spokesmen usually took pains to distinguish their cause from that of the enslaved. However, the two proved difficult to separate. White abolitionists sometimes argued that free colored citizenship would prepare the way for slave emancipation, or that free coloreds might, if driven to desperation, join forces with slaves in open revolt (doc. 22). Most perplexing was the ill-judged appeal for unity that colored merchant Vincent Ogé made in September 1789 to the white planters' club in Paris (doc. 23). After alluding in an idealistic yet threatening manner to preparing for the end of slavery, Ogé was frostily rebuffed. The likelihood of whites and nonwhites finding common ground quickly receded.

The National Assembly stonewalled the free men of color for eighteen months with dishonest maneuvers. Its deputies were fully occupied with domestic issues, and they were reluctant to intervene in a question few of them understood. As French politics grew more radical, however, popular interest in the colonial question grew (doc. 24). Then news arrived that an exasperated Vincent Ogé had launched a brief rebellion in Saint Domingue and been brutally executed. This shamed the assembly out of its evasive action, and there ensued in May 1791 one of the great debates of the French Revolution (doc. 25). The result was a compromise decree that enfranchised men of color born to free parents but not freedmen. Even this was too much for most white colonists. Their deputies walked out of the assembly. In Saint Domingue there was talk of secession, and the governor refused to enforce the decree. This caused the National Assembly to reverse course. During its final days in September 1791 it handed control over "personal status" back to the colonial assemblies.

These switchback changes in policy would create havoc in Saint Domingue, enflaming the resentments of white and nonwhite colonists. The colonial question had already irrevocably changed, however. In August 1791, the slaves became active participants in the revolution, and the focus of events shifted from Paris to the Caribbean.

The Fight for Racial Equality in Saint Domingue

During the previous two years, the colonial ministry had vainly tried to control the flow of information between France and the Caribbean. It prevented free people of color from boarding ships, and it secretly opened their mail. Meanwhile white correspondents, the major source of colonial news, deliberately covered up certain events. Historians still have a fairly hazy picture of this period of the revolution and, in particular, of the activities of the free men of color and their transatlantic contacts.

As in France, early moves toward cooperation between whites and free people of color quickly failed (doc. 26). When news of the democratic revolution arrived from Paris in the fall of 1789, and again when elections were held for a colonial assembly the following spring, free men of color mobilized in those districts where they were most numerous and requested redress of their grievances and permission to participate in the political process (doc. 27). These requests were ignored, and for some six months sporadic local clashes erupted across the colony. Free colored protests gave rise to a series of murders, executions, standoffs, and property seizures. The collecting of severed heads as trophies—a tactic that all sides in the Haitian Revolution would come to use—seems to have begun at this time.

After being intimidated into silence by the rise of the Patriots (white populists), free colored militia had the satisfaction in August 1790 of helping the governor and his white troops close down the colonial assembly in Saint Marc, which looked like it was aiming for independence. Yet royalist counterrevolutionaries would prove no more willing than the colonial radicals to satisfy the free coloreds' political aspirations. In October, just when the liberal National Assembly in Paris assured white colonists that it, too, would do nothing about the color question, Vincent Ogé slipped back into Saint Domingue and gathered 300 armed men in the mountains of the north.

Confident in the justice of his cause, Ogé thought he could impose terms from a position of strength (doc. 28). However, although free men of color mobilized in a few parts of the west and south, most declined to join him, and he rejected the idea of recruiting slaves. When the governor attacked with a large force, his followers were scattered after a brief skirmish. Hundreds were arrested and twenty-three were executed (doc. 29). Yet their deaths were not entirely in vain, because the National Assembly was forced to respond with the limited, but ultimately incendiary, decree of May 15, 1791. The rebellion may also have prepared the way for the massive slave revolt of August 1791. In the aftermath of the rebellion, whites disarmed free coloreds in some districts and thus weakened the forces of control. Certain writers have also credited fugitives from Ogé's band with inspiring the slave uprising.

Exasperated by the whites' violent reaction to the May 15 compromise, free men of color again rose up in arms in the summer of 1791, this time in the central region of Saint Domingue where they were most numerous. Using their experience as militiamen and from hunting in the forests, they inflicted humbling defeats on the forces sent by the Port-au-Prince radicals against them (doc. 30). Facing a massive slave revolt in the north and fearing it would spread further, the white colonists now proved willing to accept the free coloreds' demands (doc. 31). Just then, however, news arrived that the National Assembly had withdrawn the May 15 law, and the fighting began all over again. For months, a bitter civil war paralyzed much of the west and south, while the slave revolt continued unchecked in the north (doc. 32).

The realization that the whites could not defeat the slaves without the collaboration of the free coloreds finally brought the French government to extend full political rights to all free men in the colonies by the law of 4 April 1792. It was a milestone in the history of the Americas that most whites grudgingly had to accept. The atrocities each side had committed made reconciliation difficult, but by the summer a fragile alliance of white and nonwhite property owners was able to turn its attention to the increasingly rebellious slaves.

The Slave Insurrection

From the very beginning of the revolution, colonists and officials feared how slaves would react to all the new talk of liberty and the overturning of established order. In the fall of 1789, as rumors swirled in the colony, there were several obscure incidents in which planters brutally cracked down on their slaves (doc. 33). But for two years the enslaved mainly kept a low profile. They watched as tensions mounted between whites and free coloreds, and they saw the divisions within the white population grow deeper as the French Revolution became more radical. Amidst talk of emancipation, secession, and counterrevolution, and just when a new Colonial Assembly was gathering in Cap Français, slaves of the North Plain struck a devastating blow. The night of August 22/23, they began killing and burning on a scale never seen in any other slave revolt (doc. 36). Within a week, tens of thousands were involved, and the town of Le Cap was under siege.

The uprising had been planned by locally born "elite" slaves (coachmen, drivers, domestics) (doc. 34), but Africans made up a large proportion of the insurgents, and African-derived religious practices formed part of their preparation for revolt (doc. 35). Their goals are difficult to discern and may have varied between participants and through time. According to white observers, some claimed the king had freed them; others that they had been granted three free days per week, or merely that they demanded an improvement in their treatment. Some spoke of the rights of man, but most employed a conservative rhetoric of loyalty to king and church. In a letter to the governor, drawn up early in the revolt, the insurgents used a conservative discourse (no mention of rights) but combined the claim to have been freed with a demand that the French leave the colony (doc. 37).

In late October 1791, the slave rebels overran the northeastern mountains along the frontier with neighboring Santo Domingo thanks to the dynamism of the sadistic leader Jeannot and the collaboration of local free men of color disgruntled with the rejection of the May 15 law. Stunned by the slaves' successes, many colonists began to suspect that white counterrevolutionaries were secretly directing the rebellion using free colored agents (doc. 38). In a brief power struggle, the handsome young coachman Jean-François and Georges Biassou, a hard-drinking slave driver, eliminated Jeannot to become the main leaders of the uprising. Fearing the imminent arrival of troops from France, they opened negotiations with the whites in late November seeking amnesty for the insurgents but emancipation only for their leaders (doc. 39). Three "civil commissioners" sent by the French government sought to broker a deal, but neither the Colonial Assembly nor the mass of insurgents would accept such a compromise (doc. 40). Among the militants women were as prominent as men. Though the slaves who helped colonists escape tended to be female, women shared fully in the desire for vengeance. Some played military roles (doc. 41).

As 1792 began, a military stalemate continued in the north, while the civil war between whites and free coloreds worsened in the rest of Saint Domingue. A cordon of posts, constant patrols, and merciless reprisals kept the northern uprising from spreading, but spasmodic rebellions broke out among slaves elsewhere, often encouraged by free men of color. To boost their numbers, both whites and free coloreds began to arm select groups of slaves, which further weakened the slave regime (doc. 42). Although the estates generally remained intact, plantation work slowed or stopped in much of Saint Domingue, as whites fled the countryside.

Six thousand troops arrived from France early in the year, and another 6,000 disembarked in September, but they could not suppress the northern rebellion. As crises multiplied, they were dispersed to all parts of the colony, and they succumbed rapidly to tropical fevers, as was common in Caribbean wars. In this war, however, European soldiers also faced an elusive enemy, whose tactics and strategy were entirely unfamiliar; it was poorly armed but inured to the environment and seemingly numberless (docs. 43, 49a). Even the most prejudiced colonists came to accept they could not defeat the slaves without the military assistance of the free men of color. Most regions therefore grudgingly accepted the April 1792 law on racial equality. As the year wore on, white and colored men of property worked to overcome the bitter legacy of past conflicts and turn their attention to suppressing the slaves in rebellion.

Slave Emancipation

In September 1792, just after the monarchy was overthrown and France became a republic, two new commissars arrived in Saint Domingue to enforce the new law of racial equality (doc. 44). Unlike their predecessors, Léger-Félicité Sonthonax and Étienne Polverel were endowed with dictatorial powers to reassert metropolitan control in the colony. They quickly closed down the colonial assemblies and deported, first, conservative officers considered disloyal to the new regime, and then autonomist Patriots who opposed their actions. These conflicts held up the campaign against the insurgent slaves. Around the turn of the year, however, the French finally launched a coordinated offensive that drove the rebels rapidly backwards. They lost most of their mountain camps and several thousand people surrendered. In the West and South provinces, too, insurgents were in retreat. Yet in early February 1793, Sonthonax called off the offensive, for reasons that are disputed. This proved to be a turning point, because the simultaneous outbreak of war in Europe then abruptly tipped the balance of power against the French and reshaped the struggle for Saint Domingue.

Although the civil commissioners had no mandate to deal with slavery, the radical lawyer Sonthonax did have an abolitionist background, which he covered up (doc. 45). This fact, discovered in the 1980s, means that analyses of how the slave uprising led to the ending of slavery cannot ignore metropolitan idealism as a causal factor. Abolitionism remained a weak force in France; the Amis des Noirs continued to argue that emancipation should be only a long-term goal (doc. 46). Yet antislavery attitudes were gaining ground, and once war broke out with Britain and Spain, they were greatly reinforced by fears for colonial defense.

Both the French and Spanish governments made the extraordinary decision to recruit the insurgent slaves as soldiers, but it was the Spanish who succeeded. They offered freedom and land to Jean-François and Biassou's followers along with guns, uniforms, and cash (doc. 47). War with England meant that France could no longer safely send troops across the Atlantic, and the prospect of foreign intervention also encouraged white colonists to rebel against the civil commissioners. To outbid the Spanish, defeat the treasonous colonists, and to raise forces to resist a British invasion, Sonthonax took the desperate gamble of proclaiming slavery abolished and called on all the black population to defend the new regime of liberty. Without the likelihood of France losing Saint Domingue, the 28-year-old Sonthonax would surely not have dared act on his antislavery convictions. But no previous official facing foreign invasion had ever considered freeing all a colony's slaves. The emancipation proclamation of 29 August 1793 (doc. 48) thus emerged from the confluence of three developments: an undefeated slave insurrection, the outbreak of war, and the fortuitous presence of a radical abolitionist in charge of the colony.

A new era began. After three centuries of unchecked growth, slavery was proscribed precisely where it had most flourished. Amidst the rubble of Cap Français, burned in June, Sonthonax gathered round him a small group of free colored and white radicals who began to construct a largely black army. The challenge for Sonthonax was how to preserve the plantation regime that fueled the export economy without slave labor. His solution was a sort of profit-sharing serfdom. Most former slaves would be paid but remain tied to their old estates. As many preferred to become independent peasant farmers, the policy did not prove popular and set up a conflict that would last for decades. In those parts of Saint Domingue where the plantations remained intact, white and free colored slaveowners rejected emancipation and surrendered great swathes of the West and South provinces to British and Spanish invaders.

Most of the northern insurgents also rejected Sonthonax's offers. Under Jean-François and Biassou, they continued to wage war on the French as auxiliary troops of the king of Spain (doc. 49). In 1793, monarchical Spain looked more like a winning side than the imperiled French Republic. Moreover, neither leader had shown any commitment to the ideal of universal freedom. They had demanded freedom for their families and immediate followers, which the Spanish offered, but not the emancipation of all slaves. Indeed they sometimes rounded up slaves for sale to their Spanish neighbors. This deepened divisions within their ranks, as did personal rivalries (doc. 50), but into 1794 they continued to gain ground against the French Republicans. Most of their advances were due to the black freedman Toussaint Louverture, who emerged as a talented commander. Breaking the western cordon, he pushed south in December 1793 to seize the seaport of Gonaïves, which became a vital link to the outside world. Spanish forces, in a rare moment of activity, took the northeastern port of Fort Dauphin a month later.

In both France and Saint Domingue, Year 2 of the new republican calendar began (in September 1793) amidst extreme crisis but led through political radicalization to eventual military success. Following the first multiracial election in France's colonies, Sonthonax sent a multiracial deputation to the legislature in Paris. Out of a mixture of radical idealism and fear of losing its Caribbean possessions, the Convention responded to the commissar's fait accompli by abolishing slavery in all its colonies (doc. 51). The landmark decree of 4 February 1794 not only freed slaves but also declared them to be citizens. Even radical Jacobins had reservations about how disruptive the decree might prove (doc. 52). In practice, however, most former slaves remained subject to forced labor, as Sonthonax envisioned, and few were able to exercise political rights.

The decree nonetheless was a fearsome weapon of war. French agents used it to galvanize black resistance in British colonies, and in Saint Domingue it helped encourage some of the insurgents who had joined the Spanish to switch sides and rally to the French Republic. By far the most important of these was Toussaint Louverture. His volte-face was a turning point in the revolution, because it unambiguously united for the first time the forces of black self-liberation, antislavery idealism, and the resources of a powerful state. Among its indirect repercussions was a massacre of hundreds of colonists by Jean-François' soldiers in July 1794 (doc. 53). The massacre demonstrated the bankruptcy of Spanish policy. Most of the black auxiliaries remained loyal to Spain, but they were now a spent force. Spain withdrew from the war in mid-1795, and the former insurgents were left on the wrong side of history.

The Rise of Toussaint Louverture

Although there is reason to believe Toussaint Louverture may have been the architect of the slave uprising (doc. 54), he remained a shadowy figure during its first eighteen months, only gradually emerging as a minor military leader, subordinate to Grand Admiral Jean-François and Viceroy Biassou. A small wiry man, born in slavery to African parents, he had been free for about twenty years yet remained close to the slave population. People thought he was in his fifties, though he was probably a little younger. Unlike most slaves, he could speak some French, as well as Creole, and the language of his African parents. He could read and recently had learned to sign his name. Almost all his letters, dictated in Creole, were written by French or free colored secretaries, but they bear the stamp of a powerful personality that distinguishes them from the correspondence of the other slave leaders.

Like Jean-François and Biassou, he joined the Spanish in May 1793. Several quick successes against republican forces established his reputation. In July, he seized La Tannerie, Dondon, and Marmelade using trickery, threats, and promises of pardon. This strategy reaped rewards. White and colored planters surrendered to him, drawn by his willingness to maintain plantation production. Toussaint's conquest of new regions little affected by the slave revolt nonetheless opened up new opportunities for recruiting. As arms and ammunition fell into his hands, so his tiny army grew. Lances and machetes were exchanged for muskets. Free colored and even French soldiers joined its ranks and helped train its levies. Spanish officials found him pious, prudent, honorable, and dignified.

Toussaint rejected the overtures of the civil commissioners and maintained for a year a royalist, pro-Spanish stance (doc. 55). No genuine documentary evidence connects him to the goal of freedom for all until Sonthonax moved to abolish slavery in late August 1793. Trying to win over black opponents, Toussaint then claimed this had always been his goal (doc. 56). Some scholars ignore these statements as meaningless rhetoric, as nothing changed in his actions at this point. Yet most historians have taken them as defining the man and his mission. They assume he stayed with the proslavery Spanish because of his royalist convictions, or because he thought they would win. One should also note that the Spanish were not yet strong enough to force blacks back into plantation work in those areas where they had abandoned it. The choice between them and the abolitionist republicans was therefore not quite as Manichean as it might appear.

By early 1794, however, Spanish advances and the return from exile of hundreds of French colonists made a revival of the slave regime seem more imminent; racial tensions rose in the Spanish-occupied zone. Personal rivalries among the Black Auxiliaries also worsened (doc. 57). Meanwhile, Britain's invasion of Saint Domingue began to sputter, and the French Republic started to look like a more attractive ally, as in Europe its troops went on the offensive. Against this background, Toussaint Louverture—before he knew of France's abolition of slavery—began a cautious and protracted reversal of alliances in April. While continuing to assure the Spanish of his loyalty, and to draw supplies from them, he promised allegiance to the beleaguered French governor, Étienne Laveaux, and later to the British, too, who were threatening him from the south. His forces attacked selected Spanish targets, but he preserved "deniability" by blaming disobedient subordinates. The long-prepared Spanish march on Cap Français was immediately abandoned.

After the French emancipation decree arrived in June, Toussaint then fell on each of his opponents in turn with devastating effect. His seizure in October of the Spanish frontier towns of San Miguel and San Rafael permanently redrew the map of Hispaniola. For the next four years, his ragged soldiers fought to drive the British and their planter allies out of the western mountains and the town of Saint Marc that barred the route south to the capital. "Naked as earthworms," as he graphically described them, they continually lacked for food, clothing, and ammunition, and they died by the hundred in headlong assaults on well-entrenched positions. But in the process was forged a formidable army. The rank and file were mainly Africans; the officer corps was a mixture of black ex-slaves, *anciens libres*,[1] and a few whites. Already prominent by the end of 1794 were the youthful Moyse from the Bréda plantation, whom Toussaint called his nephew, and the grimly energetic Jean-Jacques Dessalines, both creole ex-slaves.

Governor Laveaux and Louverture established a close relationship built on mutual respect, commitment to slave emancipation, and growing rivalry with the *anciens libres* (doc. 58). In March 1796, General Jean-Louis Villatte, the ambitious free colored commandant of Cap Français, launched a coup against Laveaux, but Louverture and fellow black officers rescued him and squashed the rebellion. In a dramatic move, Laveaux proclaimed Toussaint lieutenant-governor of the colony. The French government promoted him to division general in the summer, and in May 1797 Sonthonax named him commander-in-chief of the colonial army. Throughout this period he confronted an array of foreign and local opponents.

Although Spain had made peace in 1795 and ceded Santo Domingo to France, many of the remaining Spanish colonists collaborated with the British, who now greatly expanded their military presence. Jean-François and Biassou

---

1. "Formerly free," as free coloreds were called now that all were free.

went into pensioned exile in different parts of the Spanish Empire taking 800 followers, but the soldiers they left behind proved reluctant to submit to the republicans. Plantation workers frequently rebelled, sometimes against military service or fearing the restoration of slavery, as Toussaint sought to enforce the revival of plantation agriculture (doc. 59), which financed his army. Villatte's defeat left *anciens libres* disaffected across the north, and when Sonthonax tried to assert control over the powerful André Rigaud, who was fighting the British in the south, an open rift developed between the north and the south.

Thanks to his military and political skills, Louverture thrived during this time of multiple crises and the new republican regime survived. Britain's equivocation over the issue of racial equality prevented it from winning enough *ancien libre* support, and like the French and Spanish regiments that preceded them, the British forces suffered catastrophic losses to tropical fevers (doc. 60). Between May and October 1798, they evacuated their remaining troops along with thousands of colonists, who swelled the international diaspora of exiles that had been growing since 1791 (doc. 61). The 60,000 or 70,000 slaves left in the British occupied zone were finally freed.

Louverture now controlled all of northern and central Saint Domingue. Meanwhile, he continued to eliminate any potential source of opposition, both local leaders and officials sent from France. The most startling and intriguing case was his expulsion of Sonthonax in August 1797 (doc. 62). Once the British were gone, Toussaint's sole significant rival was the *ancien libre* Rigaud, whose power base was the south coast.

The Government of Toussaint Louverture

As the black governor was consolidating his position in 1797, he faced a new threat, coming from France itself. French politics began shifting to the right after reaching a radical peak in mid-1794. By 1797 the legislature contained many who regretted the abolition of slavery and criticized the new colonial regime. Louverture responded in a number of publications that defended the colonial revolution and demonstrated his political acumen in their blending of advocacy and threat (doc. 63). A political purge of the right wing in Paris in September 1797 temporarily ended this threat, but the conservative trend in France would soon resume.

To replace Sonthonax and the system of civil commissioners, the French government sent out General Théodore Hédouville in March 1798 with the title of Agent. Tensions quickly built up between him and Toussaint. They climaxed in the autumn when he found himself shut out of the negotiations between Toussaint and the British. Louverture acted like an independent ruler, concluding a nonaggression pact and trade treaty with France's enemy. Hédouville's efforts to reduce the size of the colonial army then led Toussaint and Moyse to orchestrate a "popular uprising" that drove out the white general after only six months in the colony (doc. 64). Some observers termed this the de facto end of colonial rule.

As before, the black governor sent envoys to France to defend his actions; the government was obliged to accept his explanations, and he continued to pursue an autonomous path. His elimination of Sonthonax had brought better relations with Rigaud, which in turn had helped the two expel the British. Now without a common foe to unite them, the two revolutionary leaders faced off against each other. Hédouville had helped prepare the ground by bringing Rigaud back into French favor and boosting his pretentions to create a counterpoise to Toussaint's power.

The War of the South (June 1799 to July 1800) began as a boundary dispute between two rivals, and was at bottom a regional power struggle, but it was also shaped by class conflict and used the language of race in its propaganda (doc. 65). In the region under Toussaint's command, hundreds of *anciens libres* were arrested and killed, accused of favoring Rigaud, and in some places they rebelled against him. Rigaud's southern army of about 10,000 men and Toussaint's northern forces, which were about twice as large, each consisted overwhelmingly of black ex-slaves. Both generals were *anciens libres*; they each had African mothers and wore their hair European-style. Both were committed to slave emancipation and claimed to be defending the interests of the French Republic. But Toussaint, the son of African slaves, and Rigaud, who was freeborn with a white father and trained in France, represented the classes in which they were raised, as did their respective officer corps. The conflict was thus more than simply regional, and it proved to be extremely brutal. After a long prelude of border skirmishes during which Louverture terrorized the *anciens libres* of the west and north, Jean-Jacques Dessalines led an invasion of the south that was marked by fierce resistance and mass executions. Rigaud and dozens of other leaders fled to France and to neighboring islands.

By August 1800, the whole of Saint Domingue was under Toussaint's control. He could now extend the forced labor system Sonthonax had created in 1793 and the sequestration and leasing out of absentee property that both the Republicans and British had pursued. Senior officers became planters and formed a new black landholding class. Toussaint remained committed to the plantation system, perhaps because of his previous history as a man of property, but more certainly because only the export of cash crops would generate the revenue that funded his army and administration. This policy alienated much of the ex-slave population. Rather than labor on plantations for others, they preferred to grow food crops as independent smallholders, or they sought a new life in the towns (doc. 66). Faced with grassroots resistance, Toussaint now applied military discipline to agriculture (doc. 67), which heralded the militarization of the future Haitian state.

Admirers of the new colonial regime saw a brave new world—vibrant, optimistic, and socially mobile. They described a multiracial egalitarian experiment, defended by a citizen army, in which racial prejudice was fast disappearing, the birth rate was rising, and there was ample leisure (doc. 68). Philippe Roume, Hédouville's successor as Agent, praised the cultivators' desire for education and the character of Toussaint's leading generals (doc. 69). Louverture's success in reviving the export economy remains uncertain. Official figures from 1801 show sugar production roughly 90 percent below pre-revolutionary levels and coffee down by about half. But they included exports from regions where the British had preserved slavery down to 1798. On the other hand, the figures might have been understated, some suggest, to cover up the creation of secret accounts and the stockpiling of munitions.

In the eyes of his critics, Louverture was a hypocrite: ostentatiously pious but ambitious and ruthless, prudish in public but a private libertine. His army was more feudal than republican: officers acted like local lords, whose troops, left unpaid, preyed on the rural masses. Officials invented illegal fees to compensate for irregularly paid salaries. Racial and class tensions vitiated the forced labor regime (doc. 70). Most historians assume that Louverture envisaged a multiracial future for Saint Domingue, because he valued the managerial and technical skills of the whites. Some argue, however, that, although he invited refugee planters to return, few got their estates back, and instead they served as hostages to discourage a future French attack.

If there was any way Saint Domingue could have avoided a French invasion, after the ambitious and dynamic Napoleon Bonaparte came to power in 1799, is a vexed question, but the policies pursued by Toussaint in 1801 certainly helped make it inevitable. In January 1801 he invaded and annexed neighboring Santo Domingo. After Spain had ceded the colony to France in 1795, the Directory (France's governing body) decided to defer an official takeover until the war ended. In making himself master of the whole island, Toussaint contravened a specific directive from Bonaparte, and he imprisoned Roume, France's representative, who refused to give his assent. The governor's motive was probably to protect his eastern flank against a future attack, but in doing so, he made such an attack inevitable. In March, Napoleon quietly canceled Toussaint's promotion to Captain-General and removed his name from the French army register. In July, widening the breach further, Toussaint promulgated on his own initiative a colonial constitution (doc. 71).

Remarkably bold, the constitution made Louverture governor for life, with the right to name his successor, and it gave France no role in running what was now a colony in name only. Although sent to France for ratification, the constitution was in fact put into effect immediately. There was no chance Bonaparte would accept such an affront. If French merchants were not given a privileged position in Saint Domingue, the colony would be of little use to France. Toussaint had miscalculated. His white advisors proved reluctant to argue the matter as he became increasingly dictatorial. No doubt he thought that the previous failure of French, Spanish, and British armies in the colony would warn off a French general who, though a rising star, had recently come to grief in an overseas expedition to Egypt. It is further likely that, buoyed by his treaties with the British and Americans, Toussaint failed to appreciate how the situation would brusquely change once the war in Europe ended.

Some historians claim the constitution was a stepping stone toward the declaration of an independent state. Yet this was a step Toussaint would never take and something he always denied. It was not because he felt profound loyalty to the French Republic, but because the creation of a black state by former slaves was likely to meet with a retaliatory embargo by the British and Americans as well as hostilities with France. Far better to have autonomy in alliance with France—in other words, the substance of independence without its trappings. This intermediate solution, however, was unacceptable to Bonaparte, so the scene was set for a conflict between colony and metropole.

Just as this international crisis was about to unfold, Toussaint faced a dramatic challenge from within Saint Domingue. In October 1801, cultivators rebelled across a swathe of the North Province and massacred more than 300 white colonists (doc. 72). They were motivated, no doubt, by the forced labor law passed a year earlier that had been recently reinforced by the constitution. It seems the revolt was instigated by Moyse, the charismatic and willful commandant of the North and Toussaint's leading general. Much remains obscure, however, because the rebellion was quickly crushed and Toussaint prevented any participant from speaking in his own defense. Some historians think Moyse wanted to divide up the plantations, but it is more certain he wanted them to be run by black officers rather than Europeans. Moyse was Toussaint's wife's nephew, whom he had known all his life, so the rebellion cut close to home.

The long and rambling proclamation of 5 Frimaire, year 10 that Toussaint issued a month later hints at the personal turmoil these events caused for him (doc. 73). Linking treason, crime, dislike for agriculture, negligent parenting, and a lack of Christian morals, he again reaffirmed the labor decree of October 1800 (doc. 67), and instituted an identity card system for urban residents and a census of plantation workers. Among the stiff penalties introduced for a variety of offenses, the reappearance of the ball and chain was pregnant with symbolism.

The Saint Domingue that Toussaint Louverture sought to create combined the awkward compromise between slavery and freedom that the French Republic had pursued since 1793, and a hybrid blend of colonial status and independence that he himself pioneered. This new society was not given long to prove itself. By the end of 1801, after barely eighteen months of domestic peace, the new regime clearly faced serious internal problems, while across the Atlantic a threat of unprecedented magnitude was taking shape.

The War of Independence

Napoleon Bonaparte seized power in France in November 1799, but he could do little in the Caribbean while the war with Britain continued. For two years his intentions were unclear, and they remain so for some scholars. Some evidence suggests he kept a pragmatically open mind about slavery (doc. 74a), although he had no qualms about maintaining it in those colonies that had avoided implementing the emancipation decree in 1794. Until March 1801, he also appears to have been willing to work with Toussaint Louverture and perhaps use the black general to further his imperial ambitions. Toussaint's constitution and annexation of Santo Domingo changed that, however. When peace preliminaries were signed with the English in October 1801, Bonaparte immediately began preparing a large expedition for Saint Domingue. He assigned command to his brother-in-law, Victoire Leclerc. Yet in his public pronouncements (doc. 74b), he continued to profess support for slave emancipation.

Britain and the United States had supported Louverture as long as France was their enemy. Now they signaled their approval of the French expedition, because they feared a peacetime France less than a regime run by ex-slaves. Spain and the Netherlands contributed shipping and finance to the expedition. Cuba later supplied hunting dogs to combat guerrillas. Some have therefore called the Leclerc expedition a Euro-American crusade, although it also included André Rigaud, Jean-Baptiste Belley, and hundreds of *anciens libres*, eager to avenge the War of the South.

General Leclerc landed in early February 1802 with 10,000 troops, whose numbers were soon doubled. His orders were to proceed stealthily, to win over where possible the black generals, then disarm their soldiers, and eventually deport all black officers. But his orders made no mention of slavery (doc. 75). Leclerc published Bonaparte's assurances that slave emancipation was inviolable. Uncertain of French intentions, and anxious to preserve the property they had acquired, some generals, and most of the population, offered no resistance, leaving Toussaint, Christophe, and Dessalines to fight a desperate campaign. They burned towns and plantations, massacred hostages, and took to the mountains. Nonetheless, the massive deployment of experienced troops and their arrival in the healthy winter months brought the Europeans rapid success. Toussaint's surrender in May ended the first phase of the war.

Toussaint was soon deported to France on suspicion of plotting rebellion (doc. 76), but the other generals were incorporated into the army of occupation and used to disarm the rural masses. Resistance mounted during the summer, as it became clear that French policy was to reimpose slavery. Previously hesitant to rally to the black army, rural blacks now produced leaders of their own in the tradition of the maroons. At the same time, the spread of tropical fevers decimated Leclerc's forces (docs. 75, 77, 78). For several months, generals including

Dessalines and Christophe collaborated in suppressing popular resistance, until in October both the co-opted black generals and the *anciens libres* officers who had arrived with Leclerc finally broke with the French. They realized by then that French policy was to restore not only slavery but also racial discrimination. To maintain freedom and equality, they had to unite in a war for independence, though it took many more months before they proclaimed this as their goal.

As the French campaign of terror and deportation became almost a war of genocide against the nonwhite population (docs. 78, 79), a new sense of unity based on racial solidarity emerged. Rigaud's successor, Alexandre Pétion, accepted Dessalines as commander-in-chief. Despite his brutal behavior in the War of the South, then as Toussaint's inspector of agriculture and as Leclerc's chief collaborator, Dessalines was the ideal person to lead the struggle to expel the French. A menial slave before the revolution, he had none of the liking for French culture and white society that Toussaint and the former domestic Christophe shared with the *anciens libres*. He spoke only Creole, the language of the masses, and he exuded demonic energy; his battle cry was "Burn houses, cut off heads!"

The international solidarity that seemed to surround the Leclerc expedition soon evaporated. Fearing French ambitions in Louisiana, President Jefferson did nothing about a trade embargo on Toussaint, which he had hinted at; U.S. merchants continued to supply both sides in the conflict, as they always had. Rising tensions in Europe similarly led Britain to reclassify a black Saint Domingue as a potential ally against the French. When the European war resumed in May 1803, the British gave naval support to Dessalines, just as the U.S. navy had assisted Toussaint Louverture in his war with Rigaud. No country wanted the emergence of a black autonomous power in the Caribbean, but they now feared even more an aggressive expansionist France. Foreign policy toward the Haitian Revolution was a matter of calculating the lesser of two evils, and relations with France always determined government attitudes to Saint Domingue.

Decimated by fever, driven into a few coastal towns, and blockaded by the British, the French army evacuated the colony in November 1803 after losing more than 40,000 soldiers and sailors. The losses of local inhabitants are unknown but probably greater. On 1 January 1804, amidst popular jubilation, Dessalines proclaimed the independence of the state of Haiti at a public ceremony in the port of Gonaïves. By resurrecting the pre-Columbian Amerindian name for the island, he symbolically erased the European colonial past and gave the largely African-descended population a new, American identity. The Declaration of Independence—only the second in world history—called in blistering prose for the extirpation of all things French (doc. 80). During the following few months, most of the remaining white colonists perished in a series of organized massacres that can be seen as an epilogue to, or the climax of, the Haitian Revolution. They were explicitly an act of revenge for past treatment and a warning against any future attempt at reconquest.

Some Haitian officers secretly helped whites escape, and some official exceptions were made, as for 400 Polish troops who had deserted Leclerc's army. Yet the massacre did much to damage the new state's international image. As the killing drew to a close, Dessalines defiantly justified his actions in a proclamation that presented the massacre not only as retribution and self-defense but also as a sort of blood pact that would reunite former slaves and *anciens libres* in an act of national reconciliation (doc. 81). In banning ownership of property by Europeans, it weakened the egalitarian and universalist thrust of the Haitian Revolution and strengthened its distinctively "ethno-national" character.

Haiti thus won its independence against a background of apocalyptic destruction. With thousands of its plantations and several of its towns burned, much of its working-age population killed, and most of its literate minority eliminated, the new state was able to export barely a quarter of its previous output. It remained, nonetheless, an important coffee producer. The Vatican cut off relations after the 1804 massacre, and it took decades for foreign powers to accord diplomatic recognition, in contrast to their embrace of the Latin American states that achieved independence in the 1820s. But Haiti was never commercially isolated, despite a U.S. trade embargo that lasted from 1806 to 1810. Its rulers tried for several decades to maintain the plantation system, but inexorably Haiti became a country of peasant smallholders, unique in the Americas. The aspirations of its formerly enslaved masses were, at enormous cost, eventually realized.

A profound social cleavage separated the rural masses, about a quarter of whom had been born in Africa, from the new elite that, despite the hostility expressed in the declaration of independence, remained strongly attracted to French culture. The elite itself was divided between black officers that had risen from slavery, who were numerous in the north, and the *anciens libres* of mixed racial descent, who controlled the center and south. In 1807, the country split along these regional and class lines into two warring states and remained divided until 1820.

Because Haiti's revolution entirely eliminated the ruling class and remodeled the economy, it might be considered the most profoundly transformative of the Age of Revolutions. Yet its political message is less clear. It was unusual among the colonial revolutions of the Americas, though not unique, in the way independence became its main goal only very belatedly. And its focus on slave emancipation rather than citizenship particularly sets it apart. While the struggles of Saint Domingue's free coloreds and white colonists lay very much within the liberal republican mainstream of the Atlantic revolutions, the revolution that emerged from the slave uprising was entirely authoritarian. Other revolutions, not least the French, also ended in military dictatorships, but all the gifted ex-slaves who rose to power were unapologetically autocratic and made no pretense of espousing liberal democratic values.

Despite the popularity of the term "the black republic," the state that Dessalines created was a military autocracy, and in 1805 he took the title "emperor."

The Republic of Haiti was founded only in 1806, after Dessalines' assassination by the *anciens libres* surrounding Alexandre Pétion. The political scission that followed divided the country by ideology as well as region and class. Refusing to be a weak president in a republic controlled by his *anciens libres* rivals, the black general Henry Christophe formed a breakaway state in the north, of which he became king.

Overseas Reactions

From its earliest days, news of the revolution spread wide and fast—an inspiration for some, a nightmare for others. Slaves sometimes seemed informed ahead of their masters. Beyond the burgeoning milieu of newspapers and pamphlets, news circulated around the Atlantic seaboard in encounters between sailors and dockworkers, the animated table talk of planters and merchants, and rumors retold by their servants. Within a month of the North Plain uprising, slaves in Jamaica were singing songs about it (doc. 82). Britain and Spain's intervention in the revolution made it all the more difficult to prevent news spreading through their Caribbean colonies. Cuba and Jamaica were barely a day's sailing from Saint Domingue; each sent expeditions to Saint Domingue and received waves of refugees, white and black, bearing witness to its destruction (docs. 83, 84). As the world turned upside down, whites everywhere complained of a new "insolence" among people of color. Men and women of African descent took pride in the stories they heard and, from Brazil to Philadelphia, signaled their awareness in a variety of ways (docs. 85, 86, 87).

The French Revolution proclaimed the ideals of liberty and equality, but the Haitian Revolution proved to African Americans they could be won by force of arms, that things were perhaps not so immutable as they seemed. Contemporaries and historians have often exaggerated the importance of this factor, but a good number of the many slave rebellions and conspiracies of this period show various types of "Haitian" influence. The most striking example was a widespread conspiracy organized in Havana in 1812 by the free black carpenter José Antonio Aponte (doc. 88).

Colonial governments and planter classes were all alarmed by the spectacle of self-liberation in the Americas' most productive colony. Yet it also brought them economic opportunities (doc. 89, 90). By driving up the world price of tropical produce and creating a diaspora of refugees who settled new lands in Cuba, Jamaica, Louisiana, and Trinidad, the revolution stimulated the spread of slavery to new frontiers and the revival of older plantation economies. It was a bitter irony. Although the revolution freed a half million slaves—indirectly, more than 600,000 in all the French colonies—and it closed the Atlantic slave trade's largest market, the overall volume of the slave trade scarcely declined from its all-time peak in the 1780s. Greed everywhere proved stronger than fear. This makes it difficult to believe that fear of rebellions was a major factor in the eventual outlawing of the slave trade, which mainly occurred between 1802 and 1830.

The Haitian Revolution's impact on the development and eventual success of abolitionism remains controversial. Both sides in the antislavery debate used it in their propaganda, although most abolitionists were apologists for the revolution rather than supporters. Only a few obscure figures, in Europe and the United States, were willing to recognize that slaves had a right to rebellion (docs. 91, 92). Events in Saint Domingue seem to have convinced Thomas Jefferson, a slaveowner morally opposed to slavery, that slave revolution was inevitable in the Caribbean and the U.S. South (doc. 93). Yet, with the U.S. cotton economy burgeoning, these convictions led nowhere.

There are, however, two important instances where the Haitian Revolution made critical, if indirect, contributions to antislavery successes. In 1807 Britain abolished its slave trade, not because of fears of West Indian rebellion, but because the revolution had ended France's standing as a major colonial power. It is unlikely British politicians would have felt free to vote their consciences, if they believed their traditional enemy would be able to profit from it. The second instance concerns Simón Bolívar, the leader of the Spanish American independence movement. During his long struggle to end Spanish colonial rule, Bolívar twice had to seek refuge in Haiti. His host, President Alexandre Pétion, asked him to add slave emancipation to his political agenda. When Bolívar later began the dismantling of slavery in Venezuela, he certainly had local reasons for doing so. But without Haitian help, he might not have made a successful return to South America. Haiti thus made a major contribution to the decolonization of Spanish America as well to ending slavery there.

Bolívar nonetheless held a very jaundiced view of Haiti, which he regarded as an exemplar of tyranny and anarchy (doc. 94). Like Jefferson, he disliked slavery but feared slaves, and in pessimistic moments he claimed that Spanish America needed authoritarian government to avoid a race war. One reason he did not attempt to liberate Cuba was his fear that its large slave population might turn it into another Haiti. As this view was generally shared by the Cuban elite, one can say that the Haitian Revolution hindered decolonization in Cuba while it promoted it on the mainland.

Another area in which the revolution's impact was ambiguous was attitudes to racial difference. The achievements of Saint Domingue's slaves, and particularly Toussaint Louverture, impressed many in both abolitionist and proslavery circles. The spectacle of field hands and flunkies defeating the armies of three major powers and founding a modern state encouraged a rethinking of old attitudes, and in the minds of various writers constituted a major turning point in world history (docs. 96, 97, 98, 99). For others, however, the violence of the revolution and the political instability that followed it confirmed old prejudices.

Together with the starkly different susceptibility to tropical disease displayed by Europeans and Africans during the conflict, it may have also encouraged the growth of biological racism.

In the field of imaginative literature numerous poets, playwrights, and novelists, both famous and obscure, were inspired by the Haitian Revolution. Victor Hugo's first novel, *Bug Jargal,* and Heinrich von Kleist's novella *Die Verlobung auf Saint Domingo* offered rather negative and superficial visions of the event. William Wordsworth's fine sonnet, "To Toussaint L'Ouverture," still resonates powerfully (doc. 98). The philosophy of Georg Wilhelm Hegel also appears to have been shaped by his reading on the revolution, although scholars do not agree whether he was thrilled or traumatized by it.

The international impact of the Haitian Revolution was thus wide-ranging and impressive but also in many ways ambiguous and contradictory. Much of its ambivalent legacy is on view in the speech given by the veteran black abolitionist Frederick Douglass to eulogize Haiti a century after its richly complex revolution had first seized the world's attention (doc. 99).

Timeline

1789

Jan.–Mar. Wealthy colonial activists illegally elect deputies to the States-General in France.

Aug. White and free colored colonists form separate political clubs in Paris to press their interests.

Oct. Inspired by the Bastille's fall, white radicals force the Intendant to flee Saint Domingue. Free coloreds calling for political rights meet with persecution. Slaves voicing protests on some plantations brutally suppressed.

1790

Mar. National Assembly allows colonies to elect their own assemblies; is deliberately evasive about the rights of free people of color.

July Governor Peinier closes the autonomist Colonial Assembly at Saint Marc.

Oct. Vincent Ogé leads brief free colored rebellion in the north.

1791

Feb. Grisly execution of Ogé.

Mar. White radicals drive governor out of Port-au-Prince.

May National Assembly decrees political rights for freeborn men of color.

July White colonists discuss secession and organize to resist the May 15 decree.

Aug. Insurrections of slaves in the north and free coloreds in the west.

Sept. National Assembly annuls the May 15 decree.

Nov. Port-au-Prince burned in fighting between white radicals and free coloreds.

1792

Jan.–Mar. Slave rebellion spasmodically spreads in west and south.

Apr. Legislative Assembly ends racial discrimination in the colonies.

Sept. Arrival of second Civil Commission with 6,000 soldiers. France becomes a republic.

Oct.–Dec. Commissioners form alliance with free coloreds and deport white conservatives and radicals.

1793

Feb.–Mar. War begins with Britain and Spain.

May Spanish conclude alliance with Jean-François and Biassou.

June Civil commissioners' struggle with Governor Galbaud causes burning of Cap Français and emancipation of slave recruits.

Aug. Sonthonax abolishes slavery in the north. Abolition extended to the west in Sept. and south in Oct.

Sept. British forces begin five-year occupation in parts of south and west.

1794

Jan. Fall of Fort Dauphin completes Spanish conquest of most of north.

Feb. Jacobin government declares the slaves in all French colonies to be free citizens.

Apr.–July Toussaint Louverture turns on his Spanish allies and joins the French.

1795

July Spain makes peace and transfers Santo Domingo to France.

Dec. Jean-François and Biassou leave for exile.

1796

Mar. Toussaint foils free colored coup against Governor Laveaux and becomes deputy-governor.

May Sonthonax and Raimond return with new civil commission.

Oct.–Dec. Toussaint and Sonthonax consolidate their control of the north. British switch to a defensive strategy.

1797

May–Sept. Reactionary forces in French legislature push for revision of colonial policy, until they are overthrown in the coup of September 4.

May Sonthonax names Toussaint commander-in-chief.

Aug. Toussaint forces out Sonthonax.

1798

Jan. Law on constitutional organization of the colonies finally incorporates Saint Domingue.

Mar.–Oct. General Hédouville's mission creates friction with emergent power of ex-slaves under Toussaint.

May–Sept. British withdrawal. Toussaint signs trade and nonaggression treaty.

1799

June War of the South begins.

Dec. Napoleon becomes head of state. Colonies lose right of metropolitan representation.

1800

Aug. Completing his defeat of Rigaud, Toussaint controls all Saint Domingue.

Oct. Toussaint orders army to impose forced labor on the plantations.

1801

Jan. Toussaint flouts French orders and occupies Santo Domingo.

Feb. Toussaint announces project for a constitution. Napoleon names him Captain-General of Saint Domingue but then retracts his decision.

July Toussaint's constitution makes him governor for life.

Oct. Franco-British peace preliminaries permit the Leclerc expedition. Rebellion of Moyse.

1802

Feb.–May Leclerc conquers Saint Domingue.

June Toussaint deported to France.

Aug. News of re-establishment of slavery in Guadeloupe rekindles resistance in Saint Domingue.

Oct. Dessalines and Pétion unite in rebellion.

1803

May Franco-British war resumes.

Dec. Last French troops evacuated.

1804

Jan. Dessalines declares independence at Gonaïves.

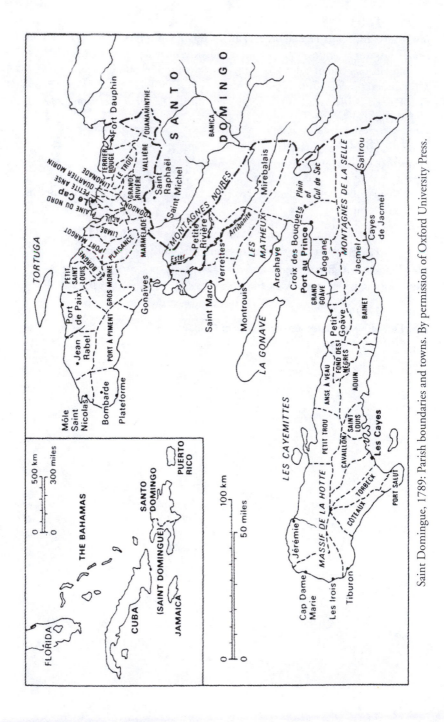

Saint Domingue, 1789: Parish boundaries and towns. By permission of Oxford University Press.

1. SAINT DOMINGUE ON THE EVE OF REVOLUTION

Saint Domingue society was founded on brutal exploitation and pervaded by a get-rich-quick atmosphere. It was in some ways a very modern society: peopled by migrants with weak family bonds; a site of intensive investment, devoted to international trade; multiracial and multicultural. Confronting unfamiliar diseases with little social support, enslaved Africans and European immigrants tended to die young and have few children. Marriage was rare in all social groups. Newcomers from France (doc. 1) found the cost of living high and generally thought that the ruling passions of the white population were sex, gambling, and hurriedly returning to Europe after making a fortune. As men outnumbered women three to one among white colonists, interracial unions, ranging from the ephemeral and sordid to the occasional marriage, gave rise to a large population of mixed racial descent.

France had the biggest population in Europe but relatively few colonies, so Saint Domingue received a large number of lower-class migrants seeking employment and escape from the economic crises that would lead to the French Revolution. Those who succeeded worked as artisan craftsmen or clerks in the towns, or as plantation overseers (doc. 2). The latter worked long hours in close proximity to the slaves they supervised. They hoped one day to become a manager and then estate attorney, while accumulating the capital to start their own plantation.

In the eyes of slave traders, who in the 1780s shipped more than 200,000 Africans to Saint Domingue, enslaved humans were merely things (doc. 3). Enslavement converted people into property as a matter of law, and a common defense of slavery was precisely that slaveowners' self-interest prevented the mistreatment of slaves. The limitations of this argument became apparent as critics, influenced by the Enlightenment and the literary fashion of sensibility, began to look closely at the institution (doc. 4). Yet the assessment of conditions is complicated. Caribbean slaves, unlike their U.S. counterparts, usually had to grow their own food on small provision grounds that they worked on Sundays. This increased their workload and exposed them to shortages, but it also gave them opportunities to market any surplus they produced and to accumulate income. Labor was at its most grueling on lowland sugar estates, but their size and complexity provided slaves a richer social life and wider variety of employment than on mountain coffee farms.

Although killing a slave was not made a capital offense until the 1780s, French law was more protective of slaves than was English law. Yet it was rarely enforced.

Most government officials thought it dangerous to undermine the authority of slaveowners, even those who committed heinous atrocities. The two trials of the planter Nicolas Lejeune in 1788 pitted an unusually vigorous, reform-minded administration against entrenched colonial attitudes, and at bottom, two opposing ideas about social control and the use of terror (doc. 5). In a few earlier cases, slaves had denounced brutal masters to the judiciary, unsuccessfully, and governors had occasionally deported sadistic colonists, discreetly avoiding a public trial. But actually prosecuting Lejeune represented a unique effort by the colonial administration. Although it failed, it strengthened colonists' desires for self-government, and it may help explain why, three years later, the slave insurgents posed as allies of the royalist government against the planters.

The plight of the free people of color was much less well known in France than that of the slaves, as there were not many of them until the 1780s. They prospered economically but, from the 1730s, faced increasing legal restrictions and segregation (doc. 6). Racial prejudice worsened in these years but had yet to harden into the biological, "scientific" racism of the nineteenth century. French colonists who might fear or dislike free coloreds as a group continued to free and endow with property their own mixed-race children. According to a Haitian historian, "They dug their graves with their penises."

As the free colored population rapidly approached parity with the whites, a few officials began to question the wisdom of discriminating against the entire group, especially as so many were slave-owning, tax-paying, Militiamen. The majority white viewpoint was that racial discrimination served as a bulwark of slavery, and that all those neither white nor slave should occupy an intermediate category in society: free but unequal. Reformers began to wonder if it might be better to accord the wealthiest or lightest-skinned equal status to whites to prevent their one day making common cause with the growing mass of slaves. Julien Raimond, a member of this elite group, privately lobbied the colonial minister testifying to the injustices free coloreds suffered in Saint Domingue (doc.7). The government tentatively investigated the matter but had taken no action by the time the revolution began.

1) **Greed and Decadence**

These observations by a French military officer stationed in Saint Domingue during the American Revolutionary War are typical of visitors' reactions in the late eighteenth century to the colony's licentious and materialistic society. Its racial hierarchy and intermixing intrigued them. Few white males failed to comment on the stylish women of color they saw in the seaports, who used their sexuality to overcome racial disadvantage.

People of a sensitive disposition would be shocked to see the licentious manners of Saint Domingue. . . . From generation to generation, the free people of color have maintained an extreme proclivity for following the dictates of love. The mulatto and quadroon[1] women, taking advantage of their debauchery, have competed with white women for the hearts of white men, and they have won. This means they have the social elite and the majority of colonists for lovers. These arrangements have caused most colonists to forgo marriage . . . [and] the inconstancy of husbands is without doubt the cause . . . of the infidelity of their wives. . . . There is no act of revenge that a creole[2] spurned by her husband will not resort to. . . . It is not enough for her to flaunt several lovers and lavish presents on them. . . . Creole women are accused of getting rid of their husbands to marry their lovers. Such women are mentioned by name . . . and the men and women, black and white, who helped them carry out their crimes are boldly identified. . . .

Fathers and mothers spoil their children. They go along with their slightest whims . . . which makes the children excessively capricious, and the fact that they never get told off makes them haughty and stubborn. . . . As they often see [slaves punished] they become hardened and come running up to watch a poor black get whipped, as if it were a game. . . . After that it is very difficult for their hearts to be moved by pity. I have heard a mother boasting that her son, at ten years of age, was strong enough to "trim a slave," that is to say remove his flesh with a whip. . . . Fortunately such examples are now rare. . . . There are many colonists who spread happiness among their slaves.

Mulatto, quadroon, and black women dress with taste, and use their appearance, their height, and their walk as an invitation to seduction. In truth, they put this stylishness to very good use as a sort of call to sensuous pleasure. Yet they avoid any other device or activity to excite men. If a woman of color went

---

1. People with one white and one black parent were called *mulatto*; those with one white and one mulatto parent were called *quadroon*.

2. In the Caribbean, "creole" meant locally born and had no connotation of mixed racial descent, as in North America. The author here means white women.

out of her way to attract men's attention, she would be considered scandalous by her fellows and certainly mocked by them. . . . The women of color who behave most like prostitutes, either by inclination or lack of resources, do not dare deviate from this sort of principle. . . .

In America, expenses are exorbitant. Meals are lavish. You have to dress with refinement. Heavy gambling is a major passion. . . . Colonists prefer to risk ruining themselves and then regretting it to the unpleasantness of living at a less extravagant level.

Agreements are rarely made in good faith. . . . How many adventurers have made their fortune in Saint Domingue by getting away with [dishonest deals]. . . . Nowhere else could the law be less observed and vice so flourishing. . . . Violent emotions take the place of principles. The heart has no other affections beyond the illusions of love, dreams of pleasure, extravagant luxury, and greed. . . . Almost no one in Saint Domingue displays passion for, or interest in, religion. . . . The churches are therefore empty. . . . Men judge everything by how it will benefit them materially. Their passion for wealth weakens their desire to be kind. . . . Deep down, they are very little concerned with who is or who will be master of Saint Domingue, as long as their economic interests are not interrupted. . . . The considerable mixture of people of different fortune and standing makes it impossible for patriotism to be the same [as in Martinique].

(Bibliothèque Mazarine, Paris, Ms. 3453, "Remarques sur la colonie de Saint-Domingue," by lieutenant-colonel Desdorides)

2) The Plantation Hierarchy

A former plantation manager, Charles Malenfant, here sketches the social hierarchy among the white employees on large plantations, which often belonged to absentee owners who lived in France. The tensions and resentment the system fostered help explain the political conflicts that would divide Saint Domingue's white community when the French Revolution's outbreak in 1789 promised a more egalitarian social order. Malenfant also alludes to the pernicious effects of absentee ownership and to the mounting debts many planters owed to French merchants.

Saint Domingue colonists put more care and effort into overseeing their slaves than do the English or Dutch; they are even excessive in their vigilance. In such a hot country this surprising activity can only be attributed to the desire to get rich. The overseer wants to become a manager; the manager to become an estate-attorney; and the latter to make more revenue than his predecessor, so as to deserve the owner's confidence and gain the reputation of being a great agriculturalist.

The young European overseer, after two days on the job, is fully aware how unpleasant his situation is, not only how tiring it is but also how little respect he gets from the owner or estate-attorney. The zealous overseer . . . gets up during the night to supervise the irrigation workers so they don't waste the water destined for the canes. On rainy days he joins them to make sure the rain falling in torrents isn't lost. He observes everything that happens on the plantation and uses a few trusted blacks as spies. He makes his report by handing a note to the owner or attorney when he joins them for breakfast. They scarcely pay attention to him. If he is . . . drenched with sweat and his shoes covered with mud, that proves he's been busy. . . . No sooner has he eaten than he goes back to the fields, does the rounds two or three times . . . and returns when the slaves finish their work. Then he goes to his hut, throw himself down on his wretched bed, waiting to be called to lunch. At the dinner table, he sits at the lower end, doesn't look up, and doesn't say a word. . . . He follows the slaves back to the fields, leaves at 6:00 p.m. and has supper at 8:00 p.m. Finally the moment of rest has arrived. He will forget his troubles . . . in the arms of an attentive African girl, whom he generally ends up buying, or at least her children, if the owner is good enough to sell them to him. This is the origin of the free blacks and free mulattoes.

The young man is a thousand times worse off than a shepherd's dog. He is even more worse off, if he is sensitive to the treatment of the blacks. If he looks like he pities them, he will immediately be told, "You don't know those scoundrels. Nature has made them to be slaves. We thought like you when we first came but we soon found out. If you want to get on in life, you must give up all those European feelings when you come to the Tropics. They aren't suited for the colonies. . . . Little by little, the poor young man gets used to [it.] . . .

After becoming a manager, he makes his tour of the fields on foot or on horseback. He relies on his overseer's diligence, having set an example himself during his three or four years on the job. His salary is 5,000 to 6,000 francs [about $1,000 to $1,200] plus the perquisites of the plantation. If he becomes an estate-attorney, he has reached the summit of his ambition. He immediately buys a coach. The black housekeeper[3] is abandoned for a mulatress, which upsets the plantation slaves; she is nearly always an insatiable goat. Every Sunday, or Saturday night, he goes into town visiting the merchants with whom he does business. All the owners and attorneys are there. A good dinner, served with taste and elegance, awaits him. He plays cards, goes to the mulatresses' ball or to the theater, and returns

3. Whether enslaved or free, the housekeeper was usually the mistress of the manager or owner.

to the plantation the next day. During the week he busies himself with accounts and correspondence. He receives 10 percent of the plantation's revenue. He goes outside only during the cool hours of the morning and evening and compensates himself amply for the fatigues he endured as an overseer. He gives orders to the slave drivers, punishes, lashes the blacks at will, chains them up, kills them if he wishes. In sum, he is the haughtiest and most insolent of despots.

His main aim is to send the owner in France the maximum revenue possible. The owner scarcely gives a thought to what is happening to the slaves on his estate. He puts himself in the hand of a man who sends him enormous sums. . . . A new attorney wants to do better than his predecessor and, at the same time, get rich quickly himself. He therefore keeps expenditure to a minimum and works the slaves in a way that, in a few years, makes his fortune but destroys the workforce. Fifty new slaves are needed. The owner protests against such an expense, but soon calms down. . . . It's on credit.

(Charles Malenfant, *Des colonies et particulièrement de celle de Saint-Domingue* [Paris, 1814])

3) A Slave Trader's View

These brutal and unselfconscious comments come from the letters of a Cap Français merchant to his partner in France. They concern the Africans arriving on different slave ships whom he was responsible for selling. Especially striking is the way he related his sense of honor to the quality of his "merchandise."

Good God! How unpleasant it is to have bad Negroes to sell and to be obliged to keep them. It's enough to make you lose your reputation and your patience. . . . This cargo is not suitable for Le Cap: old people, too many young, bad teeth, bad height, bad-looking Negroes. . . .

This sale is over, thanks be to God.

[Our agent] saw some fine Negroes, some rubbish, and not a single good-looking woman; there's smallpox on board. . . . Tell your captains to prefer young people to the aged; drooping but full breasts don't put people off, but dried up ones are disgusting.

[The sickly survivors of a nightmarish voyage] don't sell, good God, and won't die. I don't know what to do, to tell you the truth. [Of 317 blacks during a seventy-day crossing] there are 40 or so little ones who have been left without women to nurse them. Twenty men and women have scurvy and are in a very sorry state. The rest of the cargo is good. There's not a lot of old ones; 67 head died during the crossing, of scurvy and dysentery.

[Rice-eating Africans from Sierra Leone are difficult to feed and] grow melancholic when they become thin; they get lethargic and die of boredom. . . . They are Negroes who dishonor us.

(Archives Nationales, Paris, 505 Mi 85–86, Pierre-Paul Morange
to Stanislas Foäche, 1785–1789)

4) Plantation Slaves

Girod de Chantrans spent about a year in northern Saint Domingue in the early 1780s. He was therefore an outsider, like Desdorides (doc. 1), with limited experience but free of colonial bias. He depicts the slaves he saw as overworked, underfed, and cruelly punished, but like other writers he implies they were probably worse treated in the past. Like the colonist Malenfant (doc. 2), he stresses the evil effects of absentee ownership, as well as the colonists' system of "private justice" that is the subject of document 5.

There are more than twenty sugar plantations in the little plain where I am living. From morning to evening, and even during the night, you can hear there a sort of melancholy reverberation caused by the muffled noise of the cane mills and the carts that haul the crops, which is heightened from time to time by the crack of whips striking both animals and slaves. Torrents of smoke come out of the buildings where the sugar is boiled and dried, and either rise in the form of thick clouds or spread out over the countryside as they fall to earth. . . .

On a large, well-managed sugar plantation, the work never stops. Either the ripened canes need to be cut, or a field needs replanting after being harvested, or those where the new shoots risk being strangled by weeds need to be weeded. The work of the slaves begins at dawn. At eight o'clock they have breakfast and then return to work until midday. They start work again at two o'clock p.m. continuing until night, sometimes until ten or eleven o'clock.

The two hours they are allowed each day, along with Sundays and holidays, are given over to the food crops with which they feed themselves. To this end, each slave is given a small plot of land in which he plants what he wants. Manioc, sweet potatoes, dasheen, yams, pumpkins, bananas, black-eyed peas, and pineapples are the foodstuffs they prefer to grow. A slave who works hard on his little piece of land often produces more food than he needs. With his master's permission, he trades it in the closest town or village and brings back in exchange salted meat or fish, tobacco to smoke, rum, or items of clothing. This food surplus from the plantations serves to feed the domestic and artisan slaves of the towns, and even several whites who are too poor or too frugal to eat bread.

It sometimes happens that, in years of drought, the slaves in the countryside do not have enough food for themselves. Careful slaveowners deal with these shortages by supplying food from reserves they keep for this purpose. Those who fail to take such precautions are soon punished for it. Illness spreads in their workgangs and kills a large number of slaves. Others become discouraged and discontented; several run away; the pace of work slows and the plantation falls into ruin. This sort of event is only too common here. It only needs one poor mind in charge of a fine property to quickly turn it upside down, and soon in place of a vigorous workforce there is just a few sick and discouraged slaves.

You will ask if it is possible for people to act against their own interests. However, though the constant aim of most owners and their representatives is to increase their wealth, several among them are mistaken as to how to achieve this. Some believe you can squeeze *four* out of the work of a slave and only give him *half* in return. Others think on the other hand you have to give him *one* and only demand *three* for it. This variety of opinion, which always has the same intention of getting the most out of the slaves, produces, however, very different results. One will see his workforce prosper, while another will crush his in a short space of time. Add to these reasons, which are already quite enough, ineptitude, laziness, and inexperience, and you will no longer be surprised by the daily mistakes you see here in the management of properties.

There is another cause that has enormous influence on the slave gangs, and that is the discipline they are subjected to. It is generally very severe but varies according to the character of the master that imposes it. Rarely is it untainted with cruelty, and slaves are only too lucky when it does not give rise to atrocities. It is true that the royal decrees forbid slaveowners to take the life of their slaves. A slave who deserves to be put to death must be handed over to the courts. Yet this requirement is almost always avoided by a little tyrant whose pride and desire for revenge win out in the absolute power he wields on his own estate, and whose self-interest on other occasions prevents the loss of a guilty slave, as long as the slave's crime did not affect him. How can one shed light on the behavior of such a large number of whites who live isolated and scattered in the smallest recesses of the mountains? How can one penetrate the veil that often covers the evil secrets of their administrations?

You will understand therefore that, despite the very detailed laws, the colonist will be a despot as far as he is able. According to him, this is not a bad thing. His justification is always that his self-interest prevents him from abusing his power. But this reasoning is more specious than true. Allow me a few more comments to completely convince you. Although nowadays Saint Domingue's planters cannot fairly be accused of killing their slaves for pleasure, they do commonly commit acts of cruelty that do not kill, which they hope will reinforce discipline. Note also that most people in charge of properties are not their owners, and it matters little to them if a slave lives or dies, providing their salaries are paid. Are the owners themselves free from the passions that affect judgment? Self-interest is one but not the only one. Pride, anger, fear, etc. can make us unjust. Simply hearing the litany of cruelties committed is quite enough to be convinced that we are directed by other emotions besides self-interest and that the strongest override all the others. It is vain to claim that slaveowners' self-interest should prevent atrocities; experience proves that self-interest has not done its duty.

Moreover, men will inevitably treat harshly those who resist them, when they have the power to do so. Every day we see young people who have recently arrived in this colony who start out humane and sensitive, and are angry critics of tyranny, but who soon end up as hard-bitten as the oldest colonists. . . . After a certain time, once acclimated, as it were, to the New World, the European becomes a different person. . . .

Since I arrived here only a short while ago, bringing with me no other interest than curiosity and the desire to see things as they are, I think you will be interested by my account of slaves I have just been watching at work. There were a hundred men and women of different ages. They were all digging ditches in a field of cane; most were naked or covered in rags. The sun beat down on their heads and sweat ran all over their bodies. Tired by the heat and the weight of their pickaxes, and by a heavy soil baked hard enough to break their tools, they made great efforts to overcome every obstacle. A gloomy silence reigned among them; pain was visible on every face, but the hour of rest never came. The manager watched the workgang without pity, and several slave drivers armed with long whips, mixed in among the workers, dealt out harsh blows from time to time even to those who were obliged by weariness to slow down—men and women, young and old, without distinction.

Could a European fresh from the charming countryside of Switzerland gaze on that of Saint Domingue without getting angry? At the debasement of the men used here, their suffering and extreme poverty? At the enormous chains they have to drag around, if they commit a small fault (as if their daily work is not already exhausting enough)? At these iron collars fitted with long spikes that they put on slave women suspected of having abortions, which they have to wear day and night until they have produced a child for their master (as if it wasn't the master that should be punished if slaves fear to have children)? Struck with sadness and a sort of horror, I turn aside my gaze from this frightful countryside.

Colonists of Saint Domingue, boast as much as you wish about the immense productivity of your lands and the luxury in which you live, I wouldn't want it at that price.

(Justin Girod de Chantrans, *Voyage d'un Suisse dans différentes colonies d'Amérique* [Paris, 1785], letters V and IV)

5) The Lejeune Atrocity Case

Lejeune was a coffee planter whose slaves suffered a high mortality rate, which he suspected was due to poison. He tortured slaves to gain evidence, and their confessions tended to confirm his suspicions. Emboldened by new protective laws, some of his slaves denounced him to the judiciary, which took up the case. This caused a storm of protest among white colonists, which intimidated the lower court and appeal court into essentially acquitting Lejeune. The case showed the difficulty of reforming slavery. By arousing hopes it could not fulfill, it probably also increased the bitterness of the enslaved on the eve of the revolution.

Administrative reports (March–August 1788)

[Fourteen slaves from the Lejeune plantation] unanimously declared that last year Monsieur Nicolas Lejeune had a man and a woman slave burned, and that last Friday two slave women had their legs and thighs burned and that they were still on the plantation in a dungeon near the main house. . . . The [women] confessed whatever was asked of them. . . .

[Monsieur Lejeune] had long been known as someone who treated his slaves in an inhumane manner. Six or seven years ago his plantation had already been a scene of barbarity by the masters and vengeance by the slaves. The slaves were handed over to the courts and their crimes were punished with breaking on the wheel.[4] Yet the courts have never at any time, it seems, punished the inhumanity of masters. This unwise policy of severely punishing slaves and pardoning the whites everything has not had the intended effect. Slaves have continued to be insubordinate and masters to be cruel. . . .

On March 23, we received a petition from the leading colonists of Plaisance. We were dismayed to see that it was signed by several worthy planters who, without being cruel themselves, believe that good policy and the peace of the colony demand that atrocities committed by whites against slaves should be covered up. It was not without revulsion that we witnessed these planters asking us that fifty lashes should be given to Lejeune's slaves, these innocent creatures whose only crime was to seek the protection of the law against a ferocious master, their executioner . . . [It shows] how many people had an interest in playing down this despicable affair and in preventing the courts from condemning Lejeune, when each trembled at the thought that they, too, could be condemned. It pained us greatly to see such a large number of people combining to impede the efforts of the judiciary and the administration. There was even more agitation in the town of Le Cap. It seemed as if the fate of the colony depended on Lejeune's acquittal. . . .

---

4. Long used in France, breaking on the wheel involved smashing all the victim's limb bones with an iron bar.

We have a different view as to what punishment to impose and whether it should be made public. We believe that no colonist would be safe on his plantation if the slaves were not assured of the protection of the courts. They would soon turn to desperate acts, if they did not know that the law and the judiciary were watching out for their safety. If they believed that society denies them justice, they would take it into their own hands. And we know how many means our domestic enemies can use to carry out secret revenge. . . .

Lejeune's response (March 1788)

There is not a single colonist who has not been alarmed at the bold action of my slaves, who does not fear that another such event will cause a violent outburst, and who does not shudder at the thought of my slaves' winning the case. The possible consequences are enormous. . . . My cause in this case is the cause of every colonist. . . . The unhappy condition of the slave leads him naturally to hate us. It is only by force and violence that he can be controlled. . . . It is not fear of the law, or its justice, that keeps the slave from stabbing his owner; it is his awareness of the master's absolute power over him. If you remove this restraint, there is nothing he will not dare.

Administrative report (August 1788)

The depositions and everything that followed from them were declared invalid. Messieurs Lejeune, junior and Magre, were acquitted on the charges against them. It was obvious that the public had intimidated the judges. The attorney-general then appealed, and the Superior Council [appeal court] took up the case and became the center of underhand maneuvers. . . . The punishment handed down to this murderer of four slaves is to have to show his other slaves when requested, and other similarly pointless requirements, despite the fact that the lives of human beings are at stake. The only person the appeal court found truly guilty is Monsieur de Montarand [the judge who initiated the indictment]. . . .

For one hundred years, atrocities like this have been committed with impunity. They have been carried out in front of the slaves, because it is known their evidence is not admissible. . . . Finally, after so much cruelty the courts have been unable to punish, one single case comes along in which all the proof demanded by the law is present; the guilty party himself confesses and signs his confession. Nevertheless, when the judiciary was given this unique opportunity to stop with a single example this long succession of atrocities, it decided to let it slip away and used a futile pretext to come to the aid of a ferocious master, even though slaves are frequently punished with the greatest severity on the merest suspicion.

Suppose that other planters, or Lejeune himself, continue with the murders that they have been so calmly committing. Do you think that their miserable slaves will once again turn to the law courts? . . . From now on, there will no longer be any magistrates like Monsieur de Montarand willing to take actions that will expose them to slander and for which their fellow citizens will hate them. The slaves, therefore, reduced to despair, will have no other recourse but revenge. . . .

Many colonists nowadays show moderation in their treatment of slaves, and generally speaking, slavery in this colony is less harsh than it was twenty years ago. However, there are still entire districts where the old barbarity continues at full strength. The details would make you shudder with horror.

(Archives Nationales d'Outre-Mer, Aix-en-Provence, F3/90, 197–268)

6) Racial Discrimination: Official

Although all American societies discriminated against descendants of slaves, the racial climate worsened for Saint Domingue's large and comparatively wealthy free colored community in the late eighteenth century. Restrictions, petty and important, increased. The wealthiest and lightest-complexioned, who had once received favored treatment or even passed for white, no longer could do so. At the same time, their numbers and wealth increased rapidly, creating a potentially explosive situation. Grégoire was a liberal French priest who was elected to the National Assembly at the beginning of the French Revolution and joined the Friends of the Blacks (Amis des Noirs) pressure group.

The fate of people of color, especially in Saint Domingue, is to bear all the costs of society more than do the whites, while sharing minimally in its benefits. They are victims of scorn and fear, and often of violent attacks. . . .

They alone perform service in the rural police, and they do so conscientiously. . . . Every man of color has to do picket service; that is, every six or seven weeks he has to spend an entire week at the door of a commandant or other officer with a horse always bridled and ready to run whatever errands are demanded. The unfortunate farmer is thus forced to leave his plantation to the discretion of his slaves and often, when he gets back, he finds everything neglected or turned upside down. The manual worker is condemned to lose time needed by his indigent family. He has to spend at least 48 livres during this week in order to provide and feed the horse, which sometimes ends up dead from fatigue. All this to serve the whims of a man who uses the royal service as an excuse in a country where officials and especially military officers are as all-powerful as Vizirs.[5]

---

5. Vizirs were officials of the Turkish empire, a common metaphor for despotism in this period.

These burdens are aggravated by unjust and humiliating restrictions. People of color are forbidden to work in certain professions, such as that of gold-smith, . . . doctor and surgeon. . . . Priests, notaries, and other public figures are ordered to use in their official documents the terms "free mulattoes, free qua-droons, mixed-bloods," etc. . . . to mark with disapproval and keep at a distance individuals whose crime is to have skin of a different color. They are forbidden to eat with whites. . . . People of color have been shamefully dragged away from the table of a white captain who had warmly invited them. They are forbid-den to dance after 9:00 p.m., and even for dancing they need the permission of a police magistrate. They are forbidden to wear the same material as whites. Police constables designated to enforce this decree have been stationed in public squares and at the entrance to churches, where they have pulled off the clothes of members of the fair sex leaving them nothing but their modesty to cover them.

They are forbidden to use carriages under pain of imprisonment and confisca-tion of the carriage and horses. A well respected quadroon, a merchant, was trav-eling in a carriage, when a certain Mr. Prodejac stopped him in the town of Petit Goâve and forced him to get out, saying, "Must a damn mulatto like you travel in greater comfort than me?" He accompanied the question with several blows from his cane. The matter was taken to court and the first judge condemned Prodejac to a 5,000 livres fine to be *paid to the poor*. Yet it was appealed to the Council, which threw the case out despite the most authentic proof of the crime.

They are forbidden to travel to France, and can emigrate only in secret. . . . They are excluded from all public office and employment, either in the judiciary or the military. They can no longer aspire to the rank of officer, although in general they are reckoned to be very courageous. In the militia, people are opposed to their being mixed with whites. Whatever their talent or wealth, they are not allowed to take part in parish assemblies. They are segregated in the theaters, and disdain pursues them even to church, where . . . they are assigned separate seating. . . .

The author of the *Considérations sur Saint-Domingue* (Hilliard d'Auberteuil) has argued in all seriousness that "whatever derives from whites must appear as sacred to blacks and people of color." In other words, their critical faculties must be undermined so as to control their feelings and direct them like beasts of bur-den. "Self-interest and security," he says, "demand that we overwhelm the black race with such scorn that whoever is descended from a black down to the sixth generation is covered with an ineradicable stain." He adds that, "If people of color dared to strike a white man, even if he struck them, they would be severely punished. Such is the strength of prejudice against them that, in this case, their death would not seem an excessive punishment. Such severity would perhaps be unjust but it is necessary." Good God, what morals!

(Henri-Baptiste Grégoire, *Mémoire en faveur des gens de couleur ou sang-mêlés de St.-Domingue, et des autres isles françaises de l'Amérique* [Paris, 1789], 5–11)

7) Racial Discrimination: Unofficial

This extract comes from a report by the wealthy planter Julien Raimond (1744–1801), who owned more than a hundred slaves. Three of his grandparents were white, as were his father-in-law and sons-in-law, and he married a white man's widow, but in the colonies he was classed as a quarteron *or quadroon. His discreet requests for reform presented to the colonial minister in the mid-1780s were discussed sympathetically by some officials, but the French government proved too hesitant to confront colonial prejudice. Raimond's reports marked the beginning of the free colored activism that would burgeon at the start of the French Revolution.*

If a white man desires the property of a man of color, or—can I say it, my lord, or you hear it, without disgust?—his wife or daughter, they have to be yielded to him or the white will use violence and ill treatment against the man of color. He will sometimes even be beaten in his own house and the white will get off scot-free once he utters these four words, "This mulatto disrespected me." He is always taken at his word. In Saint Domingue, you hear every day these words in the mouth of a white man: "I like this woman—or this girl—I must have her!" If someone objects there is a husband or a father, he replies, "Fine, I'll give him a hundred blows with my cane, if he wants to argue," and sometimes that happens.

A white will go to the house of a person of color and enter without even knowing the person, and there, in the presence of the husband or father, will make the most indecent comments to the woman or girl. If the man of color, who has no other recourse than to remove his wife or daughter out of earshot of such propositions, does send them away, then he is sure to be badly insulted and lucky if he is not beaten in his own house. Sometimes it is a white whose official post gives him complete control over a man of color. If the white believes that the presence of the colored man stands in the way of his desires, then he orders him to perform service that keeps him away from home. If the man of color, in a fit of jealousy or worn down with fatigue, complains, then his complaints are treated as disobedience and he is punished with a few days in prison. During his imprisonment, the white brings all manner of pressure to make the wife or daughter yield, and the husband or father is often spared only at the price of his dishonor.

Forgive me, my lord, for placing such a picture of debasement before the eyes of your lordship, but it is necessary that you know of our grievances in order to be able to grant us the justice that we are calling for today.

(Julien Raimond, "Trois mémoires," Archives Nationales
d'Outre-Mer, Aix-en-Provence, DFC/XXI/129/245)

2. SLAVE RESISTANCE

Slave revolts and conspiracies to revolt were larger and more common in the Caribbean than anywhere else in the Americas. The average plantation was larger; the imbalance between slave and free, and black and white, was exceptional. The contrast with North America is especially striking. It is therefore paradoxical that the colony that produced the largest of all American slave rebellions had previously experienced, by Caribbean standards, relatively few revolts or conspiracies. While further research may yet uncover more examples, this raises questions about the causes of rebellions and how different types of resistance were related.

Slaves struck back against their enslavement in a wide variety of ways. Scholarly attempts to categorize them have resulted in various models that seek to distinguish political from apolitical acts, overt from covert, individual from collective, and the day-to-day from the exceptional. Others have contrasted self-enhancing acts like escape, sabotage, or feigning illness, and self-destructive acts such as suicide and self-mutilation. At the nonviolent end of the spectrum we find slaves' mocking of authority figures, which provided a safe mode of self-assertion and expressing grievance that was widely attested in American slave societies (doc. 8). Some slaveowners complained that urban environments encouraged slaves to be "insolent," and that urban slaves were allowed too much independence (doc. 9). Only 4 percent of Saint Domingue's slaves lived in towns or villages, but the urban markets attracted thousands from the countryside every Sunday providing cover for clandestine meetings and the elaboration of an independent culture.

Fear of poisoning reached epidemic proportions in northern Saint Domingue during the twenty years after the trial in 1758 of the sorcerer François Macandal, whose legend grew steadily after his execution (doc. 10). However, not all colonists were caught up in the paranoia. Some mocked the idea that every slave had knowledge of herbal poisons and claimed that, while a few obtained arsenic from apothecaries' shops, it was used for private vengeance among slaves more than against whites. By the 1780s white opinion more readily accepted tropical disease as the cause of sickness and death, and that torturing suspects was not a reliable tool of investigation.

Just as sorcery, the claim to directly manipulate supernatural forces, sometimes overlapped with poisoning, it also partially overlapped the religious practices that have come to be known as Vodou (docs. 11, 12, 13). Modern Vodou blends different African traditions, new ones established in Saint Domingue, and a small admixture of Christianity. It is usually thought to have contributed to the revolution by uniting different ethnic groups, by providing leadership and grassroots organization, and encouraging the belief that amulets (magic charms) could protect believers from their masters and therefore in battle. At the very least, it brought together slaves from different plantations and different backgrounds, as did the Sunday markets. If it was an intrinsically revolutionary force is less clear. Whereas Moreau de Saint-Méry, writing in the 1780s, only expressed foreboding as to its potential (doc. 11), Drouin de Bercy wrote with the benefit of hindsight after the revolution (doc. 12). Both authors noted the recent emergence of the violent Petro branch of Vodou that probably reflected the growing influence in the slave population of Kongolese culture from West-Central Africa (doc. 13).

Work strikes by slaves have received little attention from historians. It is not clear how common they were in Saint Domingue, but there seems to have been an upsurge in the North Plain in reaction to the government's attempt to implement protective reforms in the mid-1780s (doc. 14). Like the judicial activism associated with the Lejeune case (doc. 5), the reforms and the colonial hostility they provoked may help explain why in 1791 the slaves revolted in the name of the king.

Strikes took the form of collective "maroonage," a term coined to describe the activities of fugitive slaves, of whom the great majority fled singly, not in groups. European and Caribbean scholars have tended to disagree about the dimensions and significance of maroonage. The former depict it as a minor irritant to planters, a safety-valve within the system, not a threat to it. The latter present maroonage as a war against slavery, and emphasize the formation of armed bands that attacked plantations. This, however, was very rare and only a small part of the phenomenon. The correspondence excerpted here comes from a new plantation that witnessed a high rate of maroonage (doc. 15).

Saint Domingue's size and low population density favored maroonage, as did the proximity of even more sparsely settled Santo Domingo, the neighboring Spanish colony. The spread of coffee cultivation in the mountains after 1760, however, and an extradition treaty signed with the Spanish in 1777, began to reduce opportunities for fugitives. The most acculturated and those with marketable skills aimed to pass for free in the towns. The relationship between maroonage and the Haitian Revolution is controversial. A Haitian nationalist tradition claims a prominent role for maroons and Vodou priests in the slave revolution but has generally failed to substantiate its claims. Yet a few linkages can be demonstrated. Loulou, the turbulent slave driver (docs. 15, 16), later shows up in 1792 as an officer in the insurgent army of Jean-François. And the newspaper advertisements that are a major source for studying maroonage also reveal that Jean-François himself, as well as his Fulani companion Charlotte (respectively, the dashing coachman and lady's maid of the Papillon family), both enjoyed a successful career as maroons on the eve of the revolution (doc. 16).

8) Satirical Song

These contrasting evocations of work songs that employed a typically African call-and-response structure suggest how singing enhanced community solidarity while voicing discontent in different ways. They come, respectively, from a sugar planter and a coffee planter. The second description, which is perhaps sugges-tive of a proto-blues, concerns African slaves working on mountain plantations. In the first, the workforce is apparently creolized. Such improvised songs would readily adopt new content during the revolution (docs. 82, 85, 86).

A Negro singer faced a line of field slaves and sang songs that he improvised on the spot; the slaves answered in a chorus, and many with excellent pitch. The singer mixed in jokes, and all the line broke out laughing without stopping work. When I went to see them, I was an inexhaustible source of songs, in which they mixed praise and requests for things they wanted. They sang about those known as good masters, and didn't spare the reputation of those who passed for too severe. They had a refrain, repeated on all the plantations: "Happy as a slave on Galliffet."[1]

(Comte de Vaublanc, *Souvenirs* [Paris, 1838], 1:177)

The unhappy wretch normally maintains a mournful silence; or if he gives in to his natural and dominant predilection for singing, it is only to express his pain in melancholy airs. The words, in an unknown language, are an obscure enigma for the master who does not understand the curses they contain, but for his companions, who share the same feelings that move him, they are only too easy to understand. They reply with sad refrains, repeating as an echo plaintive and lugubrious sounds.

([Jean-Baptiste Laplace], *Histoire des désastres de Saint-Domingue* [Paris, 1795], 88)

9) Urban Slave Culture: Report of the Chamber of Agriculture (1785)

The planters of this government advisory body complained that urban life encouraged insubordination. Two-thirds of Cap Français' 15,000 inhabitants

---

1. The large and imposing Galliffet plantations in the middle of the North Plain would later be at the center of the 1791 slave revolt (docs. 35, 36).

were slaves, and the Sunday market brought in another 15,000 from the coun-tryside every week. Many town slaves had little contact with their owners, and they sometimes socialized in large numbers. In view of the use of royalist ideol-ogy in the slave uprising of 1791–1793, the reference to the king here is very interesting. However, although the anonymity of urban environments gave slaves opportunities to conspire, the concentration of whites in towns made urban revolts extremely rare in the Americas. The slave revolution of 1791–1793 would remain almost entirely rural.

The Negroes are so open in their insubordination that the line of demarca-tion between whites and slaves has almost vanished. What remains of it appears when one journeys away from the capital,[2] which sooner or later is going to cause ever greater problems between discipline-loving planters and their work-forces. Controlling them nowadays requires more technique, subtlety, and cau-tion [than before]. . . . The Chamber dares to predict there will be serious events that will change the face of things if . . . the minister does not give the most prompt orders to put an end to this evil. . . .

Such good intentions, however, will be useless if the Negroes are not brought under control in the towns and villages whence the evil is spreading bit by bit, and if we tolerate their nightly gatherings and gambling dens, their nocturnal dances, associations, and brotherhoods . . . and if the town of Le Cap continues to conceal quick-witted fugitive slaves . . . who obtain lodgings from ship cap-tains and many town residents, which is an enormous abuse. . . . There are in the town 2,000 slaves who pay their masters a certain sum every day, week, or month . . . but do not see their masters for two or three months. . . . They rent rooms where they please, where they can commit the worst excesses. . . . All the slaves are thieves and receivers of stolen goods.

Let us list some of the acts of insolence that will perhaps better demonstrate how far the slaves push their disobedience. . . . Monsieur Dufour, walking along Rue Espagnole at five o'clock in the evening, found his way blocked by a group of blacks. He had a lady on his arm. As none of them thought it his duty to step aside, he said to them, "Let Madam pass." One of them replied, "M—r F—r, if it was one hour later, you wouldn't dare say anything. You'd step aside your-self." . . . On Rue Royale, a man told a group of Negroes making a noise in front of his house to go away. He received the reply, "The street doesn't belong to you; it belongs to the king!" He went to raise his cane, and they threw a large stone at him just missing his chin. . . . Seeing a slave woman pass by who had just been whipped in the jail, one of M. Fouché's slaves, shouted out, "Well now! Isn't it right that slaves should kill whites? Just look what they did to this woman!"

---

2. Port-au-Prince was the administrative capital, but the writers are referring to Cap Français, Saint-Domingue's largest town and main port, known as Le Cap.

Many Negroes in Le Cap never go out without a large stick, and on holidays you find 2,000 of them gathered at La Providence, La Fossette, and Petit Caré-nage[3] all armed with sticks, drinking rum, and doing the kalinda.[4] The police do nothing to prevent these parties, and they never end without quarrels and fighting.

(Archives Nationales d'Outre-Mer, Aix-en-Provence, F3/126, 408–10)

10) Macandal the Poisoner

François Macandal was a charismatic sorcerer who sold magic charms and poisons in part of the North Province and remained a fugitive for many years. His name derives from a Kongo word for an amulet or magic charm. This account from the 1780s shows how he became a legend after his execution in 1758. As many colonists confused epidemic disease with poison, and poison with sorcery, and as they used torture to gather evidence, the true extent of Macandal's activities is unclear. What is perhaps most important about him is that, by 1789, he had already become a mythical figure, credited by whites with a colony-wide conspiracy and remembered by slaves for his supernatural powers and for outwitting the slaveowners.

The Negro Macandal, born in Africa, belonged to the Lenormand de Mézy plantation in Limbé. His hand had to be cut off after it got caught in the mill, and he was made a stockman. He then became a fugitive. After running away, he became famous for his use of poison, which spread terror among the blacks and made all of them obey him. He taught this hateful art to many others and had agents all over the colony. At the slightest sign from him, people died. Finally, as part of a vast plan, he conceived the hellish project of eliminating everyone in Saint Domingue who was not black. His steadily increasing success caused a panic that made success all the more likely. Neither the vigilance of the judges or that of the government proved able to bring about the scoundrel's capture. . . .

One day, the Dufresne plantation slaves in Limbé held a large dance. Macandal, long used to impunity, came and mingled [and got drunk. Denounced by a slave] he was arrested in a slave hut. . . . On 20 January 1758, the Cap Council

---

3. Districts on the outskirts of Cap Français.

4. A dance associated in some parts of the Caribbean with stick-fighting contests. These cudgels, sometimes fitted with metal studs and hollowed to contain magic powders, were associated with secret societies in Africa and Saint Domingue. They had been banned since 1758.

condemned him to be burned alive. As he had several times boasted that, if the whites captured him, he would escape from them in different forms, he declared he would assume the form of a fly to escape the flames. As chance would have it, the stake to which he was chained was rotten, and his violent movements, provoked by the torture of the flames, pulled out the metal ring and he tumbled out of the fire. The blacks cried out, "Macandal saved!" There was an incredible panic and all the gates were closed. The detachment of guards around the place of execution cleared the square. . . . He was tied to a plank and thrown back into the fire. Although Macandal's body was burned, many blacks believe, even today, that the execution did not kill him.

(Médéric-Louis-Élie Moreau de Saint-Méry, *Description topographique . . . de Saint-Domingue* [Philadelphia, 1797–1798], 1:651–53)

11) Vodou and Petro

Our earliest description of Haitian Vodou, penned in the 1780s, comes from the colonial lawyer Moreau de Saint-Méry. His account brings out various aspects of the religion, including its functioning as a benevolent society, but stresses its potential danger for the colonists. Although recognizing Vodou's syncretic nature, he connected it in particular with the "Arada" (Aja-Fon, who live in modern Togo and Benin) and the snake cult of the town of Whydah, still in existence today.[5] Moreau also noted the later appearance of "Don Pèdre," the violent and antisocial branch of Vodou nowadays known as Petro. He showed less interest in Vodou's relation with medicine.

According to the Arada Negroes, who are the true followers of Vodou in the colony and guardians of its rules and principles, Vodou means an all-powerful, supernatural being that controls everything that happens on earth. This being is the nonpoisonous snake. . . . This snake possesses knowledge of the past, present, and future. Yet it agrees to share its power. It makes its wishes known only through a high priest chosen by its followers and more particularly through a Negress whom the priest's love has raised to the rank of high priestess. These two ministers, who claim to be inspired by the god, . . . decide if the snake accepts a candidate's admission into the group, and they lay down the duties . . . the candidate must fulfill. They also receive presents and offerings the god expects

---

5. Live snakes ceased to be used in Haitian Vodou around the end of the nineteenth century.

in due homage. To disobey them is to resist the god itself and to risk the greatest misfortune. . . .

On selected days the Vodou king and queen preside over meetings following African practices, to which creole custom has added several variants and certain features that reveal European influence. . . . The real Vodou meetings, those that have lost least of their original purity, are held only in secret beneath the cover of night. . . . On each occasion, the king and queen administer an oath of secrecy that is the key element of the association. To make it the more imposing, it is accompanied by the most horrible things a deranged mind can dream up. . . . Each member, according to his needs and his seniority in the association, comes forward to put requests to the Vodou. Most ask for the ability to influence their master's mind. . . . Some seek more money; others want the gift of attracting a woman who is uninterested in them, or recovery from an illness, or a long life, or to win back an unfaithful mistress. . . . Requests represent every conceivable passion, and those with criminal ends are not always well disguised.

The Vodou king meditates upon each invocation until the spirit acts in him. Suddenly, he takes down the box containing the snake and has the Vodou queen stand on it. As soon as the sacred abode is beneath her feet . . . she is penetrated by the god. She trembles, her whole body goes into a convulsive state, and the oracle speaks through her mouth. . . . According to her wishes, her self-interest, and caprice, she issues in the name of the snake, like laws with no appeal, whatever orders it pleases her to make to the assembled idiots . . . who invariably obey what is prescribed to them. . . . Afterwards . . . offerings are made . . . which pay for the expenses of the meeting, and provide assistance to present or absent members who are in need. . . .

After that, the Vodou dance begins. . . . The agitation goes from one to another round the circle, and everyone begins to move as if their shoulders, head, and upper body seem to be dislocated. . . . The madness goes on increasing, stimulated by the consumption of alcohol. . . . Some pass out; others go into a sort of rage; but all exhibit a sort of nervous trembling they appear unable to control, turning round and round. . . . [T]his sort of magnetism [has caused] whites found spying on the sect's secret practices and who were touched by the member that discovered them to sometimes begin dancing and agree to pay the Vodou queen to put an end to this punishment. However, . . . no member of the police force, which has declared war on Vodou, has ever felt the compulsion to dance, which would no doubt have kept the dancers from having to flee.

Perhaps to allay the fears this mysterious Vodou cult causes in the colony, a show is made of dancing it in public to the sound of drums and handclapping. It is even followed with a meal at which only poultry is eaten. But I can assure you this is only another ruse to mislead the vigilance of the magistrates and to better secure the success of these sinister meetings. They are not for amusement and pleasure but rather a school where weak minds give themselves over to a domination that in a thousand ways could prove to be fatal. . . . Nothing is more dangerous than this Vodou cult, which is founded upon the idea that those adorned with the title of ministers of this being know and can do everything. It is ridiculous but a potentially terrible weapon.

Who would believe that Vodou is surpassed by another phenomenon that also has been labeled a dance? In 1768, a Negro of Spanish origin from Petit Goâve, taking advantage of the gullibility of the Negroes with his superstitious practices, gave them the idea for a dance similar to Vodou but with faster movements. To make it even more effective, the Negroes put well crushed gunpowder in the rum they drink when dancing. Called Don Pèdre's Dance, or simply the Don Pèdre, it has been known to kill Negroes. Even spectators, electrified by the convulsive spectacle, share the intoxication of the performers and bring on by their singing and rapid rhythm a crisis that in some degree affects both groups. It has been necessary to ban the Don Pèdre dance, imposing penalties that are severe but sometimes without effect.

> (Médéric-Louis-Élie Moreau de Saint-Méry, *Description topographique . . .*
> *de Saint-Domingue* [Philadelphia, 1797–1798], 1:46–51)

12) Vodou and the Underworld

In this planter's attempts to identify social types linked to criminal activities, we again glimpse the two dominant sects of modern Vodou, the Kongo-influenced Petro and the West African Rada. Drouin de Bercy's sensationalized description of an initiation ceremony has much in common with that of Moreau de Saint-Méry and also with later studies of Central African secret societies, whose offshoots are still found in Haiti.

The Caprelata is a good-for-nothing who goes from plantation to plantation and never works. He pretends to be a sorcerer and sells the blacks amulets and fetishes that he assures them will let them do anything without being caught or punished or even hit by bullets. He wears on his body and head twenty or so little tails decorated with feathers and birds' feet, glass beads, grains, and shells.

The Don Pedro is a Negro that goes around the plantations at night to see his women. Not satisfied with stealing vegetables, poultry, and sheep, he carries off horses and sometimes little black boys. He is lazy, argumentative, and a bold-faced liar. He wears a couple of tails on his head and a long lock of hair on each side of the face.[6] He usually carries a large stick or a large whip called an *arceau*.[7] Postillions,[8] carters, and stockmen are generally Don Pedros.

The Vodou is the most dangerous of all the Negroes. He works only when he has to; he is a thief, liar, and hypocrite. He gives the blacks bad advice and also subtle poisons with which they secretly kill livestock, poultry, and whites and Negroes they don't like. Gatekeepers, the watchmen on provision grounds, gardens, and canefields, and a great number of old Negroes are Vodou. In their huts, they always have different poisons kept in coconut shells or calabashes.[9] The Don Pedro and the Vodou constitute a combination that is all the more terrible in that its aim is the ruin and destruction of the whites and to persuade the Negroes they will never be happy unless they join. To be a Don Pedro, one must be a good pickpocket, bold-faced, stubborn, and hardened to blows, and must never reveal what happens at their meetings.

When the brotherhood believes there is nothing to fear from the weakness, cowardice, or indiscretion of a Negro who wants to become a Vodou, it informs the king of the organization. The member elect is then put through a month of tests. If he proves by his skill in larceny, his patience, his firmness, and his ability to stand being beaten that nothing can get him to tell its secrets, he is taken blindfolded into its inner sanctum. Once he kneels down, his blindfold is taken off. All around him he sees Negroes armed or decked out in a frightening manner, and in the middle of the chamber a large cloth on which there are scattered birds' claws, feathers, and bloodstains.

An appalling noise announces the arrival of the Vodou king, who emerges from under the cloth carrying in one hand a burning ember and in the other a dagger. He asks the neophyte in a ferocious voice what he wants. "I wish," he says, "to kiss the sacred serpent and to receive from the Vodou queen her orders and her poisons." To test him, the king sticks the point of his dagger into his arm and into the fat of his thigh, which he then touches with the burning ember. If the Negro complains or grimaces, he is killed on the spot. If he doesn't raise an eyebrow, the armed blacks then lead him into a spacious room with a curtain at one end and in the middle a large *Bamboula* or drum, four feet high, decorated with ribbons, leaves, and fetishes.

The neophyte crosses the room on his knees and elbows between two rows of Negro men and women. On reaching the curtain, he makes an offering of the poultry and vegetables he has stolen. The curtain is immediately raised, and he sees on a throne the Vodou king ready to pierce him with an arrow, and next to

---

6. Although presumably dreadlocks, such *cadenettes* were also a military fashion found in certain French regiments at this time.

7. Perhaps a confusion with the *asson*, the ceremonial rattle of the modern Vodou priest.

8. A type of coachman.

9. Containers made from gourds that have been hollowed out and dried.

him the queen, who is holding back the deadly weapon. As soon as his offering is made, the snake is wrapped around his body. He kisses it and then receives the orders and poisons of the queen to destroy in the next two or three months his [or: her] enemies and their animals.

Seven naked Negroes with leaves around their loins, feathers on their heads, and glass beads around their wrists take him and lead him to the sacred drum. They arm him with a stick similar to their own, and make him drink an intoxicating potion made of blood, gunpowder, and rum. After this, they sing and repeat in a chorus the following words, which they begin and end by hitting the Bamboula with a stick.

"A ia bombaia bombé, lamma samana quana, e van vanta, vana docki," which means, "We swear to destroy the whites and everything they possess. Let us die rather than renounce our oath."[10]

After the oath the men and women start to dance completely naked and drinking rum. The scene thereafter becomes nothing but an indecent orgy, with members of the opposite sex intertwined in each other's arms.

(Louis Marie César Auguste Drouin de Bercy, *De Saint-Domingue*
[Paris, 1814], 175–78)

13) Prophet or Crook? The Real Don Pedro

These letters by the judge of Petit Goâve parish reveal that the original Don Pedro was not a freedman but probably a maroon slave, and that Moreau de Saint-Méry (doc. 11) was mistaken in thinking he was Spanish rather than African. Due to Portuguese influence in Africa, Pedro was quite a common name among Kongolese, both for African kings and Caribbean slaves. Significantly, the author uses the Portuguese "Dom" not the Spanish "Don." Petit Goâve lies west of Port-au-Prince on Haiti's southern peninsula.

(1 May 1769.) In June/July 1768 and on into 1769, [I] carried out the very extensive investigation for the criminal case against the infamous black slave Pierre, of the Congo nation, who called himself Dom Pedro, and his adherents and accomplices to the number of forty-two imprisoned Negroes, mulattoes,

---

10. In the Kikongo language, the words in fact roughly translate as, "Oh honored Mbumba [rainbow snake deity], oh Mbumba! Seize, carry off, take by force. Yes! Kill, crush that witch!"

and Negresses. The Negro Dom Pedro was extremely dangerous. He went from plantation to plantation dominating the minds of the blacks by means of performing crude tricks. He informed them that they would soon be free, and he had the slave drivers of each plantation whipped, telling them that they could no longer flog the slaves in their charge and, moreover, that they would not be punished by their masters. He demanded tribute in either money or animals from initiated or compliant slaves, and he imposed it on those who did not remain loyal to him. This investigation involved some 300 documents, and it was brought to an end in February by order of the Council, because the Negro Dom Pedro had been killed in a hunt.

(15 October 1773.) [The jails of Petit Goâve were full of] the accomplices of a black slave calling himself Dompèdre who stirred up the workforces of the north and south coasts [of the southern peninsula] inciting them to rebellion and to be independent of their masters.

(Archives Nationales d'Outre-Mer, Aix-en-Provence, E 182, Ferrand de Beaudière to the Naval and Colonial Minister)

14) Slaves on Strike

(a) Like their free counterparts, enslaved workers sometimes withdrew their labor to bargain for better conditions. Such strikes usually took the form of a temporary, collective maroonage. Historians have yet to show how common or widespread this was, but there were many cases in Saint Domingue's North Plain during the 1780s. Although slavery was always a contest of wills, colonists tended to blame this self-assertion by slaves on new French government reforms (decrees of 4 December 1784 and 23 December 1786) that undermined the authority of plantation personnel by allowing slaves to denounce abuses to royal officials. In the first extract, we hear the voices of a plantation manager and the merchant-attorneys who employed him.

3 June 1785. Morange to Foäche[11]

What I predicted to you regarding the [Cabeuil plantation workforce] has just come about. The manager, Ducrot, . . . went to the fields yesterday morning to see the slaves at work. . . . Not finding them in the place they were meant to

---

11. Morange and Lefebvre (mentioned later in the letter) were partners in Stanislas Foäche's merchant house in Cap Français, which acted as attorney for several plantations, overseeing their operation on behalf of their owners living in France.

be, he went looking for them and . . . came across them committing depreda-
tions in a field of sweet potatoes. . . . He went up to them and seized one, whom
he had whipped. . . . The others took off. . . . An express messenger has just this
moment arrived from Ducrot with the letter of which I'm sending you a copy.
You can send it to Mr. Cabeuil if you think it appropriate. We won't write to
him for fear of alarming him. It's the decree [of 4 December 1784] that has made
them talk like this. They hadn't complained about Mr. Ducrot before. It's true he
controls them more by fear than by affection.

4 June 1785. Ducrot, manager of the Cabeuil estate, to Morange & Co.

A great deal of disorder continues to reign on the plantation. It would be
hard for me to guess the cause of it, which means I can't tell you what it is. All
I've been able to understand is that you can no longer compel them to keep a
manager who doesn't suit them, and that they were going to act so as to force
you to put me out like a dog (to use their expression). They say I thought only
about work and that I never gave them good food, neither meat nor codfish,
believing that that depended on me. To put their project into effect, they have
just pulled off a coup. As soon as harvesting was finished in field no. 9, they all
disappeared, on the pretext that I had had the bell rung too early, at 11:30 a.m.
Twenty-five still went to the field that afternoon, but the next morning most
of them followed the others, and that without my even looking at them, since
I deliberately did not go to the fields. I would be very grateful if Mr. Lefebvre
came and put a stop to all this. At first, I thought they would go and seek you
out. That's why I let a whole day go by. But after seeing them in the canes, it's
now quite clear they have no intention of going to see you. They surely don't
dare, as they are in the wrong. You would do me a great favor, gentlemen, if you
could come immediately. Your presence here would be a great help. Yesterday
evening I arrested a slave woman and the number one slave driver, who was in
the group that started all this. He is awaiting your sentence. It is fortunate that
this is happening at a time when there is very little to do. Don't worry about it.
It is you who will decide what happens.

8 June 1785. Lefebvre [on the plantation] to Morange, etc.

I've been busier than I expected. For four days, I haven't stopped for a second
and I haven't slept with worry. Since Monday I've been with the rural mounted
police. We have caught fifty or so of our people, who gave us a great deal of
trouble. There remains about twenty or so, whom I hope to get. I've just learned
that some are in jail in Fort Dauphin. I'm sending someone there straightaway.
The whole district was happy to give me a helping hand. I've handed out 500 to
600 lashes. I haven't killed anyone, but I aimed close. Have no concern, I think

all will turn out well. For the good of our other plantations, I am taking vigorous action. I am spreading the rumor that I am calling in twenty soldiers from Le Cap. Talk about it in front of the slaves but don't do anything.

9 June 1785. Morange to Foäche

Lefebvre has got back from [Cabeuil] after a lot of running around, staying up all night, and some hard knocks. He has rounded up the herd. He has punished those who were captured and pardoned those who surrendered. When he left, there were only four missing, who were expected to give themselves up. They had a grudge against Mr. Ducrot and were determined to get rid of him. Mr. Ducrot is a good manager. He knows the business of being a planter; he makes good sugar, but he doesn't like the Negro race. He is always on his guard against them, with the result that he is harsh, not in his actions but in his words. He always talks to the blacks in a harsh manner; he prefers severity to kindness, and he never talks favorably about them. In addition, he has done them a few small injustices, which we have corrected as best we could without compromising him, but unluckily for him the slaves have noticed. Mr. Lefebvre has given him some advice.

25 December 1785. Morange to Foäche

Ducrot is going to leave, because he dislikes the [new] attorney; unlike us he is a Negro-spoiler.

(Archives Nationales, Paris, 505 Mi 86)

(b) The following are notes taken by a wealthy absentee planter in France, the marquis de Galliffet, that summarize the letters he received from his plantation attorney in the North Plain. They show that the whites' concerns of 1785 were still present in 1789, and they are especially interesting because the 1791 insurrection would begin with an attempt to kill the manager of Galliffet's La Gossette estate (docs. 35, 36). Ending, on what would become Bastille Day, with a curious mixture of jottings, the notes pose the question of whether a new proto-revolutionary spirit was developing on the eve of the French Revolution.

16 May 1785

All the slaves of the Lombard plantation have marooned, claiming that the decree allowed them to choose their manager. The rural police have brought them back. Verret was nearly stabbed by one of his slave artisans; he parried the blow. [The slave] has just been executed. . . . The Le Cap Council has refused to register the decree; it has influenced the slaves, and it has been necessary to hand out punishments. On the Mentor plantation in Plaine du Nord the slaves refused to do the night-shift, but the attorney's firmness has restored order. Punishments were needed on my own plantations. A slave waved his fist under the steward's nose telling him he was not able to punish him; he had injured a mule, for which they are whipped. He was put in the dungeon, given fifty lashes, and was branded, which greatly humiliates creoles. The next day his father went and saw Mr. de Court [the parish commandant], who wrote back saying to pardon him. [The attorney] found this very trying, and he thought it a result of the decree.

13 October 1785

All the Chastenoy slaves went and complained to the vicomte de Choiseuil. This escapade is all the more astonishing, as they were thought to be a good workforce. The decree has also caused forty elite slaves of the Walsh estate to leave for two months . . . although the attorney says it was due to his sending the head cooper into the fields.[12]

22 June 1789

The 1784 decree is fatal to discipline and causes insurrections in part of our province. The Montaigue plantation was without its workforce for four months; it came back only after the steward was dismissed. Mr. Dumesnil gave his plantation to the manager who had worked as an assistant to Mr. Bayon. The slaves gathered together and, in the most insolent tone, said they didn't want him. Dumesnil . . . went off leaving things to work themselves out. A month ago all the Choiseuil escapees went to the vicomte de Choiseuil complaining of overwork. The viscount gave them a letter to the attorney, who was obliged to pardon them. . . . One could fill a book with examples of these sorts of disturbances that they are experiencing. What convinces [my attorney] that the workforces are not what they used to be is the maroonage on May 21 of twenty-three of my own slaves, some of them creoles, on La Gossette. Suspecting they've not gone far, he told the workforce it would have to work every Sunday until they were brought back. . . . After four days without news, he put the slave driver in the dungeon, telling him that he would stay there until their return, as he should have been aware of everything that went on. . . . They asked Mr. de Montalet to request they be pardoned. It was on condition that they would be branded and work as many Sundays as days they had been absent, and they headed back to La Gossette. The first driver has been whipped for not putting an end to the disorder. He said the second driver was unhappy with the manager and encouraged the slaves to flee so as to get him sacked. He has been given a hundred lashes.

---

12. Enslaved artisans—coopers were barrel makers—and domestic servants thought it humiliating to do the work of field slaves, just as creole (locally born) slaves were humiliated by being branded like imported Africans.

14 July 1789

The maroon Negroes of La Gossette have received their punishment and order has been restored. Fear concerning the influence of what the slaves said. The new Negroes are doing well. Drought. A diseased mule has been found and must be put down.

(Archives Nationales, Paris, 107 AP 128, Galliffet notebook)

15) Day-to-Day Resistance on a Mountain Plantation

About one hundred slaves worked on Marie Joubert's new coffee plantation in the remote northeastern mountains. Born in Saint Domingue, she was a widow in her mid-twenties with a small child. She was assisted by a white manager, Jamet, and a few artisans. Several of her slaves frequently ran off or stole food. They were badly fed and recently had been uprooted from the densely populated plain, where they had lived on an unproductive estate whose owner had died. They resented the change. Mme. Joubert's letters to her fiancé in Le Cap describe the ritual of requesting pardon that often mediated this constant struggle. Besides handing out harsh punishment, she depended on the help of planter neighbors and of her own and others' slaves to capture and return fugitives. Ironically, the domineering slave driver, Loulou, whom she needed to control her workforce, was also one of the most incorrigible offenders (doc. 16).

(18 November or December 1787) Azor ran away yesterday morning. But the same evening, they brought him back to me from the warehouse, where he had gone to rest until he could make it to Caracole. He has been given a good tanning. I sent someone to Mr. Monnier to look for a collar. They sent me a chain. Mr. Jamet yoked him together with Cassan. The slaves are alarmed and begin to work a bit better. Up to now, they were very discontented being made to sort [coffee beans] in the evenings. . . . Azor and Cassan are still chained up. I saw them today. I cannot express how that sight affected me. But I am determined to leave them like that. These slaves are such rascals. You wouldn't believe, my dear friend, how they trade everything in the village: hoes, billhooks, shirts, boilers, and even our chamber pots that Azor was going to sell. That rascal sold the shirts I gave to Cassan. Or rather, François did. They are accusing each other.

(26 December 1787) Antoine brought Jacquot back. He and his companion got their spanking this morning. Jean-Louis has been put in chains in place of Cassan. As Jacquot came back, he got off with a whipping. Mr. de Pondegault

asked me to pardon Jean-Louis and thought it would have brought back the others. Mr. Jamet wanted to make an example of him, so I didn't insist. I am, however, angry that it is not that rascal Clément we're chaining up. It is he who has corrupted the others, as they admitted. We must keep up the pursuit to try to get him back. He swore he would rather have his head cut off than come back. Jean-Louis has been told that we won't take his shackles off until Clément and one more come back. He has to help us find them; it is in his interest. . . .

I forgot to ask you by the last mail for a piece of cloth for the slaves' New Year's gifts. I'll offer it only to those I am satisfied with. That will make a great impression on them. Marie is still serving me with considerable ill-will. She is angry at seeing her brother in chains. I told her today that, at the first cause for dissatisfaction she gives me, I'll have her head shaved and make her wear a shirt and skirt made of [illegible]. You can't imagine how she is afraid of that. She can't believe I'm serious, but she will be convinced, if she has occasion to merit it.

(3 January 1788) I am going to tell you news that will sadden you as much as I. This evening my good friend Mr. de Pondegault sent me back Clément, Sénégal, and Loulou. Maybe you think that I have the latter in the stocks. No, I don't have that pleasure. He has escaped! I am going to try and tell you about it. However, I haven't yet recovered from the trouble and the fright that this wretch gave me. He came in with only Michel, who was already trembling, and his two companions. He tried to apologize for his running away by telling me that it was Mr. Comte's fault. Finally, he swore and promised me he was a decent man and he would serve me well from now on. All of that in the most persuasive tone, a knife in the only good hand that he has left. He lost a finger of the other hand at Mr. Pondegault's on New Year's day. I noticed it. I took his knife away, very bravely. When he heard the chains, he put his hand on a machete he had. I asked him for it, and he didn't dare refuse me. Then, he threw himself at my feet. Right when Mr. Jamet was putting the collar on Sénégal, and when Mr. Jamet said to take him—vain words! —he made just one jump and he bounded all the way down the hill. We didn't know what happened to him. Even if our slaves had seen him, they wouldn't have dared to catch him. He scares them terribly. And they all have noticed that it is his right arm he can still use.

You can't imagine the trouble that this escape caused me. I am sending Paul after him. He is in such a state that he can't go very far. He doesn't have his weapons any more. Perhaps we'll find him. I am still trembling. The sight of this armed rascal in my house gave me a surprise and a fright that are hard to express. I have trembled for more than an hour. I think Mr. Jamet was more afraid than me. He said he wanted to begin with Clément because he thought he was the craftiest of them. But I rather think he had seen the machete and the knife and that Loulou's air of despair ended up scaring him. I am still surprised by the courage I had. A woman disarming a rascal! Did you think I was that brave? But don't let's joke. It is a serious matter, very serious. I will feel at ease only when I know he's in the royal chain-gang. I wouldn't like at any price to keep the wretch here.

(8 January 1788) Mr. Jamet left on Sunday morning and at ten o'clock I caught Loulou in Jeanne's cabin. He is chained up, although I don't think he has either the means or the will to run away. I did it to punish him. He is really humiliated. I hope his wound won't have unfortunate consequences. Antoine has come back. I'll give him his pardon providing he behaves properly. But if he pulls any tricks, he will pay for everything in one go. Pompée doesn't want to give himself up. I think your return will bring him back. If he is a long time coming, I will send Antoine not to look for him but to catch him.

(9 January 1788) The poor devil has Monnier's thick chain around his neck and he is in the stocks. His finger is very painful. However, there is no risk of an accident. Antoine came back. I gave him his pardon. The idiot was led astray by the others. Now, Pompée is the only one who is still missing. I'll send old Antoine to catch him one of these days. . . . Though Loulou has behaved like a scoundrel, Mr. Jamet thinks we should make him slave driver again. We'll do that when Jamet comes back. I will have someone ask for his pardon. We absolutely need a driver, and he is well suited for it. The fear he inspires in the whole workforce will be very useful to us. Besides, who here could give him orders? I am beginning to believe that Mr. Le Comte is the cause of his running away. He has paid for it with a finger and a chain, and that's enough. He is very humiliated, and he cried when I chained him up. He was shaking and sweating like a man with the shivers. I assure you that upset me a lot. He feared there would be even more, but the medical attention I gave him reassured him. As for Jeanne, she daren't look at me. However, I said nothing to her, though I am sure it wasn't the first night that Loulou spent in her cabin.

(16 January 1788) Loulou surprised rather than frightened me. You told me that nobody dared arrest him in Maribaroux. That is the only reason that made me take away his machete and his knife, which he meant to use for scaring my slaves. That's all. I fear these people so little that I would have put the chain around his neck, even if he was still armed. Believe me, the white race has a real ascendancy over them. The poor devil is still chained up and very submissive. He strongly denies having been with Robert. He says he was coming to give himself up when he was injured, and that he didn't mean to be disrespectful when he approached me with his machete. He says, however, that he feels he deserves to be punished and that he patiently awaits whatever I would like to do with him. I told him that he won't be whipped. Victoire must have told her mother to go and beg Mr. Monnier to ask his pardon.[13] I will give in with a

---

13. It was customary for fugitive slaves to ask white neighbors to intercede on their behalf to facilitate their return.

lot of difficulty. So, when Mr. Jamet comes back, I will make him slave driver again. He is the only one on whom we can count. I will give him some linen and provide him with food from the big house. We must try to win his loyalty with our kindness. People of his color[14] usually respond better to it than to punishment.

I thought I told you that I forgave Jean-Louis and Azor on New Year's day. The whole workforce came and requested it on bended knee. I was happier to give it than they were to receive it. However, he was the only one who has been really punished. Clément and Sénégal dance with their collars on. Yesterday, I had the cloth handed out. Everybody got some. Sénégal came to ask me for his pardon. I told him that it didn't depend on me but on Mr. Jamet. When he comes back, he can do what he wants. This Sénégal is a little devil; we must tame him a bit. Azor is the greatest rascal that we have. It's him who destroyed the pigeon house. Beatings have no effect on him; he is incorrigible. The evening before Mr. Jamet's departure, he got fifty lashes for having eaten three hens with Cassan. The day after, he stole a stem of bananas and got the same again. The day after, he took some of Julie's meat in the night. I have put a ball and chain on him. On Sunday, he ran away and stole a stem from Mr. Mathieu's. A few days before, he stole a stew that was just ready to serve. If we could get rid of him, it would be a good bargain. He is worth about 3,000, but only for someone who doesn't know him. We never will do anything with him here, and we would get two nice slaves in his place. . . .

My turkey cocks are dying, the young ones as well as the old ones. I am going to eat all of them. As for my hens, my slaves won't let me try. They've taken a liking to them, at least Cassan and Azor.

(23 January 1788) Jean-Baptiste has been punished rather severely. I don't think we'll need to repeat it for him to mend his ways. He went away very ashamed, protesting vehemently, and with his backside smarting a good deal. . . . I had to repair my henhouse a bit. Azor went to the trouble of emptying it.

(31 January 1788) I am giving Antoine a note this evening to go and look for Pompée. He will surely bring him back. Loulou is driver with Michel. . . . I didn't give out the pardons. Sénégal and Clément keep their collars. We just exchanged Loulou's large chain for a ball and chain. Mr. Jamet wants to tame them. I didn't object. Azor is still a rascal. He is completely slashed with whip marks. He gets a ball and chain. None of this makes him change his ways. He won't be whipped any more. It is useless. There is only one way to tame him. It is to have a mask made for him to stop him eating. Then, he will never steal.

(University of Michigan, Clements Library, Tousard
Papers, Marie Joubert to Anne-Louis Tousard)

---

14. Loulou was of mixed racial descent, a *mulâtre*.

16) Runaway Advertisements

Besides being a record of resistance, the fugitive slave advertisements that appeared in colonial newspapers also provide rare glimpses of slave life. The following eight examples suggest some of their diversity. Although Africans were less successful than creoles in avoiding recapture, the first two cases show how an enterprising few could find a place in the informal economy and remain free sometimes for a year or more. The fourth case is significant because the woman's partner, Hyacinthe, was a Vodou priest who became a local leader during the revolution. Hers is one of several cases of cross-dressing by female fugitives in these years. The two following advertisements show that Loulou the slave driver (doc. 15) persistently fled his isolated mountain plantation to the plain below before becoming caught up in the slave revolution. The last two announcements establish that Jean-François, main leader of the North Plain slave revolt (docs. 38, 39, 40), had been a maroon for several years, and that his partner, Charlotte, probably joined him a few months before the uprising. In September 1791, the exultant rebel slaves would crown them "king and queen" in the fortified camp they established on the Galliffet plantations.

(a) It was announced in the *Affiches* in November 1788 that the Negro Nerestan, Mozambique, had been missing for several months. This slave is branded across the chest VALADON, and underneath St. MARC & P. AU-PRINCE, aged twenty-eight, height, 5'8" to 5'9", very stout, quite a good-looking face, the teeth of the upper jaw filed.[15] He has a scar between the heel and calf of his right leg, and speaks French with a nasal accent. He has been seen in the meantime armed with a machete and claiming to be free. There is reason to believe he is being hidden by the slaves of several plantations in the Matheux district and receiving goods that they manage to steal from their owners, paying for them with rum that he is able to buy from several sugar plantations that set up drink shops at their gates for selling this treacherous liquor that is ruining the colony.[16] Those who may have knowledge of this slave are requested to have him arrested and to notify Mr. Bonneserre, boat-owner of L'Arcahaye, or Mr. Valadon, planter in the Matheux. There will be a reward of 4 *portugaises* [$32 U.S.].

(*Supplément aux Affiches Américaines*, 26 Dec. 1789)

---

15. Africans of several ethnic groups filed their front teeth to a point for aesthetic reasons.

16. The sugar plantations were in the plain of L'Arcahaye about 2,000 feet below the mountainous district of Les Matheux; Nerestan was trading between two ecological zones.

(b) Zamore, Congo, cook, belonging to the minor Gulleman, branded GUL-LEMAN, twenty-five to twenty-six years old, 5′9″ tall, with several of his upper front teeth broken. Ran away during the night of July 13/14 last. This slave has been seen in the Port-de-Paix region beating the drum at Negro dances. It is the job he has done since he became a maroon. Send any news of him to Messrs. Poupet bros., Guymet, and Gauvain, agents for Messrs. Mazois and Co. There will be a reward.

(*Affiches Américaines, Supplément à la Feuille du Cap Français*, 30 Dec. 1789)

(c) There was lost around July 13 last a slave of the Mondongo nation, very black, branded ARLEGUY AU F. PALMISTE, aged twenty-two to twenty-three, 5′6″ in height. He was on a schooner that at the time was sailing to Plymouth. He jumped into the sea about three leagues [around eight miles] off the coast in the strait of La Plateforme after passing the cape of Môle Saint-Nicolas. His friends say he is an excellent swimmer. If it happens that he was able to reach the shore, it is requested that those who might have knowledge of him inform Messrs. Compayre and Bayle, merchants of Le Cap, Penthièvre St. There will be a reward.

(*Affiches Américaines, Supplément à la Feuille du Cap Français*, 15 Aug. 1789)

(d) Magdelaine, creole, about twenty-nine years old, extremely black, skinny, tall, and pock-marked. Has been missing about three months, presumed to have been lured away by the slave Hyacinthe of Mr. Ducoudray, with whom she has relations. She has free relatives in Port-au-Prince and Petit-Goâve, where she is from. She is in the habit of dressing up as a man and passing herself off as free.

(*Affiches Américaines, Feuille du Port-au-Prince* [1790], no. 91)

(e) Pierre, known as Loulou, mulatto, belonging to the de Paradès inheritance, aged about twenty-four, very tall, with sores on his legs. He is known to frequent the Philibert, de Pontac, and de Vaublanc plantations in Maribaroux and Ouanaminthe.

(*Affiches Américaines, Feuille du Cap Français*, 17 Nov. 1787)

(f) Pierre, called Loulou, mulatto, aged twenty-six, 5'10" to 5'11½", formerly belonging to Monsieur de Paradès; has a little finger cut off and swollen legs, scarred from sores. This slave is very well known in Maribaroux, where several plantations have become his familiar haunts. Has been missing since 15 August 1788.

(*Affiches Américaines, Supplément à la Feuille du Cap Français*, 7 Feb. 1789)

(g) Jean-François, creole, aged about twenty-two, 5′10″ in height, slim, quite good-looking, branded[17] on the right side of the chest "RB," and above "Mr. M," with a long scar under the chin. Those who might know of his whereabouts are requested to inform Mr. Papillon, Jr., merchant in Cap Français, to whom he belongs.

(*Affiches Américaines, Feuille du Cap-François*, 3 Nov. 1787)

(h) Charlotte, Poulard [Fulani], branded PAPILLON, pretty face, black and very tall, missing for five months. It is said she has a pass and claims to be free. She often moves from one district to another; is presently thought to be in Port-au-Prince or its surroundings. She dresses like a free black woman. People who come in contact with her are requested to have her arrested and put in jail. Inform Madame Papillon at Le Cap, to whom she belongs. A reward of 2 *portugaises* [$16 U.S.] will be paid, or more if it is demanded.

(*Gazette de Saint-Domingue*, 6 Aug. 1791)

---

17. Creoles were rarely branded. These marks suggest Jean-François had run away, and been sold, twice before.

3. THE RACE AND SLAVERY QUESTIONS IN THE FRENCH NATIONAL ASSEMBLY

Although the condemnation of slavery by the philosophers of the French Enlightenment was an intellectual turning point in world history (doc. 17), a popular abolitionist movement, such as emerged in England in the 1780s, never developed in France. Moreover, few antislavery writers anywhere were prepared to justify slaves' violent self-liberation, as did Diderot's anonymous contribution to Raynal's History (doc. 17c). The Amis des Noirs (Friends of the Blacks) was France's closest equivalent to the British movement. Founded in February 1788, it was a small club of generally wealthy individuals who were inspired by recent events in England and the United States and hoped to influence government policy (doc. 18). Its central figure was the journalist Jacques-Pierre Brissot, who later became a leading politician in the French Revolution, and it came to include the liberal nobles Condorcet, Lafayette, and Mirabeau, and the radical priest Henri Grégoire. Believing that slavery should be phased out gradually, they decided to focus first on banning the slave trade from Africa. The outbreak of the French Revolution soon offered the Amis a national forum and dramatically increased the possibility for reform. For a few months after the fall of the Bastille in July 1789, anything seemed possible.

The vociferous talk of liberty and sudden collapse of ancient institutions alarmed the West Indian planters who were in Paris (doc. 19). They had imagined a revolution that would merely give a political voice to the wealthy and were shocked to hear prominent figures like the comte de Mirabeau[1] denouncing slavery. Mirabeau also mocked Saint Domingue's deputies in the National Assembly for claiming to represent the whole colony when only a small number of whites had elected them. The colonists responded by forming the Club Massiac, which became a powerful lobby for white slaveholders' interests. Its planter members joined with French merchants to publicize the colonies' economic importance to France. At year's end, news of an aborted slave rising in Martinique also helped swing opinion in a more conservative direction. These and other pressures dissuaded the French legislature from even debating slavery or the slave trade for several years.

The colonial lobby almost succeeded, too, in preventing discussion of racial equality, but they had to contend with a persistent group of free colored activists in Paris, as well as the Amis des Noirs. The National Assembly's Declaration of

---

1. Honoré Gabriel Riqueti (1749–1791), constitutional monarchist and leading orator of the early revolution.

the Rights of Man of 26 August 1789 had an immediate impact on free people of color. Although the assembly apparently gave no thought to how it might affect the colonies, the declaration caused figures like Julien Raimond (doc. 7) to move from seeking minor adjustments in the color bar to demanding full racial equality among all free men. In early September, a group of several dozen people of color in Paris formed the Société des Colons Américains. They called for the complete abolition of racial discrimination and the seating of nonwhite deputies in the National Assembly. They were soon joined by the planter Raimond and another wealthy *quarteron*, Vincent Ogé, who was in Paris for a lawsuit concerning damage to his family property (docs. 20, 21).

The free coloreds were an extremely diverse group, and they and their allies were not entirely agreed on whether they should seek political rights for all their number. Most were of both African and European descent, and some blacks in Paris complained about the initial exclusiveness of the Colons Américains. Despite their quickly including free blacks in their demands, their publications and public pronouncements continued to put special emphasis on their European ancestry, probably to appeal to a white public. In time, the new egalitarian spirit effaced the traditional colonial distinctions, although they implicitly survived in the demand of free colored and white activists for the immediate emancipation of slaves of mixed racial descent.

This demand was one of several ways in which the cause of the free people of color became embroiled with that of the slaves. Grégoire and Brissot imprudently mixed up the two in their arguments (doc. 22), and Raimond also alluded to an eventual end to slavery. The most startling example of this tactical error was Vincent Ogé's speech to the Club Massiac on the future of slavery and the risks of slave insurrection (doc. 23). Whether genuine idealism or attempted blackmail—it is unclear—Ogé did not make the mistake again. When just over a year later he led a rebellion of free people of color in Saint Domingue, he insisted that no slaves be permitted to participate. This rebellion finally forced the issue of racial discrimination on to the agenda of the French Revolution.

As popular interest in the question grew (doc. 24), the campaign for racial equality climaxed in May 1791 with four days of heated debate in the National Assembly. More than fifty deputies spoke (doc. 25). After considering opposing stereotypes of free coloreds, the likelihood of white secession and of nonwhite revolt, and the relative utility of racial discrimination and of concessions to free coloreds in maintaining slavery, deputies finally agreed on a compromise decree. Retracting an earlier promise, the National Assembly asserted its right to legislate on race relations in the colonies but, in exchange, guaranteed it would never interfere regarding slavery. The decree of May 15 enfranchised only property-owning nonwhites born of free parents. In excluding freedmen, it thus kept in existence an intermediary class, as colonists wished, but one based on legal standing, not phenotype. In practice, the decree would have affected few people, as most free coloreds' parents were not married, which made a father's status difficult to prove.

Nevertheless, the decree created uproar in Saint Domingue, and the colony's deputies abandoned the National Assembly to campaign for its withdrawal. They succeeded; the assembly reversed course. The constitution completed in September excluded the colonies, whose white inhabitants had become essentially self-governing in internal matters. Slavery, the slave trade, and white supremacy all remained intact.

17) The Enlightenment, Race, and Slavery

Beginning with Montesquieu in the 1740s, French intellectuals began to criticize slavery as a cruel and unjust institution that could no longer be justified with texts drawn from the Bible or from Aristotle. Although this new trend represented a radical shift in Western culture, it had no impact on France's burgeoning involvement in Caribbean slavery. More interested in ideas than practical reforms, the critics themselves were often ambivalent on the topic. Moreover, while the Enlightenment established modern ideas about human rights, its development of biological science and undermining of Christian teachings about the oneness of humankind also encouraged the development of so-called "scientific racism" that suggested whites and blacks were different species. The brilliant satire Candide helped publicize slavery's evils in a pithy but frivolous manner. Its author, Voltaire, championed the oppressed but also invested in the slave trade. Abbé Raynal proved equally inconstant, but he was among the first to put forward a practical abolition scheme and to discuss the alternative of violent rebellion.

(a) They met a slave laying on the ground who had on only half of his costume, that is a loincloth made of a blue material. The poor man was missing both his left leg and his right hand. "Oh my God," said Candide to him in Dutch,[2] "what are you doing there, my friend, in the horrible state that I see you in?" "I am waiting for my master, the famous merchant, Mr. Vandendendur," the slave replied. "Is it Mr. Vandendendur who treats you this way?" Candide asked. "Yes, sir," the slave said, "it is the custom. Two loincloths a year, that's all the clothes we get. When we work in the sugar factories and get a finger caught in the grinding mill, they cut off our hand. When we try and run away, they cut off a leg. I found myself in both situations. It is the price of the sugar that you eat in Europe. However, when my mother sold me on the coast of Guinea for ten Patagonian crowns, she said to me, 'My dear child, bless our fetishes, always worship them, they will bring you a happy life. You have the honor of being the slave of our lords the whites and in the process you are making the fortune of your father and mother.' Alas! I don't know if I made their fortune, they certainly didn't make mine."[3]

(Voltaire, *Candide, ou l'optimisme* [Paris, 1759], ch. 19)

---

2. Placing the scene in Dutch Suriname obviously made it more palatable for French readers.

3. In his *Essai sur les moeurs*, 8:187, Voltaire wrote "A people that sells its children is even guiltier than they who buy them. This commerce demonstrates our superiority. He who gives himself a master was born to have one."

(b) The Negro race is a different species of men from our own, as the race of spaniels is different from greyhounds. Their black wool does not resemble our hair at all, and one can say that, if their intelligence is not of a different nature to our own, it is much inferior. They are not able to concentrate very much; they calculate little, and do not seem ready for either the advantages or the abuses of our philosophy. They come from the same part of Africa as elephants and monkeys. They believe that they are born in Guinea to be sold to the whites and to serve them.

(Voltaire, *Essai sur les moeurs* [Geneva, 1755], vol. 16, 269–70)

(c) So, nations of Europe, if it is only self-interest that moves your soul, listen to me again. Your slaves do not need your generosity or advice to smash the sacrilegious yoke that oppresses them. Nature's voice is louder than that of philosophy or of self-interest. There already exist two colonies of runaway blacks protected from your attacks by treaties and their own strength.[4] These lightning flashes herald a thunder clap. The slaves lack only for a leader brave enough to lead them to vengeance and carnage.

Where is he, this great man whom nature owes to her tormented and oppressed children? Where is he? He will appear, have no doubt. He will come to raise the standard of liberty. . . . Spanish, Portuguese, English, French, Dutch, all their tyrants will fall prey to their fire and sword. The fields of America will get joyfully drunk on the blood they have waited for so long, and the bones of so many victims that have piled up for three centuries will quiver with delight. The Old World and the New will join in applause, and everywhere people will bless the name of the hero who has re-established the rights of the human race.[5]

(Raynal, *Histoire philosophique et politique des Deux Indes*
[3rd ed.; Paris, 1780], 6:128–29)

18) The Founding of the Friends of the Blacks

The elite and cosmopolitan Amis des Noirs drew inspiration from the Enlightenment and the beginnings of abolitionism in England and the United States.

---

4. The British and Dutch signed five treaties with maroon communities in Jamaica (1739–1740) and Suriname (1760s).

5. The black leader Toussaint Louverture later claimed to have been inspired by this passage, which was penned by Denis Diderot.

The author of this pamphlet, Jacques-Pierre Brissot, was a liberal journalist who had visited both countries. It was written, in February 1788, at what seemed a propitious moment: several U.S. northeastern states had recently decided to end slavery; the U.S. cotton boom had not yet begun in the South, and the British Parliament, with the approval of prime minister William Pitt, was investigating the slave trade. Brissot argued that slavery was both immoral and inefficient. Although the Amis soon made a tactical decision to concentrate just on the slave trade, they attracted little support. Their opponents depicted them as naive do-gooders or dangerous fanatics who were blind to the national interest. Because of their links with the British, many thought they were paid by France's enemies to undermine French commerce.

A respectable society has been formed in London to have legally abolished the horrible trade in Negroes. It invites all those who are friends of their fellow man to join with it to bring about everywhere this work of justice. . . . Could we better fulfill the intentions of this association other than by appealing to men whose most ardent wish is to repair the mistakes, the foolishness, and atrocities of past centuries and to develop the system of peace and brotherhood that ought to unite all peoples?

You will remember how, in the free part of America, a very small effort brought about the improvement of the life of its Negroes. One man alone, almost without any help or finances, and with no other power than that of his own will, undertook to have the use of slaves abolished in his country. He went about preaching his doctrine everywhere. His brother Quakers were the first to open their eyes to the light. . . . These Quakers proclaimed that it is unjust, inhuman, and irreligious to hold men in slavery, to command their thoughts and their will, and to take the fruit of their labor. In the four states of the north of the United States, the chains fell from the wrists of 50,000 slaves.[6] It was more difficult to have such a doctrine accepted in the states of the South. The number of blacks was much greater there, and considerably exceeded that of the whites. . . .

Greedy calculation made it seem so useful to sell the product of the sweated labor of numerous slaves without having to pay them, . . . to have to hand out only threats and punishment, . . . that people easily persuaded themselves that this slavery was a law of nature that condemned some men to serve others like domesticated animals and that it was justified by the difference in [skin] color. People came to believe that there was no other way to make America's soil pro-ductive than by the labor of enslaved blacks. False reasoning thus joined with self-interest and habit to justify this horrible injustice.

---

6. He is referring to the abolitionist pioneer Anthony Benezet and the emancipation acts of the early 1780s in New England and Pennsylvania.

However, such is the empire of reason, gentlemen, when it develops under the rule of liberty, that soon after the United States gained their independence the cause of the enslaved blacks . . . was taken up and warmly defended by the best minds and most respectable persons. . . . By what right could one continue to hold other men in slavery, even those who had just cemented with their blood this eternal truth: that *all men are born free and equal*? And with what imprudence would they have kept the use of slavery, . . . [given] this general opinion that the product of forced labor is inferior to that of free labor?

Yet such is the misfortune of vicious institutions and bad habits that . . . it was feared that, once freed, the Negroes would abuse their liberty and, having been martyred for so long, they would seek revenge against their tormentors. . . . Some also thought that the conjugal union of whites and blacks, which the latter's freedom would make more common, would be social anarchy, a public disaster. . . . [But] why fear . . . the hand of the man whom one willingly frees and embraces as a brother, whom one places at one's side and to whom one returns his rights, notably those of using his reason for his own happiness? This is to ignore the prodigious influence of liberty on the development of human reason and on the founding of universal peace. . . . Give men their freedom and they will enlighten themselves; they will become good persons a thousand times more easily and more quickly than by giving them the best books but forcing them to remain slaves.

The Quakers . . . have attempted to bring the same justice to the blacks of the English colonies, where prejudices were harder to overcome. . . . The planters endlessly repeat that the sugar islands are the foundation of Great Britain's wealth. . . . [But] since the Minister himself seems favorable to [the antislavery cause], there should be no doubt it will succeed and that England, first by banning the trade in slaves and then by freeing them, will give the first great example in Europe of a nation that abandons an oppression regarded as useful. . . . In the midst of this fermentation stirring every mind in Great Britain, will decent and enlightened men in France remain inactive? . . .

The future liberation of the blacks of the sugar islands . . . will have the greatest influence on the French colonies; it can ruin them if they resist its example, it can make them wealthy if they follow it. This dual effect flows infallibly from the demonstration, from the fact, that a free person makes the soil fruitful better than does a slave. . . .

We must not limit ourselves to the publication of English works. There are some very worthy but forgotten French ones we must seek out, examine, and publicize, and republish if necessary. . . . The Society will have to make arrangements with all the gazettes and newspapers to insert information about the cause of the Negroes. . . . It must undertake research on the condition of blacks in our islands, on the treatment they receive, whether their numbers grow or decline, on the number of new recruits needed each year to maintain production, . . .

on the way of life of fugitive or maroon slaves, on how many ships the French employ in this trade. . . .

Let us recall that the Society is being formed at a moment of precious fermentation stimulated by respect for humanity, a moment when people are tired of frivolity and feel the need to be something. Remember also our nation's character, a character marked more than any other by universal kindness.

> (Jacques-Pierre Brissot, *Discours sur la nécessité d'établir à Paris une Société pour concourir, avec celle de Londres, à l'abolition de la traite & de l'esclavage* [Paris, 1788], 1–6, 9–11, 14, 16, 22–25, 31)

19) Fear of Emancipation and Revolt

This letter of 12 August 1789 was written from Paris by Saint Domingue's deputies to their constituents in the colony. It shows their panic on discovering that the libertarian drift of the French Revolution might threaten the slave regime. On August 11, the new National Assembly had abolished serfdom and aristocratic privileges in France; the Declaration of the Rights of Man, issued later that month, further heightened the colonists' fears. The letter's suggestion of seeking the support of free men of color was soon abandoned when it became clear that the whites could not easily control them. This letter was in fact intercepted by the free colored activist Julien Raimond and made public to reveal the colonists as phony liberals.

Gentlemen and Dear Compatriots,

. . . PEOPLE HERE ARE DRUNK WITH LIBERTY. A society of zealots that has taken the name Friends of the Blacks openly attacks us in its publications. It is waiting for a favorable moment to create an antislavery explosion. If we just mention the word, that might be enough for them to demand the emancipation of our slaves. Our fear of this forces us reluctantly to keep silent. The time is not right to ask the National Assembly to collaborate with us in preventing the danger that threatens. It is up to you, gentlemen, to decide on the course to follow in such a critical situation. The peril is great and it is imminent. Watch over our safety but do so with prudence. We must not lose our heads. *Let us not awaken the enemy,* but do not be taken by surprise.[7] The National Assembly is too preoccupied with the internal affairs of the kingdom to be able to think about us. We are warning Americans everywhere to fly to the defense of

---

7. A discreet reference to the slave population.

their country.[8] Most no doubt will take ship. Only a few of us will go with them, until everyone has gathered together.

Take the precautions that your wisdom suggests to you. Pay close attention to people and their actions. ARREST SUSPICIOUS PERSONS. SEIZE WRITINGS IN WHICH EVEN THE WORD FREEDOM APPEARS. Redouble your guard over your plantations, towns, and villages. Everywhere win over the free people of color. BE SUSPICIOUS OF THOSE WHO ARRIVE FROM EUROPE. It is one of your greatest misfortunes that it has not been possible, in such critical circumstances, to prevent the embarkation of those who were in France. We asked the minister [of the colonies] to do so. *The spirit of the time is opposed to our wishes in this matter.* To prevent the embarkation of slaves, even at our request, would be regarded as an act of violence that should be denounced to the nation.

Be of good courage, dear compatriots . . . the time will surely come when we can do better. WE MUST LET TEMPERS COOL DOWN. THIS CRISIS WILL NOT LAST. COUNT ON US. . . .

The deputies for Saint Domingue [signatures]

P.S. . . . You must not neglect any precaution, any effort, to maintain order, peace, and subordination among you. It seems to us that the best way to guarantee peace in the colony *is to win over to your cause the class of free coloreds.* Assuredly they want nothing better than to associate their interests with yours and to work zealously for our common security. There is therefore no question but that you should act justly toward them and treat them increasingly better. *We look on this sort as the true bulwark of the safety of the colony.* You can tell them that your deputies, who are also theirs, are working diligently to get the National Assembly to improve their lot and obtain for them the just consideration due to all citizens who behave well.

("Lettre des députés de Saint-Domingue à leurs commettants," in Julien Raimond, *Correspondance de Julien Raimond avec ses frères de Saint-Domingue* [Paris, 1793], 7–10)

20) A Free Man of Color's Complaints

This anonymous pamphlet by a self-styled "mixed blood American" was the first of the revolutionary crisis to deal with the issue of race. In unsophisticated and sometimes obscure language, it continued and made public the reformist argument privately advanced by Julien Raimond in the mid-1780s. The author sought not racial equality but an end to discrimination against people of mixed

---

8. Developing a sense of proto-nationalism, both white and nonwhite colonists were beginning to refer to themselves as "Americans."

racial descent. He draws a sharp line not only between slaves and free people of color but also between free blacks and other free nonwhites. While emphasizing wealth and culture, he makes European ancestry the key criterion. Free colored activists would soon broaden this program under the influence of the French Revolution's universalist and egalitarian ideology.

Ambition and greed gave birth in the islands to color prejudice. This fatal prejudice has plunged the mixed-bloods into the greatest of misfortunes under the convenient pretext of necessity and security. Interpreting to our disadvantage all the edicts and regulations concerning the Negroes, judging our class by a few vagabonds who roam the towns, it has continuously weighed us down with its chains . . . vexing and humiliating us. . . . It ended up misleading the [colonial] ministry into issuing several decrees in which we saw to our deep distress that our monarch was confusing with the slaves in his colonies affectionate and loyal subjects, born free and French, who are as valuable to culture, commerce, the arts, and population growth as are his European subjects. . . .

To our legal degradation and impotence are added the cruelest of humiliations, indignities, and excesses on the part of the basest of whites. . . . Victims of violent passion, crushed by the weight of invective, what exactly is our crime? . . . Can it really be supposed that we are more favorable to slavery than to freedom [sic]?

The color of blacks denotes Africa; it alone, under our laws, owes dues to their [sic] patron; its destination is known. The color of mixed-bloods denotes America. Neither this continent nor the constitution of the French monarchy had slaves among their [sic] original citizens.[9] It is therefore yet one more injustice to mix us up with the Negroes; and from this injustice derives their extreme insubordination toward us. There are Africans, released from their chains and still bearing the marks of being punished for their wickedness, who hold as slaves mulattoes, quadroons, and *tiercerons*,[10] fruits of the Europeans' promiscuity. To such straits is this unfortunate color reduced! The make-up alone of these beings ought to [be reason to] break their chains. . . . It is not fitting for the dignity of the Nation to see its flesh and blood in chains on its territory.

How much more sharp is the pain for those who are born from respectable relationships, for worthy citizens who own property and happily pay their taxes

---

9. The author here blends two claims: that the traditional (but disputed) "free soil" or "free air" argument as to why slavery should be illegal in France also applied to the Americas, and that people of Afro-European descent were analogous to Amerindians because they were similarly indigenous to the New World.

10. Some of the various Caribbean terms for describing degrees of racial intermixture. *Tierceron* meant "one-third black," typically the child of a quadroon and a mulatto. However, Grégoire, in *Mémoire en faveur des gens de couleur* (48), stated it designated the child of white and quadroon parents, a "third-generation intermixture."

and public dues, and who have always demonstrated unfailing loyalty, to see all their descendants forever condemned to disdain for no other crime than that of their color! . . .

Nature and transcendent reasons indicate where to draw the line of demarcation amidst these diverse mixtures of progeny: it is with the mulatto.

(J. M. C. Américain, Sang-mêlé, *Précis des gémissemens des sang-mêlés dans les colonies françoises* [Paris, 1789], 3–10)

21) Free People of Color Organize

This cahier, *or reform program, was drawn up in Paris in September 1789 by the few dozen free men of color who formed the Society of American Colonists. Revolutionary in its demands, it was clearly inspired by the National Assembly's Declaration of the Rights of Man and its August 14 decree that, by ending aristocratic privilege, created equal access to employment in France. Unlike the previous pamphlet (doc. 20), the cahier makes no distinction between people of African and Afro-European descent, or between freedmen and those born free. Yet by continuing to call for the emancipation of mixed-race slaves (perhaps to boost the number of free coloreds), it implicitly accepted the privileged position of racial difference and European identity in colonial ideology.*

Article 1. The inhabitants of the French colonies are divided and apportioned into solely two classes, that of free men and that of men who were born and are living in slavery.

Article 2. The class of free men includes not only all whites, also all creoles of color, including free blacks, mulattoes, quadroons, and others.

Article 3. The creole freedmen, as well as their children and posterity, must enjoy the same rights, rank, prerogatives, freedoms, and privileges as the other colonists.

Article 4. To this end, the creoles of color demand that the Declaration of the Rights of Man proclaimed in the National Assembly apply both to them and the whites, and in consequence that the articles 57 and 59 of the Edict of March 1685 be renewed and carried out according to their form and intent.[11] . . .

Article 6. In consequence, the National Assembly will be requested to declare: 1. That the Negroes and creoles of color will . . . share with the whites the

---

11. These clauses of Louis XIV's Code Noir (Black Code) established that freed slaves should enjoy the same rights as free-born persons but, like much of the code, they had been generally ignored in the colonies.

difficulties and honor of employment in civil government and military service. 2. That, to achieve this, the law courts will be open to them. They will have access to the highest posts in the judiciary and be free to present themselves for the secondary posts such as those of attorney, notary, prosecutor, registrar, court bailiff . . . both in France and the colonies. 3. That they will similarly be promoted under the same conditions to all military posts and appointments, so that their color ceases to be a reason for excluding them. 4. That, to put an end, even as a pretext, to a distinction that must not exist among free men, the Volunteer Companies of blacks, mulattoes, and quadroons shall be combined and from this time on will be recruited among both whites and men of color. . . . 8. That the priesthood, the sciences, the arts, and the skilled trades, in a word all types of employment, will be accessible to citizens of color, as until the present they have been accorded to whites. 9. That there will be founded in the different colonies schools and public colleges in which creoles of color and even black freedmen, or their children, will be admitted together with whites without any sort of preference or favoritism. . . .

Article 20. To consolidate the regeneration of the species and re-establish good manners, . . . the National Assembly will be requested to declare that, from the date of the future decree, all mulattoes and all people of color other than Negroes will be and remain free, so that henceforward there is none living in slavery. . . .

Article 30. Finally, the National Assembly will be requested to admit the deputies that the free citizens of color propose to elect and to order that, in the future, the whites together with the free citizens of color will participate in the primary, municipal, and colonial assemblies, both for the administration of their common interests and to nominate their representatives.

(Cahier contenant les plaintes, doléances et réclamations des citoyens-libres & propriétaires de couleur [Paris, 1789], 1–5, 10, 15)

22) The Abbé Grégoire's Violent Rhetoric

Very few abolitionists wanted slaves to rebel and free themselves, but the cleric Henri Grégoire used an apocalyptic rhetoric in his pamphlets that tended to set him apart and which colonists thought reckless. In both these texts addressed to and concerning free people of color Grégoire could not resist using the occasion to predict the end of slavery. The second pamphlet, written just after the voting rights decree of 15 May 1791, arrived in Saint Domingue the month before the slave uprising began and circulated widely. It infuriated colonists, who hanged Grégoire in effigy and later blamed him for the revolt.

A secret fire is being incubated throughout Europe and foretells an imminent revolution. . . . Yes, the cry of freedom rings out in the Old and New Worlds. Only an Othello or a Padrejean[12] is needed to awake in the soul of the Negroes an awareness of their inalienable rights. Seeing that the mixed-bloods cannot protect them against their despots, they will perhaps turn their blades against everyone, and a sudden explosion will cause their chains to suddenly fall. And who among us will dare to condemn them? . . .

Often we are presented with an impressive calculation of national interest, which I regard as rooted in vile and selfish maneuvers. You insist on maintaining the slave trade and Negro slavery, because the frivolous products destined to satisfy your artificial needs are the price of their freedom. They are forced to say farewell to their homelands forever. They are brought loaded down with chains from different parts of Africa to the fields of America to share the fate of domesticated animals, because you need sugar, coffee, and rum. Unworthy mortals, rather eat grass and be just!

(Henri-Baptiste Grégoire, *Mémoire en faveur des gens de couleur ou sang-mêlés de St.-Domingue, et des autres isles françaises de l'Amérique* [Paris, 1789], 36–37)

You were men; now you are citizens. . . . One day the sun will shine down among you only on free men; its rays will no longer fall on chains and slaves. . . . The National Assembly has not yet linked the latter to your fate, because the rights of citizenship granted too suddenly to those who are unaware of the duties that go with them might prove to be a fateful gift for them. Yet do not forget that they, like you, are born and remain free and equal. With the progress of enlightenment, all peoples deprived of their liberty will eventually regain this inalienable property. It is in the irresistible march of events.

(Henri-Baptiste Grégoire, *Lettre aux citoyens de couleur et nègres libres* [Paris, 1791], 1, 12)

23) Ogé Addresses the Planters' Club

A quarteron, with three white grandparents and a white brother-in-law, Vincent Ogé (1756–1791) was one of the colony's very few free colored merchants and one of its wealthiest men of color. Seeking common ground with white planters, he addressed the Club Massiac in Paris in early September 1789. He began by evoking issues of common concern like free trade, debt, and the choice

---

12. Padrejean led a slave revolt in seventeenth-century Saint Domingue.

of colonial officials but then switched to more dangerous ground. His ambiguous evocation of an eventual slave emancipation seems to have been both a reflection of his idealism and an attempt to scare the whites into combining with the free coloreds against the risk of a slave revolt. The approach backfired, and Ogé was thereafter a marked man. The extract's last sentence proved tragically prophetic.

As a property owner from the Le Cap region of Saint Domingue and a native of the island, I come to ask the Assembly to admit me to its discussions. I have no other aim than to collaborate with it in the preservation of our property and to avoid the disaster that threatens us. . . .

To bring about this happy revolution, the flame of Reason is not enough; the flame of Freedom must blend its brightness with the gentleness of the other, so that their union may produce a uniform, fierce, and pure light that will enlighten minds and enflame hearts. . . .

But, gentlemen, this word Liberty that can only be uttered with enthusiasm, this word which embodies the idea of happiness, if only because it seems to want to make us forget the harm we have suffered for centuries, this Liberty, the greatest of possessions, the primary one: Is it made for all men? I believe so. Should it be given to all men? Again, I believe so. But how should it be given? At what period and under what conditions? This, gentlemen, is for us the greatest and most important of all questions. It concerns America, Africa, France, and all Europe. It is the primary reason, gentlemen, behind my request that you hear me.

If the most prompt and effective measures are not taken, if firmness, courage, and constancy do not animate us all, if we do not quickly bundle together all our abilities, our means, and our effort, if we sleep for an instant on the edge of the abyss, let us tremble at the moment of our waking. Blood will flow, our property will be invaded, the fruits of our labor destroyed, and our homes burned. Our neighbors, our friends, our wives and children will be slaughtered and mutilated. The slave will have raised the standard of revolt. The islands will be no more than a vast and fateful inferno. With commerce destroyed, France will receive a mortal wound, and a multitude of decent citizens will be impoverished, ruined; we will have lost everything. . . . But, gentlemen, there is still time to avert the disaster. . . . If the Assembly wishes to admit me, . . . if it authorizes me to draw up and submit to it my plan, I will do so with pleasure and even gratitude, and perhaps I will be able to contribute to warding off the storm that rumbles above our heads. . . .

If my project is adopted, I propose to go and carry it out myself, to watch over the public safety, under your orders. If I risk my personal interest, my life itself is a sacrifice that I owe to the public good, and I make it willingly.

(*Motion faite par M. Vincent Ogé, jeune à l'Assemblée des Colons*
[Paris, 1789], 1–2, 5–7)

24) Support from the Provincial Jacobin Clubs

It is difficult to gauge popular attitudes to race in France. The sailors, soldiers, and civilians who traveled to the Caribbean varied widely in their behavior. That sixteen radical Jacobin clubs all over France took up the cause of racial equality in the colonies in spring 1791 and helped bring about the decree of May 15 offers some important evidence. The campaign of support, however, can be traced to one individual in the Angers Jacobin club, Claude Milscent (1740–1794). He was a maverick liberal white planter from the parish of Grande Rivière in Saint Domingue. He had favored the local free colored activists and been forced to leave the colony in June 1790.

Letter of the Society of Friends of the Constitution of Bourg en Bresse to that of Angers, 17 April 1791

Brothers and Friends,

You plead the cause of our brothers the free men of color in the colonies with too much humanity and justice for the Society of Friends of the Constitution sitting in this town not to immediately commit itself to join its most sincere wishes with those you express to us in your letter of March 9 addressed to your brothers in all the patriotic societies of the kingdom.

The clarity of your principles, based so firmly on the Declaration of the Rights of Man and the Citizen, should embarrass anyone who did not adopt them and take every measure to present them to our august legislators. Although it is impossible for us to clothe your principles in as fine and energetic a style as you in your address to the National Assembly, the society will make it its duty to draw up a petition in accordance with your wishes in favor of those French who have no other defect than to be darker in complexion than Europeans. . . .

Letter of the Society of Friends of the Constitution of Saint-Tropez to that of Angers, 30 March 1791

Brothers and Friends,

We have received your letter of March 9 concerning the men of color. It reminded several of our members who are seamen of the harassment they have often witnessed on their voyages to the Americas. All of us have shared your righteous indignation, and all of us have been outraged by the evils that continue to be caused by ignorance of the sacred principle of the equality of mankind. A difference in appearance and in exterior color cannot change this national principle. All friends of mankind, convinced of the extent of this principle, no doubt lament that, even in this century of Enlightenment, a deal is being prepared whereby the Negroes will pay the price.[13] But when the best is beyond reach, we must be satisfied with the good, and if we cannot give freedom to the Negroes, let us not forget to give it to the people of color. It will be one triumph instead of the two we would have preferred. . . .

(*Lettres des diverses sociétés des Amis de la Constitution* [Paris, 1791], 2–4)

25) The May 1791 Debates

Vincent Ogé's revolt of October 1790 and conflicts in the Caribbean between white conservatives and radicals—the "troubles" mentioned in the following speeches—pushed the National Assembly to take a more interventionist stance in colonial affairs. The debate that led to the May 15 decree on the enfranchisement of free men of color pitched liberals and radicals, who wanted to abolish all racial discrimination, against colonists (such as Malouet, Moreau de Saint-Méry) and their supporters (such as Delattre), who argued that white colonists should be allowed to decide the issue, or at least make recommendations. Should colonies be subject to the constitution that was nearing completion, or should they remain a separate legal space? Were rights universal? The implications for the slave regime hung heavily over the debate. The struggle to reconcile "justice and prudence" ended in satisfying no one: within months both free coloreds and slaves were in revolt and whites were plotting secession.

(7 May 1791)

Delattre, senior, *in the name of the united committees.* . . . We must be just with everyone: that is the great principle that has always guided your committees. But we must be so prudently. We must give attention to the men of color, but for their own sakes we must first give attention to the colonies as a whole. . . . Gentlemen, for a long time bitter conflicts have been agitating the French islands in the Americas. The seriousness of the circumstances command you to quickly adopt a measure that will end these troubles, compensate for misfortunes that have existed for too long, and perhaps prevent still worse ones. . . . The National Assembly [should state in the constitution] that it will pass no law on the status of persons except at the specific and formal request of the colonial assemblies. . . .

---

13. This apparently meant the National Assembly's agreement not to initiate any reform of slavery.

L'Abbé Grégoire. . . . We are told we must be just and prudent. I confess I can see in the proposed decree merely a vehicle for being skillfully oppressive, for perpetuating the oppression of a class of men who are naturally and legally free but whom some want to reduce to slavery by abandoning them to the domination of others. . . .

Moreau de Saint-Méry. . . . For far too long we have been the victims of numerous slanders by men who, calling themselves friends of the blacks, seek to stir up the people of color against the white colonists. Do you not fear the designs of these evil-doers? If you hesitate or delay, they will take advantage of it to spread doubts about your intentions and lead people astray. They will incite war in the colonies and cover them with desolation, ruin, and mourning. . . .

Do you believe that the constitution you have given France is suitable for its colonies? You will either have to give up your wealth and trade, or declare openly that the declaration of rights is not applicable to the colonies. The colonies do not resemble France; this is a truth known to everybody. They cannot have the same internal regime or the same organization. . . . Their trade in no manner resembles that of other parts of the empire. If they could not conduct trade in a manner different than you, they would soon cease to be your colonies. If you subjected them to the same laws, they would soon become useless and you would lose your trade with your colonies. Without them, you would lose . . . your splendor and your political rank in Europe. (*Prolonged muttering.*) . . .

I have heard talk in the assembly of the declaration of the rights of man. Well, if you want the declaration of rights, as far as we are concerned, there are no longer any colonies. (*Violent grumbling.*)

Pétion de Villeneuve.[14] Gentlemen, it has been insinuated that the troubles in the colonies were caused by the circulation there of publications that are critical of the planters' and colonists' pretensions. Those troubles, you should have been told, are the result of ambiguous decrees that everyone in the colonies interpreted in his own fashion. You should have been told that the troubles were caused by the attempt to sacrifice a class of free men who are property owners like the colonists themselves, who like them pay taxes, and who like them have irrefutable rights that were consecrated in the time of despotism. Louis XIV himself sanctified these rights in the most clear-cut and emphatic manner.[15]

So what is being proposed to you today? The free men are not seeking a favor; they are not asking for rights, which they already have. They are merely

---

14. Jérôme Pétion de Villeneuve (1756–1794), radical deputy and future mayor of Paris; friend of the abolitionist Brissot; no relation of the free colored revolutionary Alexandre Pétion.

15. Allusion to the Black Code of 1685, which gave freed slaves the same rights as other free persons. This provision was quickly contradicted by other colonial laws.

asking you not to sacrifice them. Will you sacrifice to the pretensions of a few colonists both the existing laws and the peace of the colonies? Leave the law intact and the free men of color will have all that they are asking for, and the colonies will be peaceful. . . .

It has been proposed to you to deprive the free men of color of their political rights—a terrible principle that will lead to the subversion of the colonies. . . . That is the source of the troubles. Today there is being put forward the most humiliating and dishonorable proposal, an act to which no European nation would agree: that of making one class of men judges of the rights of another, when the two groups have opposing interests.

Are the colonies a separate state? What? If a part of the kingdom demanded the right to make its own laws and reduced you [the National Assembly] to the status of merely confirming them, wouldn't you agree that such a request would lead to the break-up of the empire? . . .

Malouet.[16] After recognizing that it would be impossible to end the troubles if the colonies were not given a guarantee of the National Assembly's position on the [colonies'] internal regime, on personal status, and on property,[17] the committees, considering that the assembly had already expressed its opinion regarding the first matter, thought it essential for you to decree this principle in a constitutional form. . . .

The English colonies have their own legislatures. The French colonists, represented here by a small number of deputies, had at least the right to demand this [right to initiate legislation]. Do you want to assimilate the colonies to other parts of the kingdom? Which of the *départements* has interests different from the others? With the best and most honorable of intentions, the assembly might be led into error regarding the interests of provinces that are unknown to most of its members. (*Complaints.*) The colonists therefore will be satisfied only when you have assured them that they have this right to initiate laws [on personal status], and that thereby the colonists' property will be safe. Showing the slightest hesitation on this point would only increase their suspicions. . . .

(11 May 1791)

L'Abbé Grégoire. . . . Nothing has been neglected, gentlemen, to confuse the cause of this class of free men [of color], who are the true strength of the colonies, with that of the slaves themselves. This mistake has been perpetuated for far too long, since the blood of these most unfortunate men is constantly being shed. Let me point out in passing that, every time the free men of color have been mentioned in this assembly, we have immediately been brought back to the slave trade and to the slavery of blacks, which we were not discussing, which

---

16. Pierre-Victor Malouet (1740–1814), former colonial official, absentee planter, liberal monarchist.

17. These terms were euphemisms for race relations and slavery.

we did not want to discuss, and whose cause has nothing in common with that of the mulattoes. (*Applause.*) We are all well aware that we must not rush things and that immediately giving all political rights to men who are unaware of the duties that go with them would be, perhaps, putting a sword in the hands of a madman. It would be a despicable present for them, too. . . .

But, the white colonists will tell you, if you grant political rights to the free men of color, the slaves will revolt. The white colonists should admit rather that it is their pride and sense of privilege that will rebel against this act of justice! And why should the slaves rebel? Because they saw the men of color attain the rank of citizen? Why did the slaves not revolt at the publication of the edict of 1685 that granted freedmen the same rights as whites? . . . Let us be clear, gentlemen, this is not what the planters fear. They are afraid they will no longer be able to subject the men of color to the same despotism they exercise over slaves. . . .

Let me repeat: they are free property-owners like the whites, tax-payers like the whites, and at least as patriotic as the whites. They must have the same rights as the whites, and with all the more reason, since they are the sons of Frenchmen and they should not have a lower status than that of their fathers.[18] . . .

The unfortunate Ogé and many others . . . have just perished on the scaffold for demanding the rights granted them by your decrees. If Ogé is guilty, we all are, and if he who calls for freedom perishes on the scaffold, all good Frenchmen deserve the same fate. (*Applause.*) . . .

Malouet. What do our adversaries' arguments amount to? To the principles you have enunciated in the constitution and to the declaration of rights, whereas you have solemnly recognized and declared that the constitution of the kingdom was not suitable for the colonies. . . .

It is not a question of examining whether the institution of slavery can be justified in law and in principle: no man endowed with sense and morality professes this doctrine.[19] It is a question of knowing whether this state of affairs in the colonies can be changed without causing a terrifying parade of crimes and misfortune. . . . This love of justice and humanity that would bring about such changes . . . would result not only in the destruction of all the colonists but in the ruin of part of your naval dockyards and most of your factories. . . . If we must forbid the application of the declaration of rights . . . on some points, it is very

---

18. This tendency to present all free people of color as having European ancestry, thus ignoring the large minority of *nègres libres* (free blacks), was probably a rhetorical device designed to evoke sympathy in a white audience. Although Grégoire made much use of the term "mixed-bloods," particularly in his early works, he explicitly but discreetly included free blacks in his proposals.

19. Eighteenth-century defenders of slavery tended to argue it was a necessary evil, not a positive good, unlike in the antebellum South.

dangerous to draw attention to its principles and apply them in the colonies on other points. . . .

Lafayette.[20] We are continually being distracted from the question at hand. What, in fact, is the issue? The National Assembly has called on the colonists to discuss their concerns. Is it not obvious that men who are free, property-owners, farmers, and tax-payers in a colony are also colonists? The people of color in question are tax-payers, farmers, property-owners, and free. Are they also men? I believe so. . . .

(12 May 1791)

Robespierre.[21] . . . You are told that you will lose your colonies if you do not strip the citizens of color of their rights.

Several members. That's not correct!

Robespierre. . . . And why will you lose your colonies? It is because one part of the citizens, those called whites, wish exclusively to enjoy political rights. It is they who dare tell you, through their deputies: If you do not grant political rights to us alone, we will be discontented; your decree will spread discontent and trouble in the colonies; the results may be fatal; you should fear the results of this discontent. Here then is a faction that is threatening to set your colonies aflame and to dissolve the bonds that unite them to the mother country, if you do not support their pretensions!

First of all, I ask the National Assembly if it is dignified for its legislators to engage in transactions of this sort with the self-interest, greed, and pride of a group of citizens. (*Applause.*) I ask if it is wise to decide under threat from a particular group to traffic in the rights of man, justice, and humanity! . . .

On what ground do they base their desire to strip their fellow citizens of their rights? What is the reason behind this extreme repugnance for sharing the exercise of their political rights with their brothers? It is, they say, that if you grant the franchise to the free men of color, you will diminish the slaves' respect for their masters, which is all the more dangerous because they cannot control them other than with terror. What an absurd objection! Did the rights that the men of color enjoyed before affect the blacks' obedience? Did they diminish the influence of the violence that the masters inflict on their slaves? But let us reason according to your own principles.

In addition to the triumphant reasons already put forward against this objection, I will add that your choosing to preserve the political rights of the colored property-owners will only strengthen the power of slaveowners over their slaves. When you have endowed all the colored property-owners and slaveowners with

---

20. Marie Joseph Gilbert du Motier, marquis de Lafayette (1757–1834), hero of the American Revolutionary War.

21. Maximilien Robespierre (1758–1794), provincial lawyer, dominant figure of the Reign of Terror of 1793–1794. Although a rising radical star, he proved reticent in tackling colonial slavery.

the same interest, and made of them but one party with the same interest, that of maintaining the subordination of the blacks, it is obvious that subordination will be greatly strengthened in the colonies. On the other hand, if you deprive the men of color of their rights, you will divide them and the whites, and naturally bring together all men of color, who will not have the same rights nor the same interests to defend as the whites. You will bring them together with the class of the Negroes. In this case, any threat of an insurrection by the slaves against their masters would obviously be much more dangerous for being supported by the free men of color, who would not have the same interest in repressing it, because their cause would be almost the same.

(*Archives parlementaires de 1787 à 1860* [Paris, 1862–1896], vol. 25:636–42, 740–41, 752–53, vol. 26:8)

4. THE FIGHT FOR RACIAL EQUALITY IN SAINT DOMINGUE

Nearly six months before the Colons Américains met in Paris, and soon after wealthy whites secretly assembled in Saint Domingue to elect deputies to the States-General, free coloreds in the colony's South Province, like Guillaume Labadie and Julien Raimond's brother François, wrote to royal officials that men of color also deserved representation. Their requests were ignored. In October 1789, during Saint Domingue's first enthusiastic response to the democratic revolution in Paris, a few of the district committees that white colonists then formed did accept the presence of free coloreds, but this spirit of toleration did not last long, and it soon was submerged in a wave of persecution (doc. 26).

In different parishes across the colony, free men of color drew up in all about twenty petitions seeking equal rights and a political voice for those who met French requirements for the status of citizen (doc. 27). Although they were mainly light-complexioned landowners, like Ogé and Raimond, this assertiveness alarmed many whites, who were already panicking at the interest slaves were showing in the French Revolution. Given the rapid growth of the free colored population, full equality would mean that, no sooner had white colonists gained a political voice than they risked being outvoted by the nonwhite neighbors they had generally scorned. Some rich colonists were willing to consider concessions, if they could control the process, but in the closing months of 1789, white colonial politics took a democratic turn. The white landowners and merchants who had launched the movement for self-government were challenged by unruly white wage-earners (urban artisans, seamen, plantation employees). These working-class migrants, who competed with free coloreds for jobs and resented the wealth of successful nonwhites, spearheaded a racist backlash.

In the West Province, a humiliating oath of "respect, submission, and devotion to the whites" was imposed on free men of color. In the ensuing protests, one of Vincent Ogé's brothers was killed. In Grande Rivière, in the mountains of the North Province, tensions also ran high. To avoid reprisals, more than a hundred free coloreds took refuge for several months in the neighboring Spanish colony, and their white ally Claude Milscent was forced to leave for France. Grande Rivière was one of the few places in the North where free coloreds probably outnumbered whites. It was there that an angry Vincent Ogé headed when he secretly returned to Saint Domingue in October 1790.

Encouraged by the support he had received from French and British abolitionists in Europe, Ogé had grown frustrated with the National Assembly's dishonest maneuvers. In Saint Domingue he linked up with Jean-Baptiste

Chavanne, one of the Grande Rivière leaders who had been forced to flee to Santo Domingo. They boldly summoned the white authorities to end racial discrimination (doc. 28). It is not certain they anticipated an armed struggle, and they were attacked and dispersed before they could raise many men. Free blacks made up a significant minority of those involved, unlike in the petitioning movement of the previous year, but men of lightest complexion still dominated. Although hundreds were rounded up and tried (doc. 29), a group of these free black insurgents remained at large and a year later reemerged in the ranks of the slave uprising (doc. 38).

Ogé's sacrifice persuaded the National Assembly to issue the compromise May 15 decree, but Saint Domingue's governor refused to enforce it. Faced with virulent and widespread white opposition, Governor Blanchelande feared it might push extremists to throw off French rule and seek independence or a British protectorate (doc. 30). For the free coloreds, this was the last straw, and in the countryside around Port-au-Prince they again gathered in arms. Wearing straw hats and mounted on mules and ponies, they quickly defeated the white militia, urban roughnecks, and royal troops who marched against them. Many whites suspected that the slaves in the north and free coloreds in the west coordinated their rebellions, but there is no reason to think so. Forcing the whites to fight on two fronts, however, was clearly one reason both the slaves and free coloreds eventually succeeded.

For the free coloreds, success came in stages. Conservative rural whites with plantations to protect were quick to ally with them. Even their urban radical enemies briefly joined the movement to sign treaties, or concordats, that now went beyond the May 15 compromise and granted full racial equality (doc.31). Continued hesitation in Paris, however, encouraged a renewal of the conflict in November 1791, and a savage race war, parallel to the war over slavery, spread across the colony (doc. 32). A cycle of atrocities and reprisals escalated until the epoch-making decree of 4 April 1792 arrived from France, which finally abolished racial discrimination in the colonies.

Colonial whites reluctantly swallowed pride and prejudice and tentatively sought common ground with nonwhite property owners in suppressing the slave rebellions that had multiplied during the months of fighting, with or without free colored complicity.

---

26) Early Atrocities

Garran Coulon's four-volume report, written in the mid-1790s, was a sort of "official history" of the early revolution in Saint Domingue. The author was a French liberal deputy, close to Brissot's circle, who headed a government enquiry into the revolution. He notes how a few early instances of political cooperation between whites and free coloreds soon gave way to vicious persecution. The judge Joseph Ferrand was known for his outspoken independence and in the past had apparently handed down antiracist decisions that caused controversy.

While the rights of men of color were being contested in France, they were being violated in the most atrocious manner in Saint Domingue. They were nevertheless so obviously justified that, even there, men of color were admitted without problem into several of the local assemblies that were held when news of the revolution [in France] first arrived. Yet no sooner had the leaders of the whites had time to get together than they excluded them from all the assemblies. In several places, they even wanted to prevent their wearing the national rosette.[1] A formal order from the colonial administration was needed to allow them to do so. . . .

The men of color remained peaceful amidst all this disorder; everywhere in the colony they were respectful to the authorities chosen by the whites. The men of color of Petit Goâve nonetheless presented a petition to the whites of this commune, who were meeting to elect their representatives to the electoral assembly of the West Province. They did not ask for equal rights but merely for some improvements in their status, particularly the right to meet and send one of their own to the provincial assembly. The petition was written in the most moderate language, but it excited the indignation of the whites. Those who brought it were arrested and forced to reveal who drew it up. It was the local seneschal [judge], a magistrate of spotless character. Respected by the whites themselves for his professional behavior, he had just received a new token of their confidence, when they had chosen him to be one of their electors. All his claims to public respect now disappeared, overshadowed by the crime of listening to the voice of humanity instead of that of unjust prejudice. He was forced to interrogate the bearers of the petition himself, so as to reveal his own so-called crime. As soon as it was uncovered, he was dragged off to prison with the petitioners. The [parish] committee had the treachery or cowardice to sanction these illegal acts by setting up a sort of trial. It did not have time to complete it. The inhabitants of Petit Goâve plain were called in, and they demanded with threats that the committee pronounce on the fate of Ferrand de Baudières [Beaudière].

---

1. The red, white, and blue cockade that was spontaneously adopted by supporters of the revolution.

After some hesitation, real or feigned, on the committee's part, its president Valentin de Cullion, who later became one of the Patriots of the first Colonial Assembly, told the crowd that he thought the seneschal was guilty. The poor old man was then snatched from his prison and, despite his pleas, the executioner was summoned and publicly cut off Ferrand's head, which was carried around the town on the end of a pike. His murderers made a show of sparing the petitioners and freed them.

Thus perished in November 1789 the first defender of the rights of man in Saint Domingue. His frightful death, which friends of humanity will long mourn, foreshadowed how little the leaders of the revolution in the colony intended to found it on true liberty and the equality of rights, and what rivers of blood they would shed before it was established. . . .

It is said that a man of color named Lacombe had already been hanged at Le Cap for having also petitioned the parish committee and calling for the rights of man.[2] The accusers of Polverel and Sonthonax[3] even seem to have admitted it, but one of them who played a prominent role in the colonial troubles (Brulley) claimed that Lacombe's petition was incendiary. The proof that he gave was that it was not drawn up in the usual style of a petition but began with the words, "In the name of the Father, the Son, and the Holy Ghost."

The people who committed these murders escaped the revenge of the law, and when the magistrates of Port-au-Prince began proceedings against those who killed Ferrand de Baudières, it was denounced as a counterrevolutionary act. Such impunity produced the usual result: it emboldened the guilty. On 26 November 1789, an old man named Labadie, who was known as "the venerable one," less because of his age than because of his generous behavior, was attacked in his home around midnight by a gang of whites led by an officer in the mounted police.[4] Labadie was accused of having a copy of Ferrand de Baudières' petition or of gathering with other men of color like himself to discuss their common interests. After breaking in his doors, the whites found him alone with a young slave of fifteen, who was killed at his side, as twenty-five guns opened fire. Labadie was wounded in three places, tied to the tail of a horse, and then dragged for a distance of three leagues [more than seven miles]. He escaped death only by a sort of miracle. This old fellow was such a good man that he has continued to urge extreme moderation on the men of color. Several of his letters prove it, and mention that his writing has changed, since he did not use to tremble before this terrible experience.

---

2. Augustin Lacombe. Arrested in November, he was in fact executed in April 1790.

3. The civil commissioners whose administration of Saint Domingue in 1792–1794 was the subject of a public enquiry in Paris, where they had to face their colonial enemies.

4. A member of Raimond's circle, Guillaume Labadie was a *quarteron* who owned 150 slaves.

The same killers continued their rampage. Later that night they went to the houses of three other men of color in Aquin parish who escaped. They smashed their furniture and insulted their wives. They carried off all the papers of François Raimond, the brother of the man who has defended their cause in such an honorable manner,[5] and they found nothing that might in their eyes justify all these outrages, since they have not published any of them.

Without the extreme moderation of the men of color, such attacks would have been repeated all over the colony. The decrees of the new administrative bodies formed by the whites seemed to justify all this violence. The electoral assembly of the West allowed men of color throughout the province to take the civic oath only with the addition of words that promised "respect toward the whites." When those of Verrettes parish had the courage to refuse this humiliation, the government, at this same assembly's request, had a detachment of the Port-au-Prince regiment march against them. Several were arrested and put on board warships. They were released only a long time afterward having been forced to take the oath they had refused. Many others were jailed for this refusal or for other frivolous reasons, and the judges that freed them were called to account before the colonial assemblies. All the letters that were sent them from France were seized.

(Jean-Philippe Garran Coulon, *Rapport sur les troubles de
Saint-Domingue* [Paris, 1797–1799], 1:106–13)

27) Free Coloreds Petition the Assembly
of the North, 10 November 1789

Free coloreds mixed deference and indignation in the petitions they sent to colonial authorities in the period October 1789 to April 1790. They initially described themselves as "mixed-bloods" and later as "American citizens." This little-known early example, from the northern parish of Grande Rivière, calls for equality but does not use the word. It is uncertain if its authors had yet seen the Declaration of the Rights of Man. Alluding to the equal status granted them by the Code Noir of 1685, they base their claims on their numbers, property-owning, and especially the night patrols and arduous slave hunts they were obliged to undertake. Like Ogé in Paris, they emphasize their importance in preventing slave rebellions, which was easily read as an implied threat.

---

5. Julien Raimond, the leading spokesman of the free coloreds in Paris, who owned plantations in Aquin.

Article 1. We constitute a large proportion of the people who inhabit this colony. Its security has always been entrusted to our zealous care and loyalty. . . . We have with alacrity incurred the greatest of risks when enemies of the state needed to be repelled or when slaves who had deserted had to be brought back to their duty, which they would no doubt resist if they were assured of our neutrality.

Article 2. . . . Too confident of our obedience, our fathers [the whites] claim over us an outrageous and despotic power. They go so far as to deform the precious right to freedom bestowed on us by our magnanimous sovereigns. These fathers treat us like slaves whom they are allowed to order around without any question of recompense. Every one of them acts like a tyrant toward us. . . .

Article 4. Most respectfully, we beseech the gentlemen of the [Provincial Assembly] to deign to grant us the same rights, privileges, immunities, and exemptions which all worthy citizens have the right to expect; that we be allowed to exercise all the arts and crafts; that we be recognized as good and loyal subjects capable of commanding ourselves [in the militia]; that our captains and officers be chosen from our class; . . . that we enjoy the liberties and privileges granted to the French people, and that it be expressly forbidden to call us freedmen. . . .

Article 5. We request . . . that our class be duly and legally invited to take part in the decision regarding our rights, as once they are stated and fixed, following our assent and the sanction of our fathers, these rights will determine our future and that of our descendants. Thereafter all insulting terms of address will forever cease, and we should be known solely by our names and surnames and place of domicile, and be treated as any other citizen. . . .

At Grande Rivière du Nord, 10 November 1789

(Archives départementales de la Gironde, Bordeaux, 61 J 15, doc. 21)

28) The Rebellion of Ogé and Chavanne

The National Assembly's early legislation on the colonies avoided mentioning racial identity. With deliberate ambiguity, it referred only to "persons." Vincent Ogé naively hoped to overcome white colonial resistance, perhaps because he had witnessed revolutionary change in Paris, perhaps because his wealth had previously shielded him from the worst of prejudice in Saint Domingue. Jean-Baptiste Chavanne (1748–1791) was less optimistic and supposedly wanted to add slaves to their small force. A struggling planter, he had gained military experience in the American Revolutionary War. One of his sons was named for the North American abolitionist Benezet. After a brief panic, whites closed ranks in a spirit of vigilantism to keep free coloreds "in their place."

Ogé to the Assembly of the North Province, 29 October 1790

Gentlemen, a prejudice that has been sustained for too long is finally going to meet its end. I call on you to have promulgated throughout the colony the National Assembly's decree of March 28 that gives to all *free* citizens, without exception, the right to be admitted to all posts and employment. My claim is just, and I hope you will give it your attention. I will not raise the slaves. That would be unworthy of me.

Learn to appreciate the merit of a man of pure intentions. When I requested and obtained from the National Assembly a decree in favor of the American colonists formerly known by the insulting term "mixed-bloods," I did not include in my demands the fate of the Negroes living in slavery. You and all our adversaries have tainted my actions so as to discredit me in the minds of good people. No, gentlemen, our demands concerned only a class of free men who have been under the yoke of oppression for two centuries. . . .

Before I turn to the force at my command, I am using gentle measures. But if, contrary to my wishes, you do not accept my demands, I will not answer for the turmoil into which my just vengeance might lead me.

(Beaubrun Ardouin, *Etudes sur l'histoire d'Haïti* [Paris, 1853], 1:140)

Blaise Garnier to his father, 18 November 1790

We have received some letters from Le Cap that are very worrying for all the whites in this colony. This is why: there has been a plot among the mulattoes to cause a general uprising to put into effect the decree of the National Assembly on the rights of man. To carry it out, they gathered in arms and wrote to the assembly in Le Cap that it should keep quiet, without protest, and that, if it did not, they would force it to do so. They also wrote some extremely insolent letters to the Governor-General, which really alarmed the colony. Le Cap decided to form an army of 3,000 men, with artillery, and it marched against the traitors to put down their revolt. They shut themselves up in the mountains, but we kept them hemmed in there all the time. There were some skirmishes with some dead and wounded on each side, but most of the victims were mulattoes. . . . All the whites of the island have gathered to choose the leaders of the Patriotic Troops that we need to create to keep us on the lookout against our sworn enemies.

(Blaise Garnier, *Combats affreux arrivés à l'isle St. Domingue* [Marseille, 1791], 1–2, 4)

29) The Sentencing of Ogé and Chavanne

Although the revolt was fairly bloodless and easily suppressed, the white colonists were determined to make an example of the insurgents, who had thrown them into disarray for several days with their slaves looking on. The ritualized execution of the leaders on the main square of Le Cap was a public spectacle. The sentence of breaking on the wheel, commonly used in France for the execution of bandits, was imposed on three of them. Yet a third of the fifty-five condemned to either death or a life sentence were never caught. Some would show up as minor leaders in the slave insurrection (doc. 38).

The court has declared and declares the aforesaid Vincent Ogé, junior, duly convicted of having premeditated for a long time the project of raising the free coloreds against the whites, and of having won over and led astray the aforesaid free coloreds, notably those of the district of Grande Rivière, by his speech, false titles, and [military] decorations; to have ordered and been the main leader in the disarming of the colonists of Grande Rivière, and armed robbery of their arms, ammunition, horses, and other effects, and of the insurrection and revolt in which were committed various thefts with breaking and entering, violence and murder; to have been the main leader, at Dondon, of a group of about eighty free coloreds, and to have made an incursion into the town of Dondon, in which three whites were killed and three were wounded; to have, according to sorts of manifestoes and declarations of war sent to the Governor-General, the Commandant of the North, and the President of the Provincial Assembly of the North, engaged in open war, and to have drawn up his group in military formation against the regular troops and militia and opened fire on them, among whom a grenadier of the Cap Regiment was wounded; to have taken several whites prisoner; to have sent another group to open fire on the militia dragoons and colonists of Grande Rivière; to have himself fired two shots at the troops with a hunting rifle; to have carried off mulatto slaves from their masters' property; to have armed them and taken them with him into the Spanish colony; to have similarly carried off black slaves from their masters' plantations. . . .

In reparation for which, we condemn the aforesaid Vincent Ogé, junior, free quadroon of Dondon, and Jean-Baptiste, known as Chavanne, free quadroon of Grande Rivière, to be taken by the High Executioner to kneel before the main door of this town's parish church and there, in shirtsleeves, their heads uncovered, a rope around their necks, and with a candle weighing two pounds in their hands, they are to make amends and declare in a loud, clear voice that they wickedly, boldly, and unwisely committed the crimes of which they have been convicted, and that they repent and ask pardon of God, the king, and justice.

Thereafter, they shall be led to the main square of this town, where, on the side opposite the one used for the execution of whites, they shall have their arms, shins, thighs, and pelvis broken while alive on a scaffold erected for this purpose. The High Executioner shall then place them on [cart] wheels with their faces turned toward heaven for however long it pleases God to maintain their lives. Thereafter, their heads shall be cut off and exposed on stakes, that of Vincent Ogé, junior, on the road leading to Dondon, and that of Jean-Baptiste, known as Chavanne, on the road to Grande Rivière.

(Arrêt du Conseil Supérieur du Cap contre le nommé Ogé jeune &
ses complices, du 5 mars 1791 [Cap Français, 1791], 3–4)

30) The August 1791 Rising in the West

Garran Coulon's 1797 report faulted the weak royal governor for pandering to colonial opinion and thus pushing the free men of color to claim their rights by force. The insurgents were far more numerous than in Ogé's rebellion and, using hunting rifles not smoothbore muskets, they proved to be formidable marksmen. They also admitted into their ranks several hundred slaves. This implied threat, along with the slave revolt raging in the north, quickly brought the whites to sue for peace—first, conservative planters, and then even their bitterest opponents in the capital.

[It has been claimed that] "on 23 July 1791 the men of color gathered in the West Province and insistently demanded the May 15 decree be put into effect." The Colonial Commission has no other information on what the men of color did during the month of July, but it is proven that, from the beginning of August, they formed a political assembly in the commune of Mirebalais whose demands [Governor] Blanchelande had rejected. Its location and its large free colored population offered them greater freedom of action and the ability to defend themselves in case of attack. It is true that Mirebalais is separated from Port-au-Prince only by the parish of Croix des Bouquets, but it is protected on all sides by mountains that are difficult to penetrate, and Croix des Bouquets, one of the largest parishes in the colony, had always been strongly opposed to the supporters of the Saint Marc assembly who were dominant in Port-au-Prince.

At the very same time that the second Colonial Assembly was gathering at Léogane, the men of color assembled in Mirebalais. They were so clearly masters of the place that they held their meeting in the church on 7 August 1791. They chose as their president Pierre Pinchinat.[6] He thereafter directed all the political operations of the insurgents and, in a career that was entirely new for him, he has never failed to demonstrate, along with a worthy patriotism, a wisdom and knowledge that easily disprove all that the white colonists in France have to say about the ignorance and incapacity of the men of color. . . .

The *representatives* of the men of color of Mirebalais sent their constitution to Blanchelande accompanied by a letter that was vigorous, respectful, and well reasoned. They complained of the way he protected their enemies, who were flouting the decrees of the National Assembly, when he could not be unaware of "the threats of secession and independence, the violent resolutions, and the destructive projects aimed at [us] in response to the May 15 decree. We are appealing to you, Monsieur the governor," they said, "because the danger is urgent, because the interests of the colony imperiously demand it, because you are the head of the executive power in this *part of the French empire*, because as such you must carry out the law and help the oppressed, . . . because we cannot and must not approach *unconstitutional bodies* against which we have complaints, owing to which we can call only on your authority." . . .

Blanchelande was so completely devoted to the white colonists, or so obsessed with them, that he declared in his reply to the men of color that he "entirely disapproved of their conduct," that he "condemned their illicit assembly," as well as their discussions, and that while he had just promised the Assembly of the North he would not carry out the May 15 decree and would suspend it when it officially arrived, he ordered the men of color "*in the name of the nation and of the king* that [they were] invoking to disband and to await peacefully and with resignation *the promulgation of the laws* that might concern them . . . and never to forget *the respect and veneration* that they owed to the white citizens, who," he said, "had not forgotten the project to *improve the lot of their charges*. . . . "

The rebels of Mirebalais and of the surrounding parishes gathered on the Charbonnière mountain[7] in August 1791. There was then a first encounter between the insurgents and the dragoons that the town of Port-au-Prince had sent there. The dragoons were driven off after losing several men killed and taken prisoner. The men of color's success caused the immediate evacuation of the white inhabitants from most of the surrounding region, from where a few slaves came and joined the insurgents.

At the same time, the free coloreds told the envoys whom Jumécourt[8] had sent to them to gain information that they would not lay down their arms

---

6. A *quarteron*, like Ogé and Raimond, Pinchinat was a forty-five-year-old lawyer who had practiced in France and was known for his eloquence.

7. Present-day Pétionville, in the hills behind Port-au-Prince.

8. Hanus de Jumécourt was a white planter from the generally conservative parish of Croix des Bouquets in the plain adjoining Port-au-Prince.

until they had gained the enjoyment of their rights as citizens that the National Assembly decrees had granted them. They added that they did not expect to be opposed by a parish that had always done itself honor in respecting the laws of the National Assembly and obeying the French constitution.

Hanus de Jumécourt, who was probably by this time on the side of the men of color, called a parish meeting. There he argued the necessity of conciliation and "of concentrating power *in a single person* who would be absolutely free to act for the public good." Others wanted to set up a municipal council, to unite with Port-au-Prince, and to take refuge there if circumstances became more dangerous. Hanus de Jumécourt prevailed and was himself granted the full powers he had called for. He sent envoys both to the men of color on the Charbonnière and to the town of Port-au-Prince offering to act as a mediator. Instead of welcoming him, "Port-au-Prince launched a second attack against the men of color of which the outcome was much more disastrous and deadly than on the previous occasion, because a much larger force was used." The Port-au-Prince town council had formed a company of adventurers and sailors to which they had given the name *Buccaneers*. They doubtless thought that this name would guarantee them, fighting against men who were defending their freedom, the same success that the old pirates who had bore this name had had against the Spanish. The new freebooters were accompanied by a detachment of regular troops and national guards from Port-au-Prince, preceded by artillery. The whites were beaten on September 2 on the Pernier plantation, and the regular troops, abandoned by the national guards, were absolutely cut to pieces or taken prisoner.

The good conduct of the men of color after this victory won them the support of the whites of Mirebalais and Croix des Bouquets, who signed an initial agreement with them two days later. Each side agreed to accept without protest or restriction the precise implementation of the national decrees sanctioned by the king, including the May 15 decree, if it arrived clothed with the royal approval.

The town of Port-au-Prince was shocked by these early defeats and by the unrest of the slaves in the surrounding area. District meetings were held, in which the local agitators were at their weakest, and delegates were named to negotiate with the men of color. The latter demanded the equality of rights bestowed on them by nature and revolutionary principles, as by the national decrees and the edict of 1685 itself.[9] They called for an agreement to implement the May 15 decree as soon as it arrived in the colony, the formation of primary assemblies under the terms of the decrees of March 1790, and the right to send deputies directly to the Colonial Assembly with the same rights of discussion and consultation as had

---

9. The Code Noir of 1685 prescribed that freed slaves should enjoy the same rights as other free people. The provision was soon ignored in practice and contradicted by other legislation, as the free colored population grew.

those of the whites. They protested against the establishment of town councils and provincial assemblies formed in contravention of the decrees of the National Assembly. They again called for the inviolability of the public mail and for freedom of the press within limits to be set by the law. Clause VII demonstrated the persecutions to which they had till then been subjected. They demanded the annulment of *all the proscriptions* inflicted on them, all the legal judgments and decrees rendered against them, and of the property seizures carried out, whether by court decision or not. They further demanded the indemnities due them for their exile. They specified in this demand that various individuals were "reserving the right to protest and make claims, at a later date and before the relevant parties, concerning the sentences handed down against messieurs Ogé and Chavannes and others included in the same judgment, regarding henceforth the sentences against these gentlemen by the Superior Council as infamous and worthy of execration by present and future generations, and as the fatal cause of all the troubles that are afflicting the North Province."

To ensure that these articles were enforced, the men of color insisted that it be accepted they remain under arms until they were and that, in consequence, "that the arms, cannon, and munitions taken during the recent conflict should remain in the possession of those who had the good fortune to emerge victors, although any prisoners that were taken by either side should be freed."

(Jean-Philippe Garran Coulon, *Rapport sur les troubles de Saint-Domingue*
[Paris, 1797–1799], 2:130–31, 134–35, 142–45)

31) The Peace Treaty of 19–23 October 1791

Signed on a plantation near Port-au-Prince, the concordat of Damiens followed on earlier treaties signed in September that local whites had balked at implementing. It was a triumph for the men of color, now referred to as "gentlemen," and a drastic climb-down by their racist enemies. Whites who had rejected the May 15 compromise now had to accept the end of white supremacy. The treaty avoided mention of the slaves that the free coloreds had armed, who by a secret agreement were deported to Central America.

Demands of the Delegates of the Citizens of Color.

Article 1. The concordat of September 11 between the whites of the Port-au-Prince national guard and the national guard of the citizens of color camped at Croix des Bouquets shall be recognized as legal and in conformity with the constitution. . . .

3. It shall be acknowledged that the governor's proclamation of September 26 was obtained by the use of misinformation. . . . In consequence, the proclamation shall be suspended and the white citizens of the West Province promise to employ all the means in their power to obtain its revocation. . . .

As it is well established that the town councils and provincial and colonial assemblies are illegal, all the acts that these unconstitutional bodies have issued or will issue are declared null and they will be dissolved . . .

6. To avoid disorder and anarchy, each town council in the West Province will be replaced by an oversight committee . . . composed of members chosen from among the white and colored citizens. . . .

9. The white and colored delegates of the fourteen parishes of the West Province will request the governor to issue in a month as of today a proclamation convoking the parish assemblies, to which all active citizens[10] without distinction will be called, following the terms of article 4 of the instructions of 28 March 1790, so as to name deputies to a new colonial assembly. . . .

12. The citizens of color . . . demand that the memory of the unfortunate victims of prejudice and passion be rehabilitated; that the colony will provide the indemnities and pensions due to their widows and children; that all judicial decisions handed down before the revolution against citizens of color in respect of clashes between them and white citizens and those where prejudice triumphed over the justice due to all citizens of the empire shall be revised. . . .

14. Terms such as "citizens of color" and "the free black, free mulatto, free quadroon, known as . . . " and others of the sort shall be in future strictly prohibited. Henceforward, there will be used for all the colony's citizens only those terms used for the whites. . . .

The entire West Province will supply the needs of the army of the citizens of color wherever it is camped and for the duration of its service. . . .

18. To eliminate all reason for hatred and disunity, and to extinguish the memory of the injustices committed against the citizens of color, a solemn service shall be held in the fourteen parishes of the West Province in memory of those who have been sacrificed to passion and prejudice since the beginning of the troubles.

19. As soon as the present treaty has been signed, a deputation from the Port-au-Prince national guard, from the Artois and Normandy regiments, from the royal artillery corps, from the royal navy and the merchant marine will be invited to proceed unarmed to the Damiens plantation to carry out a perfect reconciliation with the citizens of color, who will go to the same place, unarmed, in equal number. . . . The following day a *Te Deum* mass will be sung in the Port-au-Prince parish church. A detachment of 1,500 men from the army of

---

10. Active, as opposed to passive, citizens were those who met the property and residence requirements of France's 1791 constitution to be able to vote.

the citizens of color will go to Port-au-Prince to take part; it will enter the town drums beating with its flags displayed, and it will be received with the honors deserved by citizens who are unshakably loyal to the Nation, the Law, and the King and who took up arms only to put an end to the troubles that have for long ripped apart their unhappy country. . . .

23. The governor will in addition be asked to give his approval to all the articles of the treaty of September 11 and of this one, and to have them put into effect. . . .

Speech delivered by Monsieur the mayor of Port-au-Prince after the peace treaty was read out.

Gentlemen: What a fine day it is when we can say with truth that we are all friends and brothers! . . . Citizens of color, my friends, you are now to lose this title; there no longer exists any distinction or difference. In the future, we, all together, will have but one title, that of citizen.

(*Concordat, ou Traité de paix entre les Citoyens Blancs et les Citoyens de Couleur des quatorze paroisses de la Province de l'Ouest* [Paris, nd], 6–10, 14–15)

32) Call to Arms of the Free Men of Color, late November 1791

The fragile peace established by the Damiens treaty collapsed in a vicious race riot in Port-au-Prince on November 21, in which part of the city was burned. Free coloreds soon entrenched themselves in the countryside and lay siege to the capital and to Jacmel and Les Cayes. The anger and frustration of this moment is captured in the blazing rhetoric of this proclamation issued in the name of their main leaders, Pierre Pinchinat, Louis-Jacques Bauvais, André Rigaud, and Antoine Chanlatte. Often attributed to Pinchinat, it was in fact written by the young Juste Chanlatte, Antoine's nephew, who had returned from schooling in France two years before.

Friends, the fatherland is in danger. In all directions, our brothers are marching in arms to the defense of their violated rights and to avenge the broken trust of their treaties. There is not a minute to lose. Whoever delays or hesitates to march at this moment will quite rightly be regarded with suspicion as a traitor to the fatherland, as guilty of disrespect to the nation, and unworthy of living. His property will be confiscated and his name execrated now and in times to come.

Let us fly, dear friends, to the siege of Port-au-Prince. Let us plunge our blood-stained arms, avengers of perfidy and betrayal, into the breasts of these monsters from Europe. For far too long have we served as the playthings of their passions and their insidious maneuvering. For far too long we have groaned under the yoke. Let us destroy our oppressors and bury ourselves with them down to the slightest vestige of our shame. Let us tear up by its deepest roots this tree of prejudice. Win over or intimidate as necessary; promise, threaten, or drag along with you the virtuous white citizens, but above all, dear friends: unity, courage, and speed. Bring us supplies, cannon, and munitions, and rally forthwith to our common flag. It is there that we must perish or avenge God, nature, the law, and humanity that for so long have been outraged in this climate of terror.

(*Copie d'une lettre des chefs des gens de couleur de la Croix des Bouquets à ceux du quartier de l'Artibonite* [Port-au-Prince, nd], 1)

5. THE SLAVE INSURRECTION

Although slave rebellions were much more common and considerably larger in the Caribbean than in North America or Brazil, the 1791 uprising in Saint Domingue was unique in its size, duration, and outcome. The factors that explain why it broke out, how it kept going, and why after two years it led to slavery's demise are complex and controversial, and they need to be distinguished from one another. Historical analyses tend to vary according to their emphasis on either external factors (the French Revolution, abolitionism, war) or internal ones (population growth, traditions of resistance).

In the years 1788 to 1789, slaves in Saint Domingue learned that royal officials were trying to prevent and punish slaveowners' worst acts of mistreatment; that some important figures in France wanted to abolish slavery; and that French people had rebelled in the name of freedom and equality (doc. 33). Slaves might also have heard about the abolition of serfdom and manorial dues, and the Declaration of the Rights of Man, all brought about in August 1789. News of this sort doubtless raised their own expectations, was easily distorted into more urgent rumors, and perhaps suggested there were divisions in white society that could be exploited. Slaves in the French colony of Martinique launched a brief rebellion in late summer, claiming the government had freed them. During the next forty years, there would be many more such attempts in the Caribbean and elsewhere featuring mistaken rumors of emancipation. By far the most important was the great uprising in northern Saint Domingue in 1791.

In 1791, new emancipation rumors spread across Saint Domingue, as tensions rose between whites and free coloreds and between radicals and conservatives. One of the colony's two regiments mutinied and was deported in May. News that the king had broken with the revolution arrived in August. Just when a new colonial assembly was gathering in Le Cap a massive rebellion erupted in the surrounding plain. The insurgents were perhaps hoping to seize the town in the king's name and eliminate the radical-dominated assembly. Planning involved a large meeting of "elite" slaves from local sugar estates (doc. 34), and probably several Vodou ceremonies, of which one has become famous (doc. 35). Vodou's contribution to the revolution remains controversial, but it assuredly included grassroots organization, a sense of solidarity and of invulnerability in combat, and leadership at different levels. Boukman, the rebellion's first main leader, was both a coachman and Vodou priest; so too, it seems, was Jeannot (doc. 38).

After two false starts, which alerted whites to the conspiracy, leaders hurried to execute their plan a few days prematurely (doc. 36). This is why the revolt spread piecemeal, from plantation to plantation, and rural and urban slaves failed to coordinate. Otherwise its impact would have been even more devastating. Nonetheless, in a month the insurgents laid waste to most of the North Plain and occupied the central mountains of the North Province, where a cordon of posts kept them from advancing further. Their aspirations, as reported by white observers, varied from a limited reform of slavery to the destruction of the French. Some spoke of the Rights of Man; others, of restoring the king to power. Common sense might suggest that they would not have killed and destroyed on a massive scale if they expected Saint Domingue to remain a French colony. In the first flush of success, some indeed informed the governor that the colonists should pick up their jewelry and leave (doc. 37).

Yet many slaves apparently genuinely believed they were helping the king against his colonial enemies. This was the role most rebel leaders played, and white radicals gradually became convinced that white royalists, using free colored agents, were secretly behind the slave uprising (doc. 38). Astute leaders like Jeannot happily encouraged the illusion to divide the whites and encourage their own followers. Underrated by historians, Jeannot's success as a leader may be the main reason his rival Jean-François had him executed. His death opened the way for negotiations with the whites in December 1791. Jean-François and his free colored allies offered to help drive their African followers back into slavery in return for amnesty and the emancipation of 300 (later just 50) slave leaders (doc. 39). The insurgents had suffered serious reverses in the plains and knew that troops would soon arrive from France. Many free coloreds also wanted to take advantage of an amnesty the colonists and French government were offering them (though not the slaves). Three civil commissioners sent from France did induce many of the free men of color to change sides, but they could not get the colonists to negotiate with the slaves. Jean-François, too, looked unable to impose his compromise on his followers. Fighting quickly resumed. Many radicals believed white royalists were secretly manipulating the rebel slaves in the hope that a colonial catastrophe would end the French Revolution. Many historians have subscribed to this conspiracy theory, and it later sent the governor to the guillotine, but few have noticed it was the slaves who manipulated the radicals (doc. 40).

Slave women played diverse roles, as did men. Early in the uprising, some women helped whites to flee or fled with them; others exacted revenge, lifetimes of suppressed rage spilling forth. They continued to provide food and raise families, often under perilous conditions, fleeing with their children from camp to camp and enduring extreme hunger. In early battles they danced and chanted African-style, and at least a few bore arms, dressed as men (doc. 41).

During the next year, several large but brief slave revolts rocked western and southern Saint Domingue, and whites and free coloreds also armed groups of slaves to fight for them (doc. 42). The plantation regime was severely shaken, but outside the north it generally remained intact into mid-1793. Free colored control of the countryside was a critical factor in preventing slave rebellion from spreading. In the north, however, the black insurgents remained unbeaten.

Throughout the Haitian Revolution, they suffered heavy losses in pitched battles and, lacking an adequate artillery, they rarely were able to storm fortified camps or towns, or defend their own against assault. Instead they exploited mountainous and forested terrain in their use of broken formations and ambush, and prevented whites from effectively holding the ground that they seized. Their critical edge was their ability to scatter and withdraw at a speed European infantry could not match. In the eyes of most whites, their prudence was cowardice and their courage, fanaticism (docs. 43, 49a).

33) Slaves' Reaction to the French Revolution

These tense letters by the Intendant (chief administrator) François Barbé-Marbois, who had tried to prosecute Lejeune (doc. 5), show the impotence of his moderate reformist approach faced with planter intransigence and the fear of revolutionary change. Reports of government collapse and libertarian debate in Paris, of slave rebellion in Martinique, and the emergence of an antislavery lobby, created panic among whites, which gave rise to false rumors. The one mentioned here, concerning a fugitive slave law, is significant for the way it encouraged slaves to think of their Spanish neighbors as allies, and for involving a supposed cover-up, which itself became something of a syndrome. Hated by most colonists, Marbois had to flee to France a week after writing the last letter.

(25 September 1789.) The news of what has been happening in Paris and the kingdom up to July 20 is known here through a multitude of publications, which at first caused some agitation. . . . The public went very much further than the truth in its speculations. . . . Our chief concern is with the impression this news has on the slaves. We have omitted no necessary precaution for keeping them within the bounds of obedience. Perhaps the most effective precaution is preventing all the excesses and cruelty of which they were too often the victims. Most colonists have adopted reasonable and moderate principles in this regard. Yet barbarous behavior has not come to an end everywhere, and our task is all the more delicate in that we must hide from the slaves themselves our concern for them. On the other hand, those who fail to see that the violence they indulge in will only end up pushing the slaves to despair, resent greatly our exactitude in enforcing His Majesty's laws. Yet everything that is done and written in the kingdom about freeing the slaves becomes known in the colony in spite of the precautions we have taken. We know it is the desire of those who call themselves their friends.[1] They are very humane individuals, who are rightly indignant at the many abuses they have learned about, but the actions they are taking in France are not the right ones for preventing them. They will perhaps . . . make the condition of the slaves worse. Although the government can hardly influence what happens in the organizations formed to improve the slaves' condition, it would be desirable that they knew of the care that the government is taking in this regard and that it can only do so in a manner that does not disturb the public peace or indeed compromise the very existence of this important colony.

---

1. The Amis des Noirs (Friends of the Blacks), the antislavery society founded in 1788.

(10 October 1789.) For ten or twelve days, we have avoided taking up the national cockade,[2] wary of anything that might give the slaves the idea of rallying round a symbol. . . . It attracts the slaves' attention far too much; they call it the sign of the emancipation of the whites. We are informed—and people even write us from far-flung corners of the colony—that in the accounts the slaves give one another of the revolution, they are all agreed on one point that seems to have struck them spontaneously. This is that the white slaves have killed their masters and that, now they are free, they govern themselves and have recovered possession of the land. It would be dangerous just trying to destroy these false rumors with a truthful explanation, and we encourage people everywhere to keep silent without adopting an air of mystery.

At the same time two other news items have added to our alarm. We believe that the first is false, but it has been spread due to the fear and indiscretion of those who have the greatest interest in hiding it. Some merchants and planters are writing that the Spanish government has sent the governor of Santo Domingo a decree that states that fugitive slaves from the French part of the island will be received in the Spanish part, but that the wisdom of this official has caused him to keep these orders secret[3] . . . Another rumor, still more alarming, is that of the insurrection that has occurred on Martinique. We are unable to suppress the details so that they do not reach the slaves, and if the rising had not been put down, it is probable that there would have been an extremely violent reaction here with sedition communicated from plantation to plantation like a train of gunpowder. The unavoidable result of these events has been the meting out of severe punishment on the plantations. Crimes have been committed that cry out for judicial pursuit. We hold them in check and we issue threats, but a rigorous crackdown would in truth be like shaking a burning torch in a powder magazine. However, the Council [appeal court] has taken up four different cases of which the barbarity can only be appreciated by reading the files. Judgment is being delayed. . . . Some entire plantation [workforces] are ready to commit the worst of crimes if they can remain secret; . . . fear is the sole means of restraining them.

The books from Europe concerning liberty also circulate in Saint Domingue in spite of the precautions we have taken to prevent it. There is so much contact between free people and slaves that it is impossible they don't know about the efforts being made on their behalf.

(17 October 1789.) No officials in the kingdom find themselves in such a critical position as we do. We are acting in the presence of 450,000 slaves who

---

2. The red, white, and blue (*tricolore*) rosette that immediately became the symbol of the popular revolution in France.

3. Spain had for a century encouraged foreign slaves to flee to its colonies, but Santo Domingo was an exception. It had an extradition treaty with Saint Domingue.

are perhaps only waiting for the first sign of division among the whites to throw themselves into the most terrible uprising.

(Archives Nationales d'Outre-Mer, Aix-en-Provence, C9A/162,
de Peinier and Marbois to La Luzerne)

34) Planning the Rebellion: The Lenormand Meeting

The case of François/Dechaussée supports the popular idea that maroons played an important role in the uprising. However, Jean-François and Loulou (doc. 16) provide the only known examples. The large Lenormand plantation near Morne Rouge should not be confused with the one in Limbé parish, where the sorcerer Macandal had lived (doc. 10). It was much closer to Cap Français and thus a convenient rendezvous for slaves visiting the town's Sunday market. Unlike the Bois Caïman meeting a week later (doc. 35), the Lenormand meeting was not secret but was passed off as a weekend party.

"Report of the Limbé town council on what happened in this district at the time of the slave insurrection"

. . . During the night of Saturday to Sunday, August 20/21, we were lucky enough to capture François, slave of Monsieur Chapotin, one of those who had burned the Chabauds' trash house[4] the night of August 17/18 and who had escaped. This François, known in the band of rebels sometimes as Defeau and sometimes as Dechaussée, had been a maroon for about a year. He was the one whose deposition was the most serious and the most likely to shed light on this hellish plot. . . . These were his words:

"Last Sunday (August 14) a large meeting of slaves was held at the Lenormand plantation, Morne Rouge. It was made up of two deputies from all the work-forces of Port Margot, Limbé, Acul, Petite Anse, Limonade, Plaine du Nord, Quartier Morin, Morne Rouge, etc. The purpose of this assembly was to fix the date of the insurrection that had been discussed for a long time. Everyone was more or less agreed that the plot [sic] would take place that very night. (In which case, the colony was done for.) However, the blacks changed their minds about this after reflecting that a project planned in the afternoon would be difficult to carry through that same evening. So it was put off. The public papers were read out to us by a young mulatto or quadroon, whose name I don't know and that I'd

---

4. The dried cane stalks and leaves left over after the harvest were called *trash* and were used as fuel in the sugar factories. Trash houses were highly combustible.

never seen before. He told us that the king had granted three days a week[5] and that the whites were opposed to it; that the king and National Assembly were to send troops to uphold our rights, and that we had to wait for these troops to arrive before falling on the whites. The whites would have their hands full fighting whites like that and they would be unable to resist our surprise attack.

The workforces are generally agreed on this point. Yet there are some, like those of Pillot in Acul, and Desgrieux in Limbé, that are composed of hotheads who insist we should start the war against the whites before the arrival of these troops. It was explained to us that we would be fighting for the cause and the interests of the king. We need first to seize Le Cap in a spontaneous attack. By not giving them a chance to realize what is happening, we will surprise them with the help of the mulattoes and blacks, free and slave, on our side. And as Le Cap is the heart of the colony and its stronghold, once it is taken, the rest of the colony will be easy for us. However, the slaves of Limbé and Acul will set fire to the plantations on their way to Le Cap. They will burn the big houses, kill the whites, and seize their arms and ammunition, and then join their comrades from the neighboring districts who will already be in front of Le Cap. This plot is known to all the slaves in the colony, it involves everyone, and the object is to take over the country after burning and pillaging everything and destroying the entire race of white people."

(New York Public Library, Fisher Collection, 8:5)

35) The Bois Caïman Ceremony

Written in 1793, this is by several decades the earliest description of what many Haitians regard as the foundational event of their national history in the belief that Vodou played a central role in the Haitian Revolution's success. Dalmas was the young doctor of the Galliffet estate and drew his information from the interrogation the following morning of several participants who had tried to kill one of the plantation managers (docs. 8, 14b, 36). Although the black pig is usually interpreted as evidence that this was a Petro, not a Rada, ceremony (docs. 11, 12), it was probably modeled on the West African blood-oath ceremony, used to seal pacts. It perhaps served to sacralize the political decisions taken at the Lenormand meeting, or to bring forward the date of the uprising.

---

5. That is, three days a week to work for themselves. False rumors of such a shift from slavery to a type of serfdom began to spread in Saint Domingue in early 1791.

The elements of this plan had been worked out a few days before by the main leaders on the Lenormand plantation at Morne Rouge. Before carrying it out, they held a sort of celebration or sacrifice in the middle of an uncultivated, wooded area on the Choiseul plantation called Le Caïman, where the Negroes gathered in great number. An entirely black pig, surrounded with fetishes and loaded with a variety of bizarre offerings, was sacrificed to the all-powerful spirit of the black race. The religious ceremonies that accompanied the killing of the pig were typical of the Africans, as was their eagerness to drink its blood and the value they placed on getting some of its hairs as a sort of talisman that they thought would make them invulnerable. It was natural that such a primitive and ignorant caste would begin the most terrible attack with superstitious rites of an absurd and bloodthirsty religion.

(Antoine Dalmas, *Histoire de la révolution de Saint-Domingue*
[Paris, 1814], 1:117–118)

36) The Uprising Begins

For a several days, Saint Domingue's fate hung in the balance as whites began to uncover the plot that was timed for the Colonial Assembly's opening on August 25. This account, gathered from local eyewitnesses, was taken to Paris and read to the French legislature on November 30 by envoys sent to seek assistance in quelling the revolt. The colonists failed to explain that political enmity had probably prevented the radical town council of Limbé from getting much help from the conservative Provincial Assembly in Le Cap. They stressed instead the ingratitude of elite slaves, and their atrocities, so as to reinforce their argument that it was not the violence of slavery that caused the revolt but interference by abolitionists and the hopes they aroused. The account was immediately published and entered the propaganda war over slavery. An English translation, financed by the proslavery lobby, quickly went through four editions. Barthélemy, the Desgrieux estate cook who escaped arrest, went on to become the dominant rebel leader in Limbé parish.

The General Assembly of the French part of Saint Domingue, after first meeting in Léogane, had decided to hold its sessions in the town of Le Cap. The deputies were gradually assembling there to carry out their mission. Several of those arriving on (August) 16 in the district of Limbé, six leagues from Le Cap, witnessed there the burning of the Chabaud plantation's trash house. The arsonist was a slave driver from the Desgrieux plantation. Armed with a machete, he fled. Mr. Chabaud saw him, gave chase, and caught up with him. They fought and the slave was wounded, captured, and put in irons.

Under interrogation he stated that all the drivers, coachmen, domestic servants, and trusted slaves of the neighboring plantations and surrounding districts had formed a plot to set fire to the plantations and kill all the whites. He identified as ringleaders several slaves on his master's plantation, four on Flaville's (in Acul, three leagues from Le Cap), and the Negro Paul, driver on Blin's estate in Limbé.

The Limbé town council went to Chabaud's, where they put the same questions to the black arsonist and received similar replies. The town council sent its report to the Provincial Assembly of the North Province, and they informed the Flaville plantation attorney of the names of the conspirators in his workforce, advising him to seize them and have them jailed in Le Cap. This man was of a mild and gentle disposition and more inclined to confidence than suspicion. He assembled the slaves under his command and, informing them of what the town council had told him, he told them he could not believe in such an atrocious plot, and he offered them his head if they wanted it. With one voice they replied that the Desgrieux driver's deposition was a detestable lie, and they swore unshakeable loyalty to their manager. He had the weakness to believe them, and his credulity has been our ruin.

The Limbé town council made a request to Mr. Planteau, attorney of Blin's plantation, to be allowed to examine the Negro Paul. On being interrogated, this slave replied that the accusation against him was false and slanderous; that he was full of gratitude to his master, who daily showed him acts of kindness, and that he would never take part in any conspiracy against the whites and their property. Because of this treacherous declaration and Mr. Planteau's assurance that Paul could be trusted, he was released.

This is how matters rested until August 21, when the Limbé mounted police went to the Desgrieux estate at the town council's request to arrest the black cook, who was accused of being a ringleader. The Negro fled, sought out the slave Paul on Blin's plantation, and together with the other conspirators they prepared to bring their horrible plan to completion with fire and sword.

In the night of August 22/23, twelve blacks reached the Noé plantation sugar factory in Acul, seized the apprentice refiner, and dragged him in front of the big house, where he expired under their blows. His shouts caused the plantation attorney to come out, and he was laid low with two musket balls. The wretches proceeded to the quarters of the head refiner and murdered him in his bed. They struck with their machetes a young man lying ill in an adjoining room and left him for dead. He had enough strength, however, to crawl to the neighboring plantation, where he recounted the horrors he had witnessed. Only the surgeon was spared, as other surgeons later would be whose skills the slaves reckoned they might need.

The plunderers continued to Clément's plantation, where they killed the owner and the refiner. Day began to break, which helped the miscreants to join up with one another. They spread out over the plain with dreadful shouts, set fire to houses and canes, and murdered the inhabitants.

On that same night, revolt had broken out on the three Galliffet plantations.[6] The blacks of one of these plantations, with arms in their hands, made their way into the bedroom of the refiner intending to kill him. They only wounded him in the arm, however, and he escaped, assisted by the darkness, and ran to the main plantation. The whites who lived there banded together to defend themselves. Mr. Odeluc, Galliffet's attorney and a member of the General Assembly, came to Le Cap and reported the revolt of his slaves. Escorted by mounted police, he returned to the plantation, seized the ringleaders, and took them back to town. He immediately went out again with twenty armed men to restore peace and maintain order, but the slaves all massed together and attacked him. Their standard was the body of a white infant impaled on a stake. Mr. Odeluc, seeing in the crowd his black coachman, who had become a leader, called out to him, "You wretch! I have always treated you with kindness. Why do you want to kill me?" "That is true," he replied, "but I have promised to cut your throat." At that moment, a hundred blows rained down on him, and most of the whites died with him, notably Mr. d'Averhoult, also a member of the General Assembly.

At the very same time, the Flaville workforce (that had so recently sworn its loyalty to its attorney) took up arms in revolt, entered the living quarters of the whites, and killed five of those who lived on the estate. The attorney's wife begged for her husband's life on her knees. The intransigent blacks killed him and told the unfortunate wife that she and her daughters were reserved for their pleasure. Mr. Robert, a carpenter employed on the same plantation, was seized by the slaves, who bound him between two planks and sawed him slowly in half.

We learn of these facts from a sixteen-year-old youth who escaped from the cannibals' fury, wounded in two places. The sword was then exchanged for the torch; the canes were set alight and, shortly afterwards, the buildings. It was the prearranged signal to announce the revolt, which then spread with the speed of lightning to the neighboring plantations. Everywhere whites were slaughtered indiscriminately; men and women, children and the elderly, all fell beneath the assassin's blade.

(*Archives Parlementaires*, 35:460–61)

---

6. The attack on the manager (not the refiner) of the Galliffet–La Gossette estate in fact took place on August 21. It was another false start, like the Chabaud attack. This account telescopes several days of events.

37) The Slave Insurgents Make Demands

This letter to Governor Blanchelande is the first written statement, and one of very few, that the insurgents made of their demands. It was drawn up by a white prisoner, who claimed that the free colored secretary of Jeannot (doc. 38) dictated it to him. Written 24 September 1791 in reply to Blanchelande's proclamation calling for surrender, the letter was in fact never sent and was found in the Galliffet camp, which the governor's forces seized two days later.

Sir,

We have never had the pretension of departing from the duty and respect that we owe to the representative of the king's person, nor even all those things that depend on his majesty. You have proof of it. But you, General, who are a just man, lower your gaze upon us and look at this land that we have watered with our sweat, indeed with our blood, and at these buildings we built in the hope of a just reward. Have we received it? No, General. The king and the whole world have groaned at our fate and have broken the chains that we bore. We, humble victims, were ready to do anything and did not wish to abandon our masters, or rather, as I should say, those who after God ought to have acted as our fathers but were tyrants and monsters unworthy of the fruit of our labor. But you, brave general, want us to act like sheep and throw ourselves into the mouth of the wolf. No, it is too late. God, who fights for the innocent, is our guide; he will never abandon us. And so, this is our watchword: victory or death! So as to prove to you, respectable general, that we are not as cruel as might be thought, we wish to the depth of our souls to make peace, but on condition and with the stipulation that all the whites without a single exception will withdraw both from the mountains and the plain under your inspection to return to their homes and thus abandon Le Cap. Let them carry off their gold and their jewels. We are seeking only that dear and precious object, freedom. That, General, is our statement of our beliefs, which we will uphold with the last drop of our blood. We lack neither gunpowder nor cannon. So: Liberty or death! May God grant that we obtain it without loss of blood; that would be the fulfillment of all our wishes. Please believe that it pains us greatly to have taken this route, but alas, I will end by assuring you that the entire content of this letter is as sincere as if we were in your presence. Do not take as weakness the respect that we have for you and that we swear to maintain, for we will never have any other watchword than "Victory or death for freedom!"

We are with respect, General,

Your very humble and obedient servants, the generals and leaders who make up our army.

P.S. If you will be so good as to reply to us, you can send someone as an envoy. We will receive him with pleasure provided that he carries a white flag and is unarmed and alone. We swear to you on all that is most sacred that we will respect this envoy, as we demand should be done to us. We request that he be a white in preference to a Negro, and we swear to you that he will be respected.

(Archives Départementales de la Loire-Atlantique, Nantes,
1 ET A 34, proclamation, 24 Sept. 1791)

38) A White Captive's Experiences

Gabriel Le Gros was taken prisoner when Jeannot's forces seized the northeast mountains in late October 1791. Seeking to understand the slave revolt's causes, he offers a mixture of valuable and misleading observations, leaving the reader unsure what he might have invented himself or in what degree he was the dupe of others. During two months' captivity, he witnessed a wide range of attitudes among the insurgents. Particularly evident is the fragmentation of the free coloreds. Like many colonists, Gros uses the terms "mulattoes" and "Negroes" as proxies for free coloreds and slaves, but free blacks certainly were more integrated into the slave army than were men of mixed racial descent.

Soon the ground was entirely covered with the bodies of our unfortunate brothers; twenty-one lay on the battlefield, and there were fourteen taken prisoner, who were tied up and brought before Jeannot. He ordered us to be taken to Grande Rivière. . . . We were chained two by two and put in the middle of a strong escort of blacks and mulattoes to be taken to the brigands' headquarters. Leaving our homes in this distressing state, we saw our most valuable possessions go up in smoke. These barbarians set fire to the district in an instant, and we marched by the light of the flames. The scoundrels took pleasure in forcing us to gaze at the mutilated bodies of our brothers and in regaling us with the atrocities they would subject us to on reaching Grande Rivière, which we reached the same day covering ten leagues [about twenty-five miles] barefoot, bare-headed, and in shirtsleeves. Along the way, elderly black men and women gathered at all the plantation entrances to humiliate us with insults and boast of the exploits of their warriors, who were continually beating us with sticks. . . .

The commandant of the main camp was a black slave from the Armand plantation named Michaud. He came up to us, and I thought I could detect in his features a lot of compassion. In this I was not mistaken. He lessened our suffering when he was able, and it was in part due to him that we were freed, albeit two months later. He was obliged to chain us up, however, while waiting for the implacable Jeannot, who had not yet returned from his expedition. But he promised he would help us and gave us some small grounds for hope. . . .

The day after this fatal expedition Jeannot returned to the main camp after giving orders to burn everything. He came to see us and, after reproaching us with the death of Ogé and railing at length against the revolution, he told us that, when he had set out to attack us, he had been informed by Monsieur Pichon[7] of the position of our camp and of how many we were. . . . Jeannot chose from among the prisoners the first victims of his fury and ordered that two be taken to headquarters. He had already informed us that we would be sacrificed two by two each day so as to prolong his pleasure. A foreman and an executioner, who was always on duty, took hold of my unlucky companion Antoine and stretched him out on a ladder, where he was given at least three or four hundred lashes before my eyes. After this, Jeannot's rage was still not appeased and he had gunpowder sprinkled all over Antoine's body and applied to it six lighted matches. . . .

The reader can imagine how I felt, witness to so many atrocities and expecting the same fate myself. However, unknown to me, the driver of the Monthelon plantation had already asked for and obtained my pardon. After asking me several questions, Jeannot sent me back to my chains with the assurance that, on his word of honor, I would be safe. . . .

Our dungeon was always full. People came from all over to look at us. Some, though they were just a few, seemed moved by our condition. The others, in contrast, took pleasure in it. But it was mainly at night that we grew terrified, because of the conversations we overheard and the lugubrious singing accompanied by instruments that seemed as if it would be the prelude to another execution. . . .

Our commander, Berchais, was destined for a different sort of torture. Jeannot began by having one of his hands cut off and then had him given two hundred lashes stretched out on a ladder. He was afterwards taken to the village of Grande Rivière on a cart, where he was hung up from a post by a hook through his chin. The unlucky man lived for thirty-six hours in this condition, and when Jeannot had him taken down, his heart was still beating.

This monster, whose fury knew no satisfaction, later dreamed up a new form of torture: he proposed roasting the remaining prisoners on a spit. Such was our position in the main camp when, on Sunday, November 1, we heard a commotion in the paddock. A lot of men on horseback were circling around the big house. A distant pistol shot and some rifle fire made us suspect that The Tannery[8] was being attacked. This would have caused us all to be killed on the spot. Yet

---

7. The local military commander, Pichon was a captain in the Cap Français Regiment and thus part of the royalist establishment. Jeannot often made such claims to foment conflict in the white population.

8. A hamlet at the mouth of Grande Rivière gorge.

something quite different was going on. Jean-François, the general in chief, who was known to be more humane, had become irritated by Jeannot's cruelty and had him arrested and taken to Dondon, where he was shot the same day. Jean-François came and visited us and told us of Jeannot's punishment. He promised we would be spared and that we would have all the help we might need. . . .

Closely observing everything that went on, I obviously recognized that the mulattoes had encouraged the slaves to rebel and that the government had encouraged the mulattoes. In order to raise so many plantation workforces, the former had needed to employ such devices as the king's orders that he be restored to his throne, the rumor of a massacre of Negro dandies[9] that was to take place on August 24/25, and the king's promises to reward them for their role with three free days per week. There was also the motive of religion, which seemed to inspire them when they accused us of destroying the clergy. All this accumulation of evidence led me to believe that our destruction could only be the work of counterrevolutionary aristocrats. I made up my mind to perish or to disabuse these men of the error into which they had fallen. . . .

Aubert, whom I later discovered to be an excellent mulatto, who never took advantage of the substantial confidence I, riskily, placed in him, opened up to me in a manner that dispelled all mistrust. "Our caste," he told me, "has committed excesses, but it is not as a whole guilty, and among the guilty there are several sorts. I would first of all single out those condemned in absentia in the Ogé affair. They are peculiarly guilty, for it is they who raised the slaves, and among them there were perhaps still to be found some scoundrels who, although not involved in the Ogé affair, were nonetheless intent on wrongdoing.

"The second group consists of the less bold mulattoes who did not want to compromise themselves and, with pleasure, just quietly waited the outcome of a revolution they thought would be favorable to them. Therefore, when the brigands arrived, far from withdrawing with the whites, they joined them and made common cause. The third group had good intentions but were too confident, being completely unaware of the plot. The rapid progress of the disaster took them by surprise and, after hiding for a while in the forests, they were obliged to join with these wretches. They always have sincerely intended to withdraw. They take the field as little as possible, and they discuss matters together, whenever they can do so without danger. However, gentlemen, you will see how closely we are watched and split up between the different camps. You will see how we are humiliated and how difficult it would be for us if we wanted to separate ourselves from them. As for the original causes of this revolution, you should not have the slightest doubt that they are to be found in France and with people of the highest distinction. Indeed, gentlemen, those who had this colony set

---

9. A *nègre candio* was a fancy-dressing ladies' man, regarded as disruptive by whites. Also called *docteurs*, they may have dabbled in sorcery.

aflame, live far from here. They[10] would never have undertaken such a revolution on their own initiative; they needed precise and authentic orders."

At this moment, as he was about to continue his story, he had to break off and move away, as a group of Negroes was approaching us. He told us never to approach or, especially, talk with mulattoes when there might be Negroes around.

([Gabriel Le] Gros, *Isle Saint-Domingue, Province du Nord* [Paris, 1793], 6–11)

39) The Slave Leaders Negotiate

The first document shows that Jean-François put out secret peace feelers that amounted to a betrayal of his followers even before the civil commissioners arrived from Paris. The governor and Colonial Assembly ignored them. He repeated his overtures in December, encouraged by the commissioners, but they had no power to impose a settlement. They had been sent to deal only with the race question, having left France before news of the slave revolt arrived. Most black generals were illiterate and always relied on free colored or white secretaries. However, these overtures, written by the white prisoner Gros (doc. 38), are unusual. Their dominant voice is clearly that of the generals' free colored collaborators, who were their subordinates but here spoke for them.

(a) Lieutenant-Colonel Tousard describes the insurgents' initial approach

To Monsieur de Rouvray, 27 November 1791, at Vieux Bourg camp
General,

At the moment I received the letter that you did me the honor of writing me, a deputation had just arrived in my camp. At first I thought it was sent only by the mulattoes and free coloreds of Grande Rivière and Ste. Suzanne. You can guess how astonished I was while checking their credentials, when they told me that they had come to arrange a general peace and that they had brought with them overtures from the brigand chiefs destined for the east province and the General Assembly.[11] I have just sent [to Le Cap] an aide-de-camp with a packet of papers and an account of all that I have done with the people of color of this

---

10. He evidently means the slaves.

11. He means the eastern part of the North Province, where he commanded. The Colonial Assembly in Cap Français called itself the General Assembly at this time. Tousard was an officer in the Cap Français Regiment; the planter Rouvray commanded colonial militia.

region. They have signed an agreement that is very reasonable, since they ask only for what the laws of the National Assembly, sanctioned by the king, will grant them.[12] I doubt that the General Assembly will accept the brigands' proposals. Here they are, minus the preamble which goes with them, in which they blame Jeannot for all the crimes and state that Jean-François and Biassou, far from being guilty, deserve to be rewarded. Judge for yourself the effect that will have.

1. A full and complete pardon for all the officer corps [i.e. leaders] and the legal registration of their freedom.

2. A general amnesty for all the slaves.

3. Freedom for the leaders to withdraw to wherever they wish, in a foreign country if they choose to leave.

4. The full enjoyment of the effects in their possession.

They promise that, if these conditions are met, they will immediately return the slaves to their duty and will leave it to the royal commissioners who are soon expected to decide their fate.

(Hagley Library, Wilmington, DE, Acc. 874, Anne-Louis Tousard
to Laurent-François de Rouvray, 27 Nov. 1791)

(b) Letter to the Civil Commissioners, 12 December 1791

Dear Sirs,

Infinitely flattered and grateful for the kindness and respect you showed our envoys, we are taking the liberty of expressing our gratitude to you and, at the same time, restating those points that we think are essential for re-establishing order in these critical circumstances. As we have only the general interest in mind, we dare flatter ourselves that, by virtue of your own principles expressed in . . . the proclamation that you were so good as to send us, you will welcome our views and give them your wise consideration.

When you arrived in Saint Domingue, you were no doubt shocked by the disasters of which you were previously unaware. It is not in seeking out those who caused them, or by deploying the forces the nation has entrusted to you, that you will be able to redress the balance that has been upset. On learning of your arrival, we hurried to inform you of our satisfaction, but it would be reprehensible on our part if we did not share with you during this interval before you make known your final decision, the results of our thinking about the situation and our extensive local knowledge. If we remained silent, we could be rightly blamed for great misfortunes. We owe you, therefore, these important details.

We were impressed by the spirit of your proclamation and admire its moderation and wisdom. We feel compelled to inform you, however, that you have

---

12. Tousard is referring to an agreement signed four days earlier with the free men of color of the northeast region.

misunderstood our position, and that you have only a vague idea of the nature of the revolution of which we, as well as the whites, are the unfortunate victims. In ordering us each to return to our homes, you are demanding something both impossible and dangerous. One hundred thousand men are in arms, of whom we make up no more than an eightieth part.[13] Most of us are heads of families, and you will understand that that makes us entirely dependent on the general will. That means on the will of a multitude of Negroes from Africa, most of whom scarcely know two words of French but who have been accustomed to warfare in their native countries, and what sort of warfare! You have certainly heard reports about it.

We must therefore urge you, as much for our sake as for yours, to grant freedom to a number of leaders that we will take the liberty of naming to you. We have carefully examined the situation. The generals,[14] who have very good intentions and were eagerly awaiting your arrival, are the only ones who can, with the help of a certain number of the main leaders, bring about without great losses what a large army could accomplish only with great difficulty, slowly, and by causing the ruin of the planters. It is thus important that this gesture should not be delayed. As soon as you have granted the first article of the address to the colonial assembly that we take the liberty of sending you, we will begin the job with the help of our officers.

However, we make no secret of its being a dangerous business. False ideas, such as that the king has granted the slaves three days a week, will make them very stubborn. They will say they have been misled. The operation might turn out to be disastrous if the greatest precautions are not taken. For this reason, we believe it important to grant freedom to all the senior officers, and to have them chosen by the generals, because they know those who have influence with the Negroes, either through the fear they inspire in them or for other known reasons. Next, to make things go more smoothly, it would be sensible if you yourself wrote to the generals that all the main commanders who behaved well, by fully assisting in returning their followers to order, can certainly expect to be favored by the king. This would have a great effect. But that is not all. Even supported by you, the general assembly, and the governor, the business will only be completed if we are assisted by royal troops. They will not attack anyone but merely show themselves in the countryside at a prearranged time. If it is known that you, sirs, are leading them, everyone will cooperate, and we who at this moment will join forces will carry through the rest. We cannot hide from you the fact we will have to camp out across the different parishes for a very long time. Many Negroes will

---

13. They apparently are saying that the main slave leaders and their free colored allies—perhaps just the latter—numbered at most 1,250.

14. Jean-François and Georges Biassou. Third-person references such as this give these letters a sort of "them and us" message in which the dominant voice is that of the free men of color, despite the slave leaders' being their main signatories.

contaminate the forests, where they will hide out, and constant pursuit of them will be necessary, braving danger and fatigue. Yet the generals and the commanders whom we ask you to emancipate for this important purpose will share the burden with us, and public prosperity will be reborn from its ashes. . . .

We have the honor of respectfully being your most humble and obedient servants,

Jean-François, general, Biassou, general

Manzau, Aubert, Toussaint, Deprès, commissioners[15]

(Archives Nationales, Paris, Dxxv/1/1, document no. 6)

40) The Negotiations Break Down

A month of tentative negotiation culminated in a personal interview between Jean-François and the three French commissars in mid-December. It led to the release of Gros and other white prisoners the following day. Yet no further progress was made, and hostilities soon recommenced. This was because the Colonial Assembly refused to make any concessions and, as Gros' account demonstrates, the mass of slaves in rebellion refused to be sold out by their leaders. Gros was convinced, however, that white counterrevolutionaries subverted the agreement. The publication of his narrative in summer 1792 helped make this the standard interpretation among French radicals. He failed to appreciate that his key piece of evidence was merely hearsay recounted by the enigmatic freedman Toussaint, who, like Jeannot, saw how political passions were dividing their white opponents.

Biassou was delighted with the reply of the national civil commissioners. He decided that we would be handed over and that the meeting would take place on the Saint-Michel plantation. A sort of rivalry emerged, however, between him and Jean-François as to which of them would meet the civil commissioners to conduct negotiations. For a moment, we thought that this disagreement would turn out badly—Biassou's character made him someone to be feared—but the main leaders decided the matter, and Jean-François, as "generalissimo," took precedence.

This supreme leader of the African army was always well dressed in an outfit that consisted of a suit of fine gray cloth with yellow facings set off with a neck ruffle. He wore a cross of Saint Louis on a red ribbon and had twelve bodyguards

---

15. These commissioners represent the free men of color among the slave insurgents. This letter marks the first appearance of Toussaint Louverture during the revolution and bears his first known signature.

who wore sashes decorated with fleurs-de-lys.[16] He was liked by all the free people and by the better sort of slaves. His orders were respected, and his army was well disciplined. . . .

The moment of our departure had arrived. Carters were arriving from many different directions, and we had even been ordered to take up our packages, when suddenly Jean-François revoked the order. After deciding to take us with him, he then gave in to the urging of some of the leaders and sent us away until the following day. . . . At ten o'clock in the morning the black general and his leading officers set off, but scarcely had they reached The Tannery when a messenger brought the news that the whites were massing on all sides and that they looked like they would advance. Hearing this, Biassou mounted his horse and, together with seven or eight hundred dragoons, escorted Jean-François far out into the plain. After seeing nothing, he retraced his steps and let Jean-François continue on his way.

At ten o'clock at night the entire camp seemed worried. It was planned to kill us, if Jean-François and his officers were not back by the next morning. They swore to march immediately on Le Cap and to kill and burn wherever they could break through. In the middle of this ferment, two distant gunshots informed us of the procession's return. The returnees seemed to us very pleased for the most part and told us we would be sent back to Le Cap the next morning. Indeed, we set out at ten o'clock accompanied by 150 dragoons, who were almost all men of color or free blacks and camp commandants. Imagine our surprise when, on reaching The Tannery, we saw blacks gathering and then crowd round us armed with sabers and threatening to send our heads to Cap Français. They cursed the peace and their generals. We survived on this occasion solely because of the firm countenance of our escort. These events convinced us of a great truth: that the slaves would never return to their duty without the use of force and the destruction of some of their number.

Thanks be to the one who watches over the destiny of mortals: we finally reached the Saint Michel plantation, where we had the sweet consolation of seeing and embracing brothers and friends. In particular, we had the consolation of announcing the end of the time of troubles, because, in view of what we had just gone through, we were definitely expecting peace to be restored. As all the brigand leaders wanted it, who could have possibly prevented something so beneficial and needed by both parties? Only a monster was capable of inventing such a project. Yet, the monster, or monsters, not only invented but carried out the project, and the flames that had died down during the negotiations once again lit up this unhappy colony. Raids and murders increased, and Le Cap itself, which had become the refuge of citizens who had escaped the assassin's blade, was now attacked.

---

16. Lilies, the symbol of the monarchy.

I, who had worked on all the arrangements made between the two groups, was firmly convinced that Jean-François would not have changed his attitude without the strongest of reasons. I had various suspicions along these lines, when the deposition of Mr. Laroque finally removed any doubt. This is the deposition of this resident of Grande Rivière, who spent eight months among the brigands. . . .

"He was beginning to get worried when he saw Toussaint Bréda . . . who, with tears in his eyes, told him that everything had fallen through: the twenty or so prisoners who had been brought together from different camps on the generals' orders would no longer be going to Le Cap, and the fighting was to begin again. He added that the sole reason for this change was the arrival during the night of an officer with silver epaulettes; he was tall and lean, swarthy, and with hollow cheeks.[17] After chatting with the generals for half an hour, this officer left. The next day, which was the date fixed for the last meeting and the conclusion of the treaty, Jean-François, he said, no longer seemed the same man. After calling together his council, they all agreed to continue the war and finish off the destruction of what remained standing both in the plain and the mountains."[18] Since that moment, not a day has gone by that has not been lit up by flames.

([Gabriel Le] Gros, *Isle Saint-Domingue, Province du Nord* [Paris, 1793], 25–28)

41) Women in Rebellion

Contemporary documents provide little information on women slaves. The revolution was led and fought mainly by men. Among slaves who took refuge in the towns or abandoned rebel camps women apparently predominated. The following extracts, however, offer some rare and tantalizing glimpses that add nuance to this picture. So do some, even rarer, reports of female bodies in men's clothing found on the battlefield.

(a) (August 1791) [The rebels] went to citizen Flaville's plantation, where they found all the whites fast asleep. They killed four in the most barbarous manner. . . . A fifth white, a young refiner, was left for dead after he'd been shot twice with a pistol, in the wrist and high up on the shoulder. Afterwards some

---

17. The description was that of Captain Poitou of the Cap Français Regiment.

18. François Laroque was a Grande Rivière planter who escaped a week after Gros' release. Until mid-1793, Toussaint Louverture was known as Toussaint Bréda.

slave women gave themselves the barbaric pleasure of making him smell their private parts. The poor white then had the misfortune of showing some sign of life, and he was attacked again by these terrible harpies, who hit him with floor tiles. They kept threatening him and said, "If we knew you weren't dead [sic], we would go and get the men to finish you off." Finally, he had the strength of mind to play dead so well that they thought he was. They then went off leaving him racked by terrible pain.

(Archives Nationales, Paris, F3/141, 211, memoir by the Clément plantation attorney)

(b) (Fall 1791) The slave driver shot [the Galliffet estates' attorney] Ode-lucq dead. He went to the kitchen, got an ax, and chopped off his head. Some slave women hit the head with bricks either out of hatred or out of fear that he might recover. An overseer hid in a slave woman's hut. She helped him escape in disguise. . . .

[In the camps] slave women mocked white women prisoners: "You are now my slave." They made them serve them, and in particular they undressed them and whipped them on a ladder for minor offenses and on the slightest pretext. There was no outrage or torment to which the white women were not exposed by the Negroes. The least of which was nudity and all that concerns modesty. . . .

[In battle,] they sometimes came forward dancing, shouting, and singing, preceded by a great number of women and children, who served as ramparts. They then let out a terrible yell seeking to intimidate.

(Médiathèque, Nantes, Ms. 1809, ff. 188, 193, 195, history by Listré)

(c) (Fall 1791) They revived the savage practices of their homelands. The women were the most cruel. They used rocks to kill off the dying, mutilating them in a thousand ways and ceasing only when the body was in pieces.

(Service Historique de la Marine, Vincennes, Ms. 113, f. 657, history by Tanguy)

(d) (Late 1791) We must give credit to the leaders of the Dondon camp; they never gave us cause for complaint. They allowed us a great deal of freedom, but it was not the same with the other Negroes, who vexed us on every possible occasion. The slave women were infinitely more insolent, harsher, and less willing to return to their duties than were the slave men.

([Gabriel Le] Gros, *Isle Saint-Domingue, Province du Nord* [Paris, 1793], 12–13)

42) Arming Slaves: The Caïmittes Rebellion

The arming of slaves by slaveowners during wartime was never exactly rare in the colonial Americas, but its incidence greatly increased during the Haitian Revolution. This self-congratulatory speech describes an early stage in the process. It was made to the Colonial Assembly on 21 December 1791 by envoys from the southern district of Caïmittes. For slaves, military service brought freedom. For slaveowners, being defended by their slaves made good propaganda. The context for this development was the struggle between whites and free people of color in the South and West provinces. All sides committed terrible atrocities in the revolution. The one described here, like many others, was at least exaggerated— Mme. Pinquet and her children survived—but it served to enflame existing hatreds and make reconciliation more difficult.

At Fond d'Icaque on December 4, the people of color again took up arms under the leaders Noel Azor, the Lafont brothers, and Page, all mulattoes and owners of large plantations. They raised and armed their workforces promising them their freedom, and the next day they began to burn the plantations and murder all the whites . . . without regard for either women or children. They invented tortures unknown until this day and treated their victims with the most barbarous cruelty. Mme. Séjourné, a young attractive woman six months pregnant . . . was disemboweled by these monsters . . . the fruit she carried within her was thrown to the pigs! Mme. Pinquet and her young children suffered the same fate! . . .

Between the 6th and 7th, about twenty-five whites, men, women, and children, and thirty plantations had already fallen prey to these treacherous serpents! Nothing would have stopped their criminal progress, if they had been able to corrupt our slaves . . . and persuade them to march with them against us. Yet on the contrary we learned that some workforces, without the help of their masters and even unarmed, had repelled the brigands and put out fires. Everywhere our slaves asked us insistently to be armed to fight the brigands. Because of our weakness and our distance from help, our position and our distress were extreme. We therefore decided . . . to put our slaves' loyalty and courage to the test. On December 8, we armed about 200 slaves with machetes and pikes. We had no other arms. We put them under the orders of 126 badly armed whites . . . and in the afternoon we went to the Davezac ranch, where the brigands were camped.

Our position was not favorable; the brigands lay in ambush in the undergrowth, in the forest, and in buildings. Four whites were soon killed; others were wounded, and our little army knew it was in trouble. Then our loyal slaves, indignant at seeing the brigands get the upper hand, and angry at seeing their masters in danger, asked insistently for our guns, and we allowed them to take them. Immediately they slipped into the undergrowth and made a carnage of these brigands, and we saw them come out only to ask for more ammunition saying, "Me kill one, me kill one!"

The fight lasted three hours. For lack of ammunition, and overcome with hunger and fatigue, our little army was obliged to withdraw and leave the brigands masters of the battlefield. . . . However, we have heard since . . . that they were furiously annoyed at seeing our slaves march with us. . . . A large number of their slaves have abandoned them.

(*Procès-Verbaux de l'Assemblée-Générale*, 350–51)

43) Black Tactics, White Responses

Whites were frustrated by the military tactics of the slaves and angered at being bested by their former flunkies and field hands. As many of the Africans were enslaved prisoners of war and only a minority of French troops in 1791 had seen combat, the slaves may actually have had more military experience than their opponents. In an age of highly formalized warfare, European armies were only just beginning to learn "backwoods" practices like firing from behind cover or in a prone position, and scattering instead of standing upright when being shot at. With ambushes, psychological warfare, and hit-and-run tactics, the insurgents compensated for their lack of firearms.

A northern planter's account

Their [military] undertakings had something truly frightening about them, simply in the way they drew up and began an attack. They never fought out in the open or bunched together—a thousand blacks would never confront a hundred whites in open country—but they would advance making a terrible noise at first, preceded by a large number of women and children singing and screaming in a chorus. Having got quite close to their enemy, but still out of range, they would fall completely silent. They distributed their troops by platoons in all the overgrown places, so that they seemed six times more numerous than they really were. A weak man, already intimidated by this apparent multitude of enemies, was even more so by their grimaces and play-acting, and by the efforts the blacks made to surround their enemy when they could. . . . During these maneuvers, which were carried out amidst an imposing silence, solitary sorcerers could be heard singing and dancing and writhing like demons; they would cast spells to ensure the success of the attack, and often they would advance within gunshot range, confident that the enemy couldn't reach them and so as to convince the blacks of the power of their charms. Attacks used to begin with yells and screams that themselves alone could scare a weak man. Woe to him who at this moment flinched; at the slightest sign of their enemy being afraid and ready to flee, they would become extremely bold, and they were as agile in running down and killing all those put to flight as they were in fleeing themselves whenever we went straight at them in a confident manner. In those cases, even if they outnumbered us twenty to one, nothing could keep them in the fight. They fled abandoning [everything] the better to run. Sometimes they also used surprise night attacks, which often succeeded because of the panic they caused among the always heavily outnumbered whites but which courage could always defeat. Whatever their number, there is no example of blacks attacking hand-to-hand whites who stood their ground. . . . They never attacked whites except when hidden in woods and undergrowth, where the only sign of them was the firing of their weapons.

([Jean-Baptiste Laplace], *Histoire des désastres de Saint-Domingue* [Paris, 1795], 192–23, 213)

Journal of the La Phalange paramilitaries, Léogane[19]

(12 February 1792) The number of slaves in rebellion is increasing excessively. . . They are well armed. . . They are not disciplined and don't know how to make war, but they are excellent hunters and they use cowardly tricks. . . . They know no other laws than their own whims, and have no other motivation than a continual drunkenness that strengthens their desire to pillage and the need to brave death to find food and clothing. They look on the pillaging of our towns as a right owed to their strength, and they are so convinced of it that they even regard it as an act of justice, telling themselves that they are the cause of our wealth.

(19 February 1792) [constantly patrolling with other Léogane citizens,] we divide and beat back small groups of slaves who continually attempt to get closer so they can join up in a huge mass and fall on the town. . . . Each plantation workforce is a platoon that tries to link up with another, and the continual surveillance needed to prevent or interrupt this communication is as dangerous as it is exhausting, since these men are well armed and even have cannons. They handle them badly, but unfortunately they will soon gain experience through the

---

19. These were white royalist planters holed up in the small town of Léogane, west of Port-au-Prince. The paternalist alliance they had formed with the free coloreds in 1790 to oppose racist white radicals had weakened in late 1791, as the free coloreds grew more militant and divided along class lines, and the shaman Romain Rivière, known as La Prophétesse, rose to power in the Léogane mountains. A mixed-race smallholder, he progressively encouraged local slave rebellions and, on March 12, he launched a massive attack on the town that killed hundreds. It was beaten off thanks to white–free colored cooperation but ended white control in the region.

treacherous advice of the evil-doers who arm them against us, who themselves will soon become their victims. . . .[20]

What a situation we are in! Who will ever be able to describe it to future generations? Could one give an idea of it without describing the courage that sustains us and which we transmit even to the souls of the few women that are with us? History has never recounted anything so dramatic, and it will never dare tell all that we have suffered. It would not be believed. We would be taken for . . . barefaced liars. . . . The peace we feel in our souls is truly remarkable. . . . We are much closer to death than to life but, after the initial terror that it is normal for people to feel, there came to us a general spirit that seems a sort of heroism. . . . When you can wait for evil without worry, it's almost a way of overcoming it. . . . A bullet or a cannonball causes a lot less suffering than being sick in bed.

(18 March 1792) Most of the rebel slaves are Africans. . . . The creoles join them only because they are forced to by the Africans, who kill anyone who resists. The bravery of these Africans is unbelievable. As lazy and cowardly as they are in other aspects of their lives, they are vigorous, stubborn, and full of rage in this war that they are being made to fight.

(Archives Nationales d'Outre-Mer, Aix-en-Provence, D2c/99, "Livre d'ordres")

Commissioner Polverel to Lieutenant-Colonel Desfourneaux

Although they do not stand their ground in a fight like we do, they are no less brave and will learn our ways.

(Archives Nationales, Paris, Dxxv/12/116, letter of 3 Aug. 1793)

A colonist's teenaged daughter

Papa left last Monday with three hundred men of the national guard, which was sent at La Cul in order to chase the brigands that are there. . . . Papa went with the national guard by water. They arrived at five o'clock in the afternoon and landed at six. . . . At eight o'clock in the evening, Papa was attacked, but the brigands were conquered in the attack. . . . [Some of the guardsmen] through'd [sic] themselves in the sea. . . . Papa's guide, a Negro man, was pulling them out by the feet and crying. . . . ["Get hold] of yourselves. Is it possible that it is white men who behave in so infamous a manner?" Indeed I am not surprised that they were terrified, as they [had] arrived but three days . . . from France and were not used to fighting Negroes. Figure to yourself, my dear Mama, about four or five hundred of those black creatures, almost all naked, screaming with all their might, "Kill them, tie them, now we have them." You must know, my dear Mama, that they are never above half armed, but gather together as much as they can; some have horns, others old broken kettles, and they try to make as

---

20. He is alluding to the free men of color, notably Romaine la Prophétesse.

much noise as possible in order to confuse, and frighten whites. Papa says that it was impossible to hear oneself. The night they were attacked, they made the noise of wild beasts and behaved like mad dogs. . . . The rest of the night Papa and his troops hunted everywhere, but did not see one brigand, for they were beaten and ceased in the attack.[21]

(Martine St. Martin Tousard to Anna Geddes, nd, Tousard Papers, Clements Library, University of Michigan)

---

21. This letter from 1802 testifies to the continuity of fighting styles through the revolution. The author, a sixteen-year-old French creole, was writing to her American stepmother. She was the "small child" mentioned in doc. 15. Cf. doc. 68.

6. SLAVE EMANCIPATION

The emancipation of Saint Domingue's slaves in August 1793 was a landmark in the history of the Americas. It was the first abolition of slavery in a major slave society and the only case that was primarily a response to slave rebellion. The slave uprising, however, was a necessary but not sufficient cause of emancipation. There were two other essential developments, without which it was unlikely to have occurred. One was the outbreak of war between the colonial powers in February and March 1793, which radically changed the balance of power between France and the insurgent slaves. The other was the arrival in Saint Domingue of Commissaire Civil Sonthonax, who had an abolitionist background and dictatorial powers. Sonthonax's emancipation decree, which contemporaries compared to an electric shock, emerged from the interaction of these three factors: slave resistance, international rivalry, and metropolitan idealism. Narratives that fail to do justice to all three cannot properly explain this momentous turning point.

Sonthonax and Polverel had no instructions from the French government to change the slave regime, but when they disembarked in September 1792, many colonists feared that was their secret mission (doc. 44). Historians attributed this to colonial paranoia until, in the 1980s, they discovered that, as a journalist, Sonthonax had been an early advocate of slave emancipation (doc. 45). This makes it impossible to attribute his later actions solely to political calculation and desperate military circumstances, which hitherto had been the dominant interpretation. It also raises doubts about why, in February 1793, he stopped a successful campaign against the northern slave rebellion. Perhaps, as he said, French losses were too heavy and he was needed elsewhere. But perhaps his sympathy with the insurgents caused him to prefer a political to a military solution. Perhaps also he sensed that attitudes in France were changing.

Abolitionism made very slow progress in revolutionary France. News of the North Plain uprising failed to make even the leading abolitionist, Jacques-Pierre Brissot, alter his position that slaves deserved freedom but were not yet ready for it (doc. 46). Nonetheless a few figures, like the radical Jean-Paul Marat and the planters Claude Milscent and Julien Raimond, soon began to argue that slavery should be at least gradually ended. The government that guillotined the king in January 1793 had moved far from the positions of the National Assembly of 1789–1791. Even so, the most important development that occurred at this time was the outbreak of war in Europe.

Up to that point, the insurgents in northern Saint Domingue had already achieved far more than any other slave rebels in the Americas. They had survived longer, destroyed more, and had fought an epic combat. Yet they were little closer to being recognized as free, still less to ending slavery, than they had been eighteen months before. Maroon communities in Jamaica and Suriname had already shown that colonial regimes could be fought to a standstill; this was not new. Indeed, Saint Domingue's insurgents had in a sense accomplished less, as those maroons had won recognition of their freedom in a series of colonial treaties. War between the colonial powers, however, quickly changed the balance of power in Saint Domingue.

War with England made it difficult for the French to send more troops to Saint Domingue, because of the strength of the British navy. War with Spain brought the immediate danger of invasion from neighboring Santo Domingo. This was greatly magnified, as the Spanish took the dramatic step of recruiting the slave insurgents as auxiliary soldiers (doc. 47). Lastly, the prospect of British or Spanish invasion encouraged French colonists to rebel against the authoritarian commissars and the new regime of racial equality. In June 1793, the city of Le Cap was burned in internecine fighting, and thousands of colonists fled to the United States. In these desperate circumstances, and after failing to attract many insurgents with offers of freedom, Sonthonax moved to emancipate all Saint Domingue's slaves, so as to keep the colony French (doc. 48).

The emancipation proclamation of 29 August 1793 applied only to the devastated North Province at first, but it was quickly extended to the rest of Saint Domingue, where planters were welcoming Spanish and British invaders. Although it declared ex-slaves to be citizens, it offered them a very circumscribed freedom. Hoping to preserve the plantation economy, Sonthonax proposed to replace slavery and the whip with remunerated forced labor and lighter forms of corporal punishment. The model proved unpopular with the rural masses, henceforth called "cultivators," but it would be maintained through the rest of the revolution and into the national period.

The insurgents had little reason to rally to the beleaguered French, when the Spanish had already recognized them and their families as free. They were expected to maintain in slavery those who had not taken up arms like them, but under wartime conditions the issue was not yet pressing; in most of the north, plantation work had largely ceased. Governor García of Santo Domingo hoped to influence them by using Catholic priests as intermediaries, and Spanish officers swallowed their pride and treated them as equals (doc. 49). Once Jean-François and Biassou saw how much the Spanish depended on them, they settled into a life of independent mercenaries living it up at the king of Spain's expense. Nonetheless, Sonthonax's decree clearly affected some of their subordinate officers; several wavered in their allegiance, and in their correspondence they referred to freedom as their goal in a way the insurgents generally had not done before (doc. 50).

In the aftermath of emancipation, Sonthonax organized elections in Cap Français that sent three deputies to Paris—one black, one white, and one mulatto. Their arrival inspired the National Convention to pass the law of 16 Pluviôse II (4 February 1794), which abolished slavery in all France's colonies (doc. 51). One of the French Revolution's most radical acts, it occurred at the radical high point of the revolution, with the Republic fighting for survival and the Reign of Terror in full swing. As with Sonthonax's decree, historians debate the relative influence of idealism and political calculation in its passage. With the Jacobins in power, property rights counted for less than they did before, but slave emancipation was also explicitly adopted as a weapon of war that could be turned against Britain's colonies. The economic risks of colonial experimentation had also decreased; since war had closed down France's transatlantic trade, there was less to lose. Yet emancipation was always controversial and, in the following years, it would increasingly need to be defended against colonialist critics (doc. 52).

Still controversial is the role the French emancipation decree had in changing the allegiance of some of Spain's black Auxiliaries. Petit Thomas (doc. 50) and the number three leader, Toussaint, had by May 1794 joined the French, but this was before the decree was known in Saint Domingue. Once the decree was proclaimed, however, it cemented this alliance and changed the course of the revolution. The volte-faces of Thomas and Toussaint were in part provoked by the return from abroad to the Spanish-occupied zone of numerous slaveowners. Their desire to regain their property obviously created alarm among the black soldiers. Both of the leaders massacred local whites, at Port Margot in February and Gonaïves in April, when they rallied to the Republic. Jean-François followed suit in July with a much larger massacre at Fort Dauphin, although he remained loyal to the Spanish (doc. 53). As a political force, the planter class was finished. So was Spain's attempt to revive slavery using freed slaves. The black revolution henceforth held center stage. The French Republic retained possession of Saint Domingue, but it was increasingly dependent on one extraordinary black general.

---

44) The Colonists' Fear of Sonthonax, September 1792

*This pompous restatement of the traditional planter demand for political auton-
omy by lawyer and radical leader, Louis Constantin Daugy, was made when the
civil commissioners Sonthonax and Polverel reached Le Cap. Daugy alludes to
the commissars' dictatorial powers that threatened to override the constitutional
pretensions of the colonial assembly, which the commissioners would soon abolish.
The speech is also notable for its prescient fear of slave emancipation, although the
commissioners had no instructions other than to enforce racial equality.*

We are in your hands like a clay vessel that can be broken at any moment. It
is therefore also the moment, and perhaps the only one, to make known to you
an important truth that was poorly apprehended by Messieurs the national civil
commissioners, your predecessors.

This truth, belatedly realized by the Constituent Assembly, is that there can
be no agriculture in Saint Domingue without slavery. We did not go and buy on
the African coast 500,000 enslaved savages to bring them into the colony with
the status and title of French citizens. Their being free is physically incompatible
with the existence of your European brothers.

Determined as you might be, Messieurs, in accord with instructions that
you might have received, to make the mother country lose the produce of our
fields, this fertile source of wealth and power, rather than suffer there to be slaves
in these lands, you at least could not, without adding to the most outrageous
injustice a ferocious and deadly barbarity, fail to transport these slaves to the
place whence your European brothers took them. . . . No one can impose on
us a law to tolerate in our lands beings whom freedom would immediately lead
into vagabondage, pillage, devastation, and murder. That is why the National
Constituent Assembly delegated to us by the constitutional law of 28 September
1791 legislative power regarding the status of unfree persons. . . .

The slavery of the blacks must be maintained as much for their personal interest as for the maintenance of agriculture and the safety of their masters. . . . They
would become the most unhappy, the most miserable of men, if they were left
to themselves. This truth, already demonstrated by the experience of a century,
is even more strongly confirmed by the countless misfortunes which overwhelm
them in their current state of revolt. . . . Fortunately the colony needs adopt
no other measure than to enshrine in law the time-honored customs regarding
the management and conditions of slaves. Maintenance of this tutelary law can be
efficiently entrusted only to the cultivators [i.e. colonists] themselves, who have a
personal stake in overseeing these things. The law would fail, if the slave saw an
outside authority interpose itself between him and his master that could remove
him from the master's authority. It is against the essence of the servitude of the

blacks, against their happiness and security, to infringe in the slightest on the beneficent power of the cultivator by provoking the intervention . . . of indiscreet government activity or the formalities of judicial tribunals.

(*Moniteur Général de la Partie Française de Saint-Domingue*,
vol. 2, no. 131, 22 Sept. 1792)

45) Sonthonax's Early Advocacy of Slave Emancipation

This long-ignored text shows why planters feared Sonthonax's arrival as Civil Commissioner in September 1792. Although he had no mandate to abolish slavery, and he had never joined the abolitionist Amis des Noirs, the aggressive young lawyer had been an early advocate of slave emancipation in his radical journalism. His actions in Saint Domingue were therefore not just the impro- vised result of political calculation.

As for the slave trade and the enslavement of blacks, the governments of Europe will in vain resist the cry of philosophy and the principles of universal freedom that are sprouting and taking root among the nations. They should learn that revealing the truth to people bears fruit, and that once the impulse is given there is absolutely no choice but to yield to the torrent that will sweep away old abuses. The new order of things will arise in spite of all the precautions taken to delay its establishment. Indeed, we dare to predict, and with confidence, that a time will come—the day is not far off—when a frizzy-haired African,[1] without any other recommendation than his good sense and virtue, will come to partici- pate in the making of laws in our national assemblies.

(*Révolutions de Paris*, no. 63, 25 Sept. 1790)

46) Abolitionist Reaction to the Slave Insurrection

Brissot, the leading French abolitionist (doc. 18), made a long speech to the French legislature on 1 December 1791, responding to the colonial envoys who

---

1. Sonthonax would fulfill his prediction in September 1793 by having African-born Jean-Baptiste Belley elected deputy to the Convention (doc. 52).

had spoken the day before (doc. 36). It was a sizzling indictment of the colonists that claimed that racial intolerance went hand in hand with financial irresponsibility and secessionism. Underestimating the dimensions of the slave revolt, he implied it was a maneuver by indebted planters who wanted to seek British help and throw off French rule—a variant form of conspiracy theory that paralleled the counterrevolutionary version (doc. 38). The brutality of the insurgents should therefore be blamed on their masters' cruelty and treason. The slaves' conditions should be improved in preparation for an eventual abolition. Brissot restated two of the Amis des Noirs' central arguments: that granting equality to the free people of color would reinforce, not weaken, whites' control over the slaves (which finally produced the decree of 4 April 1792), and that slave emancipation had to be a long-term process.

Brissot de Warville. Gentlemen, a frightful event has just thrown Saint Domingue into uproar. The revolt of the blacks, the largest yet seen in the French colonies, suddenly broke out at the end of last August. Only slowly were precautions taken to stop it. . . . The danger was at first deliberately exaggerated. The Colonial Assembly called on foreign powers for help. . . . All these considerations, gentlemen, behoove you to seek out with the greatest care the cause of the troubles that have disturbed Saint Domingue since the revolution, the guilty persons who may be behind them, and the appropriate means for preventing a repetition of such a catastrophe. . . .

It is not just a revolt by blacks that you have to punish but a revolt by whites. The revolt of these blacks has merely been . . . a tool in the hand of these whites, who wanted to free themselves from their subordination to France and, in so doing, to free themselves from laws that offended their vanity and from their debts that got in the way of their dissolute pleasures. The truth of this is what I hope to prove to you. . . .

White colonists . . . who have large properties and who owe little because they control their expenditure . . . love France; they are loyal and obedient to its laws, because they feel they need it to keep order and to protect their property. Such colonists like and support the free men of color, because they . . . regard them as the best able to put down slave insurrections. . . . The dissolute colonists, burdened with debts, like neither French laws nor the free men of color. They realize that, [in] a free state . . . the law will sooner or later compel them to pay their debts, and compel them with greater rigor than in a despotic state, because despotisms allow themselves to be won over by the flattery of aristocrats. . . . These indebted and extravagant colonists like the citizens of color no more than they like the blacks, because they can see that these men of color, almost all of them debt-free and punctual in their business dealings, will always be inclined to uphold the law. . . .

This class of colonists, indigent despite its enormous properties, extravagant in spite of its poverty, proud despite its grave incompetence . . . has a very great influence on another class that is no less dangerous, known as *petits blancs* [poor whites]. It is composed of adventurers, uncouth men, almost all without morals. This class is the true scourge of the colonies, as it is recruited solely from the scum of Europe. These men are jealous of the men of color, both the artisans, who are better and cheaper workers and therefore more sought after, and also the property-owners, whose wealth they envy. . . . After independence, when they control the colony, the poor whites hope to divide among themselves what they have pillaged from the men of color. . . .

I will not pause, gentlemen, to describe to you the fate of the unfortunate [slaves] brutally parted from their freedom and their homeland to water a foreign soil with their sweat and blood without hope and beneath the lash of barbarous masters. Despite the double torture of slavery and the spectacle of others' freedom, the slaves of Saint Domingue remained calm until these last disturbances, even in the midst of the violence that has shaken our islands. Everywhere they heard the seductive word of "liberty." Their hearts were touched, for the heart of a black also beats for freedom, (Applause) and yet they remained silent. They continued to bear their chains for two and a half years without thinking of breaking them, and if they have shaken them, it is at the instigation of evil men whom you will come to know. . . .

On 23 [August 1791] it was learned that a few plantation workforces had rebelled. Those who know the West Indies might think that the center of revolt would, as usual, have been attacked, and troops sent to the plantations to put down the rebellion. However, if that was done, the revolt would have been over too soon, and envoys could not have been sent on the 25th to Jamaica and the United States to ask for help. . . .

Why, instead of going straight to the rebels, did this brave general [Governor Blanchelande] busy himself with barricading and entrenching himself in a town that was already fortified, when he had nothing to fear from an undisciplined enemy that had no weapons or ammunition and knew nothing of siege tactics? Was it not to give the rebels time and means to increase their numbers and to ravage all the plantations in the plain? . . .

Yes, gentlemen, everything is unbelievable in this affair. Should it be attributed to cowardice, to ignorance of the terrain, or to treason? We don't know. But it is obvious that the person who suggested waiting in Le Cap for the enemy instead of seeking him out in the plain or on the plantations is the main instigator of the horrible catastrophe that has devastated Saint-Domingue. . . .

You have been told of atrocious acts that would make anyone shudder.[2] This was not without purpose; the intention was to evoke your sympathy and to distract you from the crimes of the Colonial Assembly. For this reason the

---

2. He is referring to the report read to the assembly the day before by the deputies sent from Saint Domingue (doc. 36).

[colonial] deputies had to make sure they touched sensitive souls with their portrait of the atrocities committed by their rebellious slaves. We have had vicious deeds described to us. "Give me a dumb beast," Mirabeau[3] used to say, "and I will soon make it a vicious beast." But who is to blame for this beast's crime, if it is not the one who keeps it in its wretched state?

You shudder and you are moved by the terrible description of this child who had been impaled! You would not be human if your soul did rise up against the impaler. But who is the real killer of this unfortunate child? Is it the black? No, it is the white who first threw a black into a lighted oven; the white who first snatched a black from his mother's breast and crushed him before her eyes; the white who first made a black eat his own flesh. . . . Yes, even if you list all the misdeeds of the black race they pale beside the ferocity of the white monsters, beside the ferocity of the conquerors of Peru and of Saint Domingue itself. A million Indians perished beneath their daggers. With every step you take, you trample their bones that cry out for vengeance, and you complain of their avengers![4] (Repeated applause)

Color, gentlemen, does not cause crime; crime is caused by the thirst for despotism and the fury of all the passions that devour the human heart. And in whose hearts are they more extreme than in those of the whites? Ah, gentlemen, in this frightful contest between crimes, if any are the most terrible it is those of the whites, because they have been created by despotism, whereas among the blacks they result from the desire for vengeance and the love of freedom. . .

Give thought, therefore, not to suddenly freeing your slaves, but to preparing for it and to improving their lot.

(*Archives Parlementaires*, 35: 474–76, 486, 488–89)

47) Spain's Offer to the Insurgent Slaves

This letter, marked "top secret," from Spain's minister of justice to the governor of Santo Domingo, began a bidding war between France and Spain for black support and helped push Sonthonax toward an outright abolition of slavery. Many believed the Spanish government had secretly supported the slave uprising from its beginning, although its declared position was one of neutrality. Inhabitants

---

3. See above, section 3, note 1.

4. This may be the first appearance of what would become a familiar trope: depicting the slave insurgents as avenging the cruelties of the Spanish conquistadors of three centuries before. See docs. 80, 91.

of Santo Domingo certainly traded with the black insurgents, and local officials were at pains not to offend them, but only with the outbreak of war did these relations become official. This question greatly envenomed relations between inhabitants of Hispaniola's two colonies, who were already divided by politics, religion, and national rivalry. Spanish policy needs to be understood in the light of its long history of using black troops and of making treaties with maroon slaves, and its desire to regain land lost to France in the seventeenth century.

His Majesty has approved all the measures your lordship has taken as being fitting in the island's present condition and circumstances, and in conformity with the orders this ministry has sent you and with the good relations that formerly existed between this government and that of France by virtue of the conventions and treaties that were in force. However, as the French nation, forgetting its most sacred duties and giving free rein to capricious passion and fury, has suddenly trampled under foot the respect owed to this crown and to all those of Europe in committing on the august person of its legitimate sovereign the atrocious and horrible attack now known to all,[5] His Majesty wills that, at the time you receive this present dispatch, by when war will probably have been declared on this nation, you use all necessary and suitable means, and with the greatest speed, efficiency, and secrecy, to win over and gain the alliance of the Negro and mulatto brigands, as well as royalists discontented with the new government established by the French nation. . . .

To this end, it will be necessary to win over Jean-François, Hyacinthe, and the other leaders of the blacks to fight against the troops and inhabitants of the French colony who support the new constitution until you have achieved their complete extermination and brought it back under our rule. You will grant them therefore all necessary help, and promise them the royal protection of His Majesty, assuring both to Negroes and mulattoes, in His Majesty's name, from the present time forward and forever: freedom, exemptions, favors, and privileges like those of his own subjects, and to all of them you will promise advantageous settlement on the lands of either the French or Spanish part [of the island] or maintain them on those they have already acquired. . . .

In order to inform the royalists, Negroes, and mulattoes of these arrangements, you will need to use loyal and discreet envoys who can employ cunning and secrecy to notify them so that they are able put the plan into effect before any resistance to it can be organized. The most reverend archbishop [of Santo Domingo] may contribute to this project, both personally and through a few discreet and zealous priests, who will enflame the minds of those who wish to take our side with appropriate exhortations and the hope of a better fate. I am informing the archbishop of these arrangements. It might also be advantageous

---

5. The beheading of Louis XVI on 21 January 1793.

to use a few Negroes from our own colony whose loyalty is beyond doubt to go to the brigand camps and try not only to assist them in their enterprise, but also to persuade them and reassure them of the promise of freedom and settlement under his rule that His Majesty is making them.

(Archivo General de Simancas, Guerra Moderna 7161, Pedro de Acuña to Joaquín García y Moreno, 22 Feb. and 26 Mar. 1793)

48) The Emancipation Proclamation of 29 August 1793

After France declared war on England and Spain early in 1793, Saint Domingue faced imminent invasion. Most of the French troops sent to the colony had already died of tropical fevers. The Civil Commissioners tried to recruit the slave insurgents with offers of freedom, but most preferred to join the Spanish instead. Pretending to have government approval, Sonthonax then took the dramatic step of freeing all slaves in the North Province. Sonthonax's partner Polverel was shocked, although he had just issued his own, less radical emancipation proclamation in the West Province. The desperate military/political situation, Sonthonax's radical past, and growing support for emancipation in France, all contributed to this turning point. The freedom offered the slaves, however, was only a revenue-sharing quasi-serfdom that kept most of them attached to the plantations and denied their own aspirations to become independent small farmers.

Men are born and remain free and equal in rights. There you have it, citizens: the Gospel of France. It is high time it was proclaimed in all the departments of the republic. Sent to Saint Domingue by the Nation as civil commissioners, our mission was to ensure the enactment of the law of April 4, to fully enforce it, and to gradually prepare without upheaval the general emancipation of the slaves.[6] . . . The French Republic wants all men without distinction of color to be free and equal. Kings are only happy amidst slaves. . . . Do not believe, however, that the liberty that you are going to enjoy is a state of sloth and idleness. In France, everyone is free and everyone works. . . . After becoming citizens by the will of the French nation, you must also become zealous observers of its laws, and you shall defend the interests of the Republic against kings . . . out of gratitude

---

6. The law of 4 April 1792 ended discrimination against free nonwhites. Sonthonax's pretense of having orders to prepare the ground for emancipation confirmed for some their fear he had brought secret overtures from the abolitionist Brissot.

for the beneficence it has showered on you. . . . Have the courage to want to be a people, and soon you will equal the nations of Europe. . . .

Article 1: The Declaration of the Rights of Man and the Citizen will be printed, published and posted everywhere necessary by the municipal authorities in the towns and villages and by military commanders in the camps and posts.

Article 2: All Negroes and people of mixed blood currently enslaved are declared free and will enjoy all rights pertaining to French citizenship. They will, however, be subject to a regimen described in the following articles. . . .

Article 9: Slaves currently attached to the plantations of their former masters will be obliged to remain there and to work the land. . . .

Article 11: Former agricultural slaves will be hired for one year, during which time they will not be able to change plantations without the permission of a magistrate. . . .

Article 12: The revenue of each plantation will be shared into three equal portions after the deduction of taxes on the entirety.[7] A third will be attached to ownership of the land and will go to the proprietor. He will have use of another third for running costs. The remaining third shall be divided between the cultivators. . . .

Articles 14-18: The slave drivers, who will henceforth be called foremen, will have three shares in the third of the revenue going to the cultivators. . . . The other cultivators aged fifteen and above will have one share. Women aged fifteen and above will have two-thirds of a share. Between the ages of ten and fifteen, children of both sexes will receive a half-share.

Article 23: The crops will be shared out at each harvest between the owner and the cultivator either in kind or in cash at the market rate. . . .

Article 24: In each district there will be a justice of the peace and assessors, whose job will be to adjudicate in disputes between the owner and cultivators, and between cultivators. . . . They will ensure that the cultivators are taken care of when sick, that all do an equal share of the work, and they will keep order in the workforces.

Article 27: Punishment by whipping is absolutely forbidden and will be replaced, for problems of disobedience, by one to three days in the stocks, as necessary. The strongest punishment will be the loss of a part or the entirety of the salary. It will be imposed by the justice of the peace and assessors. . . .

Article 29: Cultivators cannot be made to work on Sundays. They will have two hours per day to work on their provision grounds. . . . [8]

Article 31: Women will not work in the field after their seventh month of pregnancy and will not return to work before two months after giving birth. . . .

---

7. As the tax rate was 25 percent, the workers actually received one-quarter of the revenues.

8. Slaves had been expected largely to feed themselves, raising food on small plots of land they were given.

Article 33: Two weeks after the promulgation of this proclamation all men who do not own land, are not soldiers, and are not attached to agriculture or employed in domestic service, and who are found wandering will be arrested and put in prison. . . .

(Léger-Félicité Sonthonax, *Proclamation au nom de la République* [Cap Français, 1793], 1–6)

49) The Black Auxiliaries of Carlos IV

Although the Spanish empire had a long history of using black militia and of making treaties with maroons, recruiting the men who had devastated northern Saint Domingue was a controversial experiment. It was particularly fraught, because the Spanish simultaneously appealed to French planters willing to take an oath of loyalty, and many insurgents were their former slaves. Insurgent leaders, like Biassou's adjutant Bellair, learned early on to use the church and king rhetoric favored by conservative Spanish but, once recruited, they proved independent, demanding, and assertive. Spanish commanders like Armona, who was a Cuban planter, were irritated by their familiarity but feared offending them.

(a) A Spanish officer's orders to his commanders, 15 August 1793

You should consider our black auxiliaries as skirmishers and not as line-of-battle troops. They are good for laying waste the enemy's countryside, burning and robbing, and for firing at them from behind trees and rocks and from the undergrowth, and that is the type of warfare we have to wage at the moment, so as to force our enemy to surrender by spreading hunger, anarchy, confusion, and disorder. However, you need to stress that they should not kill, burn, or rob on the plantations belonging to those who have joined our side and wish to recognize our king. Our role is to back up our allies and supply them with arms and munitions (albeit reluctantly, because without these things we cannot make war and defeat the enemy).

(Antonio del Monte y Tejada, *Historia de Santo Domingo* [Santo Domingo, 1892], 4:83)

(b) An insurgent black officer addresses the Spanish governor

For two years we fought without receiving any help and experienced all the fatigue and misery that anyone could ever imagine. . . . We withdrew into a confined space in the mountains determined to die rather than betray our holy religion. We were overwhelmed by the loss of our monarch and filled with the greatest despair, when a sad voice moved Señor the President [of Santo Domingo] himself.[9] Touched and moved by our misfortune, he deigned to come to our aid. Soon, we learned to make Spanish arms triumph, and to force the French to reconsider the ideas that they had gained from a long experience of the art of war, which had raised them to greatness.

(Archivo General de Indias, Audiencia de Santo Domingo 1031,
Gabriel Bellair to Joaquín García y Moreno, nd [Nov. 1793])

(c) A Spanish officer meets the insurgents

[Biassou] has set himself up as a monarch. Jean-François is his subordinate [he claims] and is called his admiral. . . . He has created military ranks and distinctions, and I will add that he has a harem, he gets drunk, and he cuts off heads like the Emperor of Morocco. . . . His camps begin to the west of Hinche and north of the Artibonite river and stretch as far as the Grande Rivière, or Río Grande, opposite San Rafael and El Peñon. According to what I have managed to find out, they supposedly have some 16,000 blacks under arms, or capable of bearing arms.

This man is about forty years old. He has formed a state or military monarchy decked out with abundant personnel, medals, and military honors. He has a lavish personal guard that is supplied from the enemy colony and from our royal treasury. He sits imperiously in judgment in oral trials with a council of war made up of his generals (none of whom can read or write, but who have low-born white men for secretaries) or he simply consults the opinion of those guards and their officers who are present. Everything is an imitation of what they have seen or learned among the French, mixed with the savagery they brought from Africa. It's the same with their religion. Last Sunday they rang the bell for high mass in Dondon, and because there was no priest present, one of them dressed up and acted as one.[10]

This potentate came to talk with me accompanied by his generals and guards on the morning of the 27th. He then went off to visit his camps, as they are called, between Grande Rivière and Dondon, leaving me with one of his marshals and aides de camp and a white Frenchman, who was one of his secretaries, so that they could eat with me and then be sent to Santo Domingo to negotiate with you. In all haste and before sitting down to dinner, I sent off a message so that your excellency should not be taken by surprise. . . . Be careful in how you receive them and in the marks of respect you show them, because they are always

---

9. That is, the governor, who was also president of the appeal court.

10. This was possibly Toussaint Louverture, whom some later accused of conducting services.

watching everything and very suspicious of the whites. I have found an equality established here that I did not think it prudent to change, owing to our complicated and difficult situation. Biassou holds court and gives banquets which are attended by both his and our officers on ceremonial occasions.

(Archivo General de Simancas, Guerra Moderna 6855, Brigadier Matías de Armona to Governor García, 20 and 30 Aug. 1793)

50) Royalism, Republicanism, and Freedom

Barthélemy, the insurgent leader in Limbé parish (doc. 36), was among the few to join the French republicans in response to Sonthonax's abolition proclamations. "Little" Thomas, a former slave driver from the same parish, was one of Biassou's leading subordinates but had flirted with the republicans and just fought with his fellow Auxiliary and rival Toussaint Louverture. Here Barthélemy rejects Thomas' invitation to join the Spanish. Unlike the proclamations of Jean-François and Biassou, the letter emphasizes freedom as a shared goal, although without specifically addressing the issue of freedom for all. To judge from Barthélemy's argument, republican ideology seems to have made little sense to the insurgents, but their respect for royalism appears to have been genuine and shared. Nonetheless, four months later Thomas did abandon the Spanish in the name of liberty. In 1799, Toussaint had both Barthélemy and Thomas executed on suspicion of disloyalty.

Citizen Barthélemy, Commander-in-Chief . . . to Citizen Thomas, brigadier in the Spanish army

Friends and Brothers . . . we believe that, up to this moment and similarly to yourselves, we have always been fighting to enjoy a right we were not born with and to throw off the horrible yoke . . . that was forced on us. After obtaining this liberty, what more can we want or have to fight for? We are ready to fight for a king, but only if France (whose sons we are) recognizes Louis XVII.[11] Therefore we cannot accept your proposals. Spain is trying to maintain slavery, not to free slaves. For this reason, we stay under the protection of the French Republic, as the representative of the king whom you mention. We have always recognized the respect, submission, and obedience that we owed to a sovereign when one existed, but there is no sovereign, and his rights have now been transferred to the French Republic.

(Archivo General de Simancas, Guerra Moderna 7157, letter of 24 Oct. 1793)

---

11. The eight-year-old son of the executed Louis XVI, who was imprisoned in Paris.

51) France Abolishes Slavery

In September 1793, Sonthonax organized in Le Cap the first multiracial election in France's colonies. Of the six colonial deputies chosen, three reached Paris in February 1794 after a difficult journey dogged by exiled colonists in the United States and France. Taking their seats in the legislature, they sparked a lengthy debate that produced the decree of 16 Pluviôse (February 4). In effect ratifying Sonthonax's fait accompli, the decree abolished slavery in all French colonies and made the former slaves citizens. The decree was passed amidst high emotion, and two weeks later it was celebrated in a public ceremony at Notre Dame cathedral. Many, however, feared it would disrupt colonial production. Its referral to the Committee of Public Safety was an attempt to delay its implementation, and since the constitution had been suspended, politicians were able to spend the 1790s discussing how to modify its political impact.

Decree of the National Convention . . . which abolishes the Slavery of Negroes in the Colonies, 16 Pluviôse II

The National Convention declares that the slavery of Negroes is abolished in all the colonies. In consequence, it decrees that all men, without distinction of color, domiciled in the colonies, are French citizens and will enjoy all rights guaranteed by the constitution. This decree is referred to the Committee of Public Safety, which will report immediately on measures for its implementation.

(*Décret de la Convention nationale, de 16me jour de Pluviôse* [Paris, 1794])

52) Belley, the Black Deputy

In this printed speech from late 1794, Jean-Baptiste Belley (1747–1805), deputy for northern Saint Domingue, defends the February 4 (16 Pluviôse) decree against Benoît Gouly, who represented the Indian Ocean colony of Isle de France, where colonists refused to implement the decree. At issue was the decree's political impact; it was still too early to know what its economic impact would be. Belley had been both a slave and slaveowner. He had purchased his freedom and long worked as a hairdresser in Cap Français. France's first black legislator, Belley's imposing presence was captured three years later in a now-famous portrait by the painter Girodet.

Legislators of a free people, you are told and some people dare write that your sublime decree of 16 Pluviôse is an ill-judged and barbaric disaster. The colonists shout from the rooftops that they will get it withdrawn. You have given back their freedom to two million men[12] snatched by greed from their homeland, and you have broken their heavy chains, the instruments of their misery and torture. . . .

Citizen colleagues, do you believe that Nature is unjust, that it has created some men to be the slaves of others, as the colonists claim? Do you not see in this shameful assertion the true principles of these detestable ravagers of the human species? I myself was born in Africa.[13] Brought in childhood to the land of tyranny, I won through hard work and sweat a liberty I have honorably enjoyed for thirty years while cherishing my country.

The executioners of the blacks impudently lie when they dare to claim that these oppressed men are brutes. If they lack the vices of Europeans, they have the virtues of Nature; they are sensitive and grateful beings. It is in their name, the name of all my brothers, who were invigorated on hearing the unexpected sound of happiness and freedom, that I urge you to maintain your beneficent laws. These laws, as I can testify, struck fear into their oppressors. You have struck a death blow to their avarice and greedy cruelty, and you have returned to life and happiness unfortunate men whom the colonists . . . have for a long time classed among the animals and treated with great inhumanity.

Citizen colleagues, do not believe the lies with which the [the colonist] Gouli has supported his hateful and corrupt principles. Even if a few colored citizens, who were large planters and slaveowners, joined with the colonists out of common interest to betray the Republic and sell several parts of Saint Domingue to the enemy, who have protected slavery, the great majority of men of color and former slaves are devoted to the French Republic out of duty and gratitude. Could it possibly be any different, when the fate of the blacks depends on France's prosperity? . . .

Yes, I admit that those parts of Saint Domingue occupied by the English and Spanish were surrendered to them by colonists *of all colors*, slaveowners. The whites in particular, who are born to domination, used perfidy and guile to lead into rebellion colored property owners, whose self-interest responded to their criminal suggestions. I also admit that the reason the English have not succeeded in taking over all of Saint Domingue is because the blacks who have become free and the French have made a rampart with their bodies to boldly defend the rights of the Republic against this invasion. There is no doubt that, if these brave patriots had arms and ammunition, the English and the

---

12. In 1789 there had been about 700,000 slaves in France's Caribbean colonies, roughly half born in Africa and half in the colonies.

13. His death certificate, however, states he was born in Saint Domingue.

traitorous colonists would water with their unworthy blood the soil their presence has soiled for too long.

(Jean-Baptiste Belley, *Le bout d'oreille des colons ou le système
de l'Hôtel de Massiac* [Paris, nd], 4–7)

53) The Fort Dauphin Massacre, 7 July 1794

Spain's policy was to revive the slave regime using emancipated black insurgents and armed white colonists. The return of hundreds of vengeful colonial refugees, however, steadily raised tensions in the Spanish camp. Toussaint Louverture's desertion in late April left the Spanish more dependent than ever on Jean-François and suspicious of their French colonial allies. When Toussaint trounced his army in early July, Jean-François allowed his men to vent their anger on the colonists in the town of Fort Dauphin and appease their concerns about a return of slavery. The Spanish garrison, decimated by fever and commanded by officers with little liking for the French, did not intervene. Some believed Spanish officials colluded with Jean-François to steal the local treasury, which disappeared in the chaos. This extract intercalates two eyewitness accounts given several days later by survivors who took refuge in the British-occupied zone.

Messieurs Belin de Villeneuve, Bayon de Libertat, Petit des Champeaux[14] . . . have made their appearance and the following declaration . . . That,

They were living at Fort Dauphin for some time past having come from North America or other parts of the colony, as the said place was under Spanish dominion.

That, on Monday, the 7th day of July, at noon, the Negro Jean-François, chief of the *Révoltés* who had begun to burn, plunder, and murder in the month of August 1791, came into the town. This Negro and his troops have been for some time with the Spaniards acting against the Commissary.[15] He is the general of the Auxiliary Troops in the pay of the king of Spain, with rank of Lieutenant-General and adorned with a gold medal.

This chief of the Brigands was followed by near 600 Negroes armed with firearms. . . . [T]heir number being every minute increasing, some of the French

---

14. Three prominent colonists. Toussaint Louverture had once worked for Bayon de Libertat.

15. Léger-Félicité Sonthonax, the most prominent of the civil commissioners.

people looked for their safety by going into the houses that they might be protected by the Spaniards, the French being without arms, except 50 men who
were to form a company of guides; some others came under the protection of
the Spanish chiefs. In the meantime, the Negroes of the town having joined
themselves with Jean-François' Negroes, were running about the streets crying
out: "Long live the king of Spain! Let us kill the French people and spare the
Spaniards!" Very few of the town Negroes have remained faithful to their masters. The massacre began in several parts of the town one quarter of an hour after
the arrival of Jean-François and his troops.

During the first moment, Mr. de Mont Calvo, Lieutenant-Colonel of the
Havana Regiment, commander-in-chief of the troops, hastened to meet on the
square the pickets of the several guard houses and draw them up in order of
battle, part before the King's House and part on the side of the square. In order
to save some of the French, Mr. de Mont Calvo put them amongst the soldiers
and dressed them with Spanish clothes. Many of the deponents were so saved.
In every part where this gallant officer could not be, the Spaniards pushed the
French among the assassins. By order of Mr. de Mont Calvo, the guns were
charged and two pieces of cannon carried to the square, intending to fire in
order to drive back the villains, but he was doubtless prevented doing so by
Casasola, the commander of the place; and the troops, to the number of 700
men, remained immoveable without once firing during the whole time of the
massacre in the town.

A little after the Spanish were in order of battle, Jean-François came and drew
up his troops in a like order of battle; and after a conference between Casasola,
a Spanish priest called Vasquez, and Jean-François, the last, by a whistle, gave
signal for a general massacre: for till now it was done by sundry detachments
and the Negroes of the town. (It is to be observed that the priest Vasquez, a
mulatto, has great influence on the minds of the Negroes, for Jean-François
humbly kissed his hand, when he came near him.) . . .

[When Jean-François] went to the commander's, . . . he was heard to complain in the name of his army, that proprietors had been permitted to return.
He insisted on their being all reembarked in the space of two hours. On being
informed that this was impossible in so short a delay, he answered that they
should immediately be put to death. "Death, death!" repeated his troops, who
understood the signal given. (Observe, sir, that this negotiation between the general and the commander did not take up more than three minutes.) His troops
then filed along the shore to prevent the escape of their victims, mowing down
without distinction men, women, and children. . . .

This atrocious massacre continued three hours, till no person was found
in the houses and streets. Some good Negroes had drove near fifty persons
into Jean-François' house, and from thence they came before the commander
Casasola. Their lives were granted on condition that they should be embarked

soon, and under escort of some Negroes with arms they were driven to the seashore and again plundered and some of them killed.

Montez, the commander of the navy, sent some boats to protect them. They were embarked onboard of several vessels. A greater number of white persons were in the King's House. They were confined in several rooms; some others were concealed in the garrets. At eight o'clock in the night, Mr. de Mont Calvo and some other officers sent for them, and they were placed amongst the soldiers, as they were retreating into the fort. The town remained in the possession of the Negroes and has been entirely plundered. The lodgings of the Spanish officers, till now spared, have been likewise plundered and some Spaniards, but very few, killed. . . .

The deponents think proper to say it was known that the Negroes were dissatisfied with the return of the proprietors. The president himself[16] was remarkably sorry to see their arrival, as they were, he said, the cause of inquietude to the Auxiliaries. For a fortnight, the faithful Negroes did forewarn the French of their being unsafe. The president received the same information, and after his departure from Fort Dauphin, as these informations were increasing, the commandant de Mont Calvo had taken some measures to prevent any misfortune, and he did design to give arms to the colonists in order that they might serve as it would be proper and fit. The president had agreed with that measure, and after many delays, the order arrived the same day of this dreadful massacre.

Besides, the president had left the town carrying with him the treasury, the goods and furniture of his house. The priest, the wife of Jean-François, and the principal mulattoes' and free Negroes' women were living at Laxabon, where they had carried all their baggage and furniture. The president had given arms to fifty mulattoes, instead of giving them to the whites. The priest Vasquez was just arrived a quarter of an hour before the villains and by the same road. According to the report of Jean-François, the number of killed amounted to 771.

> (The National Archives, London, CO 137/93, 182, 236-237, report by Paul Cadusch, and "Examinations taken before the Council of the Môle respecting the massacre at Fort Dauphin" [spelling and punctuation modernized])

---

16. The governor of Santo Domingo, whose titles included president of the appeal court.

7. THE RISE OF TOUSSAINT LOUVERTURE

Toussaint Bréda first appeared as a public figure during the December 1791 negotiations between the Civil Commissioners and the northern insurgents (doc. 39b). Although not yet a prominent leader, he stood out because of his protection of white prisoners in the rebels' camp and his discreet advocacy of making peace, even at the price of freeing only fifty leaders. The man whom history remembers as the liberator of the slaves paradoxically enters the historical record as a proponent of selling out the slave insurgents. Less noticeably, he also deftly promoted the rumors of royalist involvement in the slave insurrection that bitterly divided the colonists (doc. 40).

Little hard evidence survives of Toussaint's early life. Most of what was known until quite recently can be found in an 1801 report by the French general, Kerversau (doc. 54). Born to African parents on a sugar estate near Cap Français, Toussaint worked as a coachman and learned to move easily between different social worlds: African, creole, and French. Some time before the revolution, he gained his freedom. Historians assumed this meant an unofficial freedom—from plantation labor—and that he remained part of the slave elite. Then, in the 1970s, it was discovered he had long been free and had owned and rented land and slaves. He thus belonged to the free colored middle class. Recent writers have exaggerated this finding and depicted Toussaint as a wealthy planter, but in fact he owned very little; most of his family were enslaved, and he continued to work for his former owner.

Like many who knew Toussaint, Kerversau thought him exceptionally devious or elusive. His career contains various enigmas, chief of which was his role in the 1791 uprising. Most historians have believed he cautiously waited several months before joining the insurgents. Kerversau, however, reported that Toussaint was the hidden mastermind behind the rebellion, as the key intermediary in a counter-revolutionary plot. The idea that white royalists were secretly behind the slave revolt had been popular among French radicals since 1792; Kerversau's account inserted Toussaint into this older and broader theory. Some have concluded it was a rumor spread by Toussaint after his rise to power, so as to write himself back into the revolution's founding moment. It remains a tantalizingly open question.

Two similarly controversial issues are Toussaint's commitment to slave emancipation and to monarchism. His pursuit of a compromise peace in December 1791, that would have returned most of the insurgents to slavery, is usually interpreted as a temporary aberration provoked by the imminent arrival of troops from France. Once the negotiations failed, his admirers assert, Toussaint became an unwavering champion of freedom for all. This is not exactly true, as he and Jean-François made similar proposals eight months later. The context was similar, however: the imminent arrival of a French army. His actions might thus be interpreted as pragmatically flexible rather than callous betrayals. Unlike Biassou and Jean-François, he did not round up blacks for sale to the Spanish, and as a freedman, he was obviously not fighting for his own liberty. This constitutes the best argument for an altruistic interpretation of Toussaint, rather than the forged documents on which most historians have inadvertently relied.

Many of the free coloreds involved in the slave revolt broke away to join the whites, when offered amnesty by the National Assembly or when racial equality was granted, but Toussaint remained with the insurgents in the northern mountains through 1792 and the disastrous campaign of early 1793. When the Spanish recruited them in May 1793, Toussaint Bréda was Biassou's leading officer, independent but subordinate (doc. 55a). He then quickly distinguished himself in a series of engagements that reversed their earlier losses and punched holes in the republicans' Western Cordon. In early August, he adopted the name "Louverture" (the opening). The name echoed comments on his military ability, but also hinted cryptically at a new beginning.

Up to this point, Toussaint presented himself as a loyal defender of monarchy like the other insurgent leaders (doc. 55). Although Louis XVI had been executed in January, many (wrongly) assumed that the Spanish monarchy would uphold the rights of its French cousins and that the year-old republic was on the verge of collapse. In late August, however, in two now-famous letters, Toussaint adopted an apparently new persona. While not abandoning his royalist stance, he claimed in slightly mystical language to have been the first to support "general liberty," as the French called the abolition of slavery (doc. 56). Written to small groups of free coloreds, these letters were not the public proclamations historians have sometimes claimed. Repetitive, rambling collections of various arguments, they are not the lapidary statements they seem in printed abridgements. Nor was their timing fortuitously parallel to Sonthonax's emancipation decree, as some would have it; they clearly were a response to the decree then known to be impending. Yet these texts are fundamental to idealist interpretations of Toussaint and his reputation as a precursor figure in the struggle to end slavery. In the event, they had no immediate consequences; Spanish correspondence would not associate Toussaint with general emancipation until early 1794.

The new year brought a worsening in Toussaint's personal situation in the Spanish camp, where he remained stuck in third position behind the less talented Biassou and Jean-François (doc. 57). At the same time, the Republic's position began to strengthen in France and in Saint Domingue, where a few minor black and free colored leaders deserted the Spanish. Some historians have therefore seen Louverture's decision to follow suit in late April as an opportunistic act, motivated by ambition rather than antislavery. However, the two are not easy to separate. Tensions in the Spanish camp were partly due to belated moves to restore slavery, and in opposing them Toussaint found a vehicle for expanding his army. His change of allegiance, moreover, was a process, not an event; he approached the French before he knew of the emancipation act, but he broke openly with Spain only after it was clear slavery was abolished.

Beginning with a massacre of colonists in the strategic port of Gonaïves, Louverture quickly seized for the Republic the districts he had conquered for Spain a year before. For almost the next four years, he faced off against the British in the broad Artibonite valley. With Sonthonax away in Europe between June 1794 and May 1796, Louverture's relationship with Governor Laveaux[1] became the lynchpin of the new regime, the point where the French and Haitian revolutions met. It gave rise to a remarkable correspondence; about one hundred letters from the former slave to the aristocratic radical have survived (doc. 58).

The new republican regime faced not only foreign invaders, but remnants of the black Auxiliaries who fought on in the name of the king, and rebellions by local *anciens libres* commanders who jealously guarded their own fiefs (doc. 58). Some probably resented their loss of control over their former slaves and the rising power of black officers; some perhaps aspired to rule an independent Saint Domingue themselves. Plantation workers also rebelled, especially in the northwest, where plantations had remained largely intact. They resented the forced labor system the government was trying to impose and feared a restoration of slavery. New grievances regarding revenue sharing or military service were added to old ones, like being cheated in the urban markets where they sold their own produce (doc. 59).

Despite these internal divisions, France held on to Saint Domingue, because of the catastrophic losses to disease suffered by the British and Spanish invaders (doc. 60), and because of the discipline of Toussaint Louverture's army (doc. 61). By the end of 1796, Toussaint controlled all the North Province, and after the British evacuated their surviving troops in 1798, all of the West as well. The general's rising power increasingly led some to believe he would eventually overthrow French rule. Named lieutenant-governor, then commander-in-chief, he progressively eliminated all potential rivals. In summer 1796, he had Laveaux elected to the French legislature. A year later, he deported Sonthonax, ironically claiming the Frenchman wanted to make Saint Domingue independent (doc. 62). Sonthonax's replacement, Hédouville, quickly met the same fate. The French government, entirely dependent on the black governor, had to accept his diplomatic explanations and ardent protestations of loyalty.

---

1. Étienne Mayneaud (1751–1828), a former *comte*, whose manorial estates included Laveaux.

54) Toussaint's Early Life

This description consists of rumors collected by the French general François de Kerversau (1757–1825) during the five years following his posting to Saint Domingue in spring 1796. Written when Toussaint was at the height of his power, and Kerversau had just fled to France fearing Toussaint's increasing ambitions, it is not a friendly portrait and reflects the anticlerical, republican officer's distaste for the old regime in France and the new one in the colonies. But it represented a serious attempt at fact-finding. Several of its assertions, such as Toussaint's planning the slave uprising, receive support from earlier pieces of evidence, but remain unproven.

Toussaint . . . was born on the Bréda plantation at Haut du Cap. He was brought up in the master's house by the plantation's attorney Baillon de Libertat,[2] who was himself a rich planter in Limbé, and he was shown a tenderness and care that people in Europe would scarcely imagine that slave children in Saint Domingue could have received. He repaid his benefactor's goodness with affection and loyalty, and he stood out because of his superior intelligence and exemplary conduct; thus he really only knew slavery by name. Put in charge of the livestock, he amassed a degree of wealth thanks to his frugality, his master's generosity, his skill in breaking mules and horses, and the knowledge he acquired of creole remedies used in their treatment. Respected by the Africans as a sort of *Macanda*,[3] considered as upright and hard-working by whites, and cherished by his master, who completely trusted him and often consulted him even on plantation work and his own affairs, he seemed to have nothing more to want to be happy, for he had gained his freedom by the time the revolution swept him into a new sphere, unleashing his passions that were up till then held in check, and turning him into a new man.

Trained by a long experience of slavery in the school of flattery and duplicity, he knew how to mask his feelings and conceal what he was doing. This made him all the more deadly a weapon in the hands of subversive people. It was he who presided over the gathering that proclaimed as leaders of the insurrection Jean-François, Biassou, and a few others whose height, strength, and other physical attributes appeared to equip them for command. He, weak and puny, and known to his friends as Skinny Stick, was only too honored with the post of Biassou's secretary. In this obscure position that he chose for himself, hidden behind the curtain, he pulled all the strings, preparing and organizing the revolt that was about to erupt.

---

2. Antoine François Bayon de Libertat (c. 1731–1801).

3. See doc. 10.

He was the only one who knew how to read and write. This gave him an enormous advantage and made him the oracle of the conspirators. He was, or claimed to be, entrusted with papers that authorized the rebellion and its atrocious tactics. His box of tricks included letters from the princes,[4] orders from the governor, and royal edicts and proclamations. It seems clear that the government was not unaware of these early maneuvers and that it wanted to carry out the plan drawn up at Pillnitz and Pavia[5] to destroy Saint Domingue, so as to bring about a counterrevolution amidst the total anarchy that would inevitably result from the loss of its trade. It is fairly probable that the government made almost all these documents. We do not know for how long, and to what extent, Toussaint was taken in by these political games. What is certain is that he skillfully used them to mobilize the Africans, who were naturally disposed to monarchist idolatry and more impressed by royal panoply and the name of a king than by the majesty of a republic, a concept which most of them are incapable of grasping.

It would be equally hard to say what opinions and aspirations may have plunged this man into a revolutionary career, when his already considerable age, his cold and cautious personality, and his advantageous position seemingly should have kept him away from it without question. There is no doubt that, at the beginning, the rebels' aims were very limited, for a deputation, of which Toussaint himself was the spokesman, asked only for the freeing of fifty slaves and a modest sum to share among the leaders as the price of surrender and sending the workforces back to the plantations. It appears that, at first, some powerful figure exploited his vanity, that his religiosity succumbed to the advice of priests, and his pride to the desire to play a major role. The prospect of financial gain and the lure of pillage perhaps also excited in him a greed that until then he had not known, and that as his hopes grew with his fortune, so did his ambition and to such a degree that the honor of being a general remained beneath him. His avarice grew greater than all the wealth of the colony, and nowadays the Bréda plantation stockman finds the vast domain of Saint Domingue too small for him.

(Archives Nationales d'Outre-Mer, Aix-en-Provence, CC9B/23,
"Rapport au Ministre," 1 Germinal an 9 [22 Mar. 1801])

---

4. Louis XVI's two brothers, who fled into exile in 1789 and were organizing a counterrevolution to restore the old regime in France.

5. Cities in Italy and the Habsburg Empire where counterrevolutionary émigrés gathered.

55) Toussaint the Royalist

These two letters show Toussaint maintaining the royalist stance the slave rebels had adopted early in the uprising. Letter (a) replies to Sonthonax's first emancipation proclamation, that of June 20, which offered freedom to insurgent slaves who would defend the Republic. Toussaint is on campaign leading the army of Biassou, whose military role was negligible. It marks the first appearance in the historical record of Thomas (doc. 49) and Toussaint's "nephew" Moyse (docs. 57, 69, 72). The second extract (b) comes from a long, rambling response to the republicans two months later. It shows that the rebels' resentment of their past treatment by the French and their expectation that the Republic would be defeated in Europe gave them strong reasons, beyond the question of political ideology, for supporting monarchical, proslavery Spain.

(a) The Commander-in-Chief and Officer Corps of the Army camped at Bassin Caïman reply in the name of the army to Monsieur de Neuilly, Commander-in-Chief of the Western Cordon, and to the officers who signed with him: that the aforesaid army has chosen the protection of, and is under the orders of, His Catholic Majesty [the king of Spain] and that, in consequence, it will never treat with the Civil Commissioners, whose authority it does not recognize. It could also declare that, having fought up to the present jointly with its other brothers for the rights of the king, they will all shed up to the last drop of their blood to defend the Bourbons, to whom they have sworn an inviolable loyalty until death.

At Camp Bassin Caïman, 25 June 1793.

Toussaint, general of the king's armies, Moyse, brigadier of the king's armies, . . . Thomas, commandant de la Crête Rouge, . . . Biassou, governor-general for the king . . .

(Archives Nationales, Paris, Dxxv/20/200)

(b) . . . Perfidious republicans! You hold out to us the prospect that justice and the Republic will guarantee us freedom in the midst of a free people among whom perfect equality reigns. . . . You tell us that triumphant France is sensitive to our suffering and sends us representatives to protect us. . . . What misleading lies! . . . Crime and carnage reign in France and a great king is needed to save the state. It will not be long, because France itself holds out to us its faltering hands. [The king of Spain] protects us and saves us from your traps. We expect from him further signs of his loyalty, of which he has already given convincing proof. He is a king and is incapable of deception. . . . As for me, my sole desire is to die for my king and for freedom. . . .

Have you forgotten the suffering you inflicted on us shortly after your arrival in the colony? Instead of dangling before us the promises you now offer, you pursued us like wild beasts. What torture and hardship you made us endure, when we lacked strength! Spain was our refuge. . . . As long as God gives us strength and the means, we will obtain another freedom, different from the one you tyrants want to impose on us. You treat the Spanish as hypocrites; you claim they believe they impress us with their promise of freedom in the name of God, and that serving the king is to serve God and religion. . . . Your religion orders you to shed innocent blood in the name of the Republic and to choose scoundrels to put us in chains. It commands you to seize the fruits of our labor, to put to death an innocent king on a wretched scaffold, and to destroy thousands of desperately poor people. . . . You will perish as tyrants. . . .

[signed] Toussaint Louverture, General of the King's armies, approved by all our royalist officers and troops. 27 August 1793

(Archives Nationales, Paris, AA 55/1511, "Réponse sentimentale pour servir au sujet de la lettre sur la révolution de St. Domingue, Jeudy 8 Aoust 1793")

56) Toussaint the Abolitionist

These two letters, written to win over groups of republican free coloreds, do not discuss the difference between general emancipation and Spain's policy of freeing only soldiers and their families; Toussaint, a Spanish officer, merely asserts that he and his opponents are fighting for the same cause. He claims, moreover, to have been its originator, and obliquely denies the rumor that linked him to a royalist plot. His reference to landowners working safely on their estates suggests that the liberty he advocated would not free slaves from plantation work, but much remains obscure in these texts, in which clumsy writing adds to the lack of clarity.

(a) Brothers and Friends,

What, then, are your intentions? . . . You stubbornly attempt to resist your brothers, who work only, and have never worked other than for you and your greater advantage. Who is it who laid the foundation for this general liberty, the cause for which you are fighting against your friends? Are we not its originators? You cannot deny it, now that you are fighting for general liberty, which you say has been granted you. Since it has been, why do you people of Le Cap, . . . fight against your friends, your brothers, and your own color? . . . Only you can reject those things in which you completely trust and which lead you astray because of a mass of very vague promises. . . . Now the Republic is no more and the kingdom of France is once again a monarchy, everything points toward peace. Lowering yourselves to the level of destroying your comrades is not the way to win it. Dear friends, which of God's commandments orders you to shed blood in this way? Remember, friends, that, if the fear of men cannot restrain you, you have a God who leaves nothing unpunished and before whom you will have to account for your actions, good and bad, in this world down here.

The time has come—I tremble to announce it—when we are going to strike a great blow against all the enemies of peace. So, dear comrades, join our side. . . . Come, brothers, you will not be harmed any more than all the others were. Make enquiries and you will see that our conduct has been fair.

You remember the feelings expressed by your General Chanlatte in favor of freedom and equality.[6] Freedom is a right given by Nature; equality is a consequence of this freedom that has been upheld and granted by this national assembly. You say that you and your general now want these two things. It is for me to work for them. I have been given the right to do so, because I was the first to favor a cause that I have always upheld. I cannot yield my position; having begun, I will finish. Join me and you will enjoy your rights sooner.

Neither the whites nor the colored have ever advised me on a plan. I must give thanks to the Supreme Being for the inspiration into which I was plunged for this cause. The whites and the more educated men of color have always been mistaken, and unfortunately you can't see it. We have begun, have been able to hold firm, and having begun, I will finish. Who threatens with the sword will die by the sword.

You men of color, why do you want to fight for a cause that you didn't manage to support when Ogé arrived from France? He was commissioned by the king for the same thing as that for which you are fighting against your brothers and friends, who work only to protect you and uphold your rights.[7] Return, dear friends, do not delay. It will pain me if, forced by your stubbornness, . . . I will be obliged to act out of character. . . .

Your most humble servant,

Toussaint Louverture, General of the royal armies.

Headquarters, 25 August 1793.

(Archives Nationales, Paris, Section Moderne, AE II 1375)

---

6. Antoine Chanlatte (1752–1815), free colored supporter of the civil commissioners.

7. Ogé, of course, had no royal commission and did not seek slave emancipation (doc. 28). It is uncertain if Toussaint thought he did, or whether he pretended, as Jeannot seems to have done, using Ogé as a symbol that would jointly inspire slaves and free coloreds.

(b) Brothers and Friends,

I can only groan at the state in which you have been plunged for so long and at the misfortune that might occur after you have persisted with such unity in defending laws that can offer no more than an apparent happiness, but which you believe to be very real. You do not know the person who is addressing you. Be assured that he is a true brother who thinks and can see that you are among enemies without realizing it. Goodness, integrity, and humanity are the foundation of our characters. The wise advice I am giving you will leave you no doubt of it.

Do you remember, dear comrades, brave Ogé who was put to death for having taken the side of liberty? Weep. He is dead. But those who are now defending him were perhaps his judges. I am Toussaint Louverture. You have perhaps heard of my name. You are aware, brother[s], that I have undertaken this vengeance, and that I want freedom and equality to reign in Saint Domingue. I have been working since the beginning to bring it into existence to establish the happiness of all of us. But alas! You unfortunately cannot see it. Look at yourselves. Look well at the character of those leading you. Open your eyes and you will see, first and foremost, manipulators, untrustworthy men who seek only to destroy all of you. . . . You do not know what state France is in. They can't give you any news except what they make up to support their party. We can, on the other hand; we get news and always will.

I have to mention the question of our fighting. You say you are fighting for liberty and equality? Is it possible that we are tearing each other apart for one and the same cause? It is I who have taken this on and want to fight for them until they are established and recognized among us. You want nothing of that, being our enemy. Equality cannot exist without liberty, and for liberty to exist we need unity. And there can be no unity as long as you form a separate party. You know that as well as I . . . but unfortunately you let yourselves be led into error. They lay traps for you and have already caught you by one foot. They are working to seize the other so as to trip you up, but you don't notice. Come to me. . . . I am not asking you to surrender. I only want you to recognize your mistakes, like citizen commandant Vernet and J. Baptiste Paparel.[8] They kept up their fight against me for a long time, but fortunately they have had the good fortune to have the blindfold lifted from their eyes; they learn of their errors and have surrendered together with all their men. What has been done to them? They have been welcomed like true brothers who, once blinded, recognize their mistakes, and confidently mingle with their brothers to form one body and defend their own interests. . . . They are all able to remain on their properties and work in security. . . . If you need to discuss things, it is with me, the one who governs everything. Do so with confidence, and may this confidence banish any fears

---

8. Free colored officers who surrendered Marmelade and Ennery to Toussaint in late July.

that may intimidate you. God will punish the wicked and have pity on the innocent who have been led astray. . . .

Your most humble and obedient servant,

Toussaint Louverture, General of the armies for the public good.

Headquarters, Turel plantation, 29 August 1793.

P.S. If lots of whites surrendered to me in the battles I fought at Marmelade and elsewhere, I accorded them all possible honors. . . . I assisted those who wanted to return to France by having them taken to the Spanish colony, where they can take ship to the port of their choosing. Those of the landowners who wanted to stay are on their properties and working. I leave it to you to decide if it is not more advantageous for you to be on my side and achieve your well-being than to fight against your own interests.

(Archives Nationales, Paris, Section Moderne, AA 53 d. 1490)

57) Rivalry with Biassou

In these two angry, self-righteous letters to the Governor of Santo Domingo, Toussaint Louverture lays a series of charges against his erstwhile superior. The letters were taken from the Santo Domingo archives by the nineteenth-century historian Ardouin and are now lost. They are invaluable for the light they shed on mounting conflicts within the Spanish camp and form the basis for the "cynical" as opposed to "idealist" interpretation of Louverture's volte-face—that it resulted from personal rivalries rather than the French emancipation decree. However, they also show that Toussaint's hostility to slave trading and Spain's move to restore slavery were central to these conflicts.

General Biassou has always had agents in all districts who laid ambushes to carry off the women and children of the unfortunate men who were away, gun in hand, fighting the enemy while their houses were burned and pillaged and they were robbed of all they possessed. . . . I had to deal with the results of his wrongdoing and bore the brunt of it. As a result, Thomas went to Marmelade and stirred up my troops telling them I was selling their wives and children to the Spanish. He opened fire on me, killing my brother and seven others who were with me. I had to flee to San Rafael amidst a thousand dangers, abandoned by everyone. And now Biassou wants to blame this affair on me. . . .

Now that the president has allowed all the émigrés to return to French territory that has been conquered, these impatient and imprudent individuals have been trying to return immediately to their own districts, to establish camps there, and make all the slave gangs return to work, and to disarm all the Negroes who are armed. . . . They do not realize it is not yet the time to put such a project into effect. . . .

No, I will never submit to him. I am telling you that General Biassou is not my superior and never has been.

General Biassou, has been insistently encouraged by his treacherous secretary, who is a dangerous man that seeks only to spread confusion among us, . . . He is the cause of all our disunion. Yes, he is behind everything, making Biassou believe that I want to replace him—God forbid I should want such a thing. General Biassou is a simple, vulnerable man without much knowledge, and he is easily led astray by the scoundrels surrounding him. He has sworn eternal hatred for me, and for some time now he has been trying to destroy me using whatever means he can. But God, who sees everything, from whom nothing is hidden, and who reads our most secret thoughts, knows the purity of my intentions, my love for my king and for supporting his cause; he has not allowed me to fall victim to human wickedness. . . .

No sooner had Biassou arrived in [Dondon] than he began to disarm, rob, and lock up all that was most dear to me. He seized the cattle and rum that the commandant-general[9] had given me to feed my troops in Marmelade and also everything that my people brought back from the Spanish colony. . . . Placing a camp on the main road from Gonaïves to inspect everyone going to or from Marmelade, he took everything they brought from Gonaïves, robbing and mistreating them, and putting them in irons. . . .

When I reached Bassin Caïman, I was warned by people I trust coming from Dondon to avoid the main highway, because General Biassou had laid a large ambush at Vincent's Crossroads to open fire on me. . . . After getting to Marmelade, I found the troops in a great uproar; . . . tempers were so worked up and frayed that I couldn't get them to obey or even listen to me. . . . My prayers and protests couldn't restrain them. Against my will, they attacked the town of Dondon. They pillaged and devastated everything, and what is worse, there were people killed and wounded. The same thing happened at Ennery, where the Larivière plantation was sacked. . . .

Immediately after these unhappy events, some ill-intentioned persons went and assured the commandant-general that I had taken up arms against my master, the king, and was going to attack San Rafael. The commandant-general, perhaps trusting what he was told, straightaway arrested my nephew, Moyse, who was in San Rafael, because of his wounds, and he put my family under guard. . . .

Ah, my lord, it is indeed painful for me to find myself thus under suspicion, I who have always fought the enemies of our great king, who watches over and

---

9. Colonel Juan Lleonart, frontier commandant based in San Rafael.

works ceaselessly for the general good. . . . Although the wicked constantly persecute me, I am enduring with constancy and patience, for the suffering that our Lord Jesus Christ suffered for us. . . . I shall end, my lord, in assuring you of my blind obedience and complete submission to your orders and those of your representatives, and rest assured that I will shed up to the last drop of my blood to support the cause of God and my king.

(Toussaint Louverture to Governor García, 20 and 27 Mar. 1794, in Beaubrun Ardouin, *Études sur l'histoire d'Haïti* [Paris, 1853], 2:419–26)

58) Toussaint and Laveaux

These two letters date from the aftermath of Villatte's failed coup against the governor. As Toussaint was at least five years older than General Laveaux, and militarily more powerful, his addressing the Frenchman as "papa" seems strange. Yet such an address was not unusual in this milieu and probably reflects black Americans' proclivity for "fictive kinship" terms. Toussaint's extravagant flattery comes across as insincere, but most historians interpret the two men's relationship as one of genuine revolutionary fraternity. Laveaux had been an obscure provincial nobleman and career army officer, who enthusiastically welcomed the Revolution and earned rapid promotion in Saint Domingue. Like Sonthonax, he had early on expressed antislavery views.

(a) General and dear papa: It is impossible for me to find sufficiently strong expressions to convey to you the satisfaction that my soul experienced in reading your comforting letter of the 26th. It filled my heart. . . . I cannot think of you without shedding tears of emotion. There are, no doubt, pure friendships, but I am not convinced that any surpass the one I have for you or that any are more sincere. Yes, General, Toussaint is your son! You are dear to him. Your tomb will be his. He will risk his life to defend you. His arm and his head are always at your disposition. If ever he were to succumb, he would take with him the sweet satisfaction of having defended a father, a virtuous friend, and the cause of freedom.

I was pleased to learn of Gagnet's return.[10] I have already written to him suggesting a meeting at Dondon or Saint Michel. I will do my best to make sure

---

10. Leading some 2,000 men in the northern mountains, Jean-Baptiste Gagnet was a former officer in Biassou's army who accepted British aid after Biassou's departure in January 1796.

he continues following correct principles and to turn him into a perfect republican. . . . Thank you for the cloth that you purchased for the Dondon garrison.

The soldiers of the army that I command assure you of their loyalty, and I embrace you a million times.

(Bibliothèque Nationale, Paris, Manuscrits, Fonds français 12104, Toussaint Louverture to Étienne Laveaux, 28 ventôse IV [18 Mar. 1796])

(b) Governor-General, do not worry in the slightest about Delair's[11] threats. I will be able to foil all his criminal operations, and those of his associates, too. . . . Be calm, my dear father, your son Toussaint maintains a ceaseless surveillance of the evil-doers, and he will report to you on all his operations and whatever may arise.

I embrace you a million times.

(Bibliothèque Nationale, Paris, Manuscrits, Fonds français 12104, Toussaint Louverture to Étienne Laveaux, 21 germinal IV [10 April 1796])

59) Toussaint and the Ex-Slaves

For much of 1796, African plantation workers repeatedly rebelled against the Republic's forced labor regime, especially in the northwest region previously isolated from the slave revolution. Its white population was now decimated. The insurgents expressed concrete grievances, and also fear that France would restore slavery. Toussaint thought his anciens libres *opponents were behind the unrest; some thought British agents were involved. At a time of multiple crises, Louverture had to leave the Artibonite battlefront and dash across the country to restore calm. He used a public diplomacy of reconciliation, deploying a paternalist rhetoric that appealed to racial solidarity and sought to convince rural blacks that their revolution was over. His successes were short-lived. After further rebellions, the Port de Paix leader Datty was executed in September. In the long term, the rural blacks' fear that France's commitment to slave emancipation would be ephemeral proved correct.*

(a) Two officers coming from Gros Morne informed me that the disorder in the parish of Port de Paix was at its height and that the number of victims was large. . . . I reached the town of Gros Morne at midnight. . . . A large number of citizens of all colors who had been fortunate enough to escape the killing came

---

11. Jean Delair, commandant of Jean-Rabel parish, one of several *anciens libres* leaders sympathetic to Villatte's attempted coup. He was deported several months later.

to see me and gave me an horrific account of it. My horses and my cavalrymen were tired; I ordered them to unsaddle, remain ready, and distributed rations at 3:00 a.m. . . . .

At 7:00 p.m. Étienne [Datty] arrived, as I had ordered, with about 500 men, of whom a large number were armed. I had my horse saddled, and ordered Étienne to form a circle of all the citizens. . . . I mounted up and entered the circle. After preaching to them morality and reason, and reproaching them for the murders that they had committed, I told them that, if they wanted to keep their freedom, they had to obey the laws of the Republic, be submissive, and work; . . . and that Jesus had said, "Ask and you shall receive," not "Commit crimes to request what you need." I asked them if they knew me and if they were happy to see me. They replied yes, and that they knew I was the father of all the blacks. They also knew that I had constantly worked for their happiness and their freedom. . . .

They said . . . "Unluckily for us, there are bad men among us who commit crimes, but we have nothing to do with that. Alas, General, people also want to make us slaves. There is no equality here, like there seems to be where you are. See how the whites and men of color with you are good people and friends of the blacks. They are like brothers with the same mother. That, General, is what we call equality. It's not the same round here; we're disrespected and really vexed, and we're not properly paid for the crops we make. When we go to town to sell our chickens and pigs, we're forced to give them for nothing. If we complain, the police jail us without any food, and we have to pay to get out. You see, General, being treated like that is not freedom. . . ."

I asked all the others if everything the one who had just spoken said was true, and they responded all together that it was true. I quieted them and said: "My friends—I ought not call you this, because the shame that you cause me, and all men of color, shows me that you are not my friends—all the reasons that you give seem to me just, but even if you had a whole houseful of them,"—I used this expression to tell them that, even if they had all the possible reasons there are, then they had still made themselves guilty in the eyes of God, the law, and men. "How is it possible," I said to them, "that I who have just sent deputies to the National Convention to thank it in the name of all the blacks for the beneficent decree that gives them their freedom, and to assure the Convention that they will strive to merit it, and that they will prove to France and to all the nations that their submission to the laws, their obedience, and work make them worthy of it, and that I was taking responsibility for everyone, and that soon with the help of France we will prove to the whole world that Saint Domingue will regain its riches with free labor,—what will I reply to the National Convention when it asks me for an account of what you have done? Tell me! My shame will reveal that I have been deceived. It will prove that the enemies of our freedom have demonstrated that blacks are not fit for liberty, and that if they are freed they will no longer want to work and will commit murder and theft.

They all replied that they had been wrong, and . . . with one voice, "Pardon us, General, we will become so good that everyone will forget what we have just done."

(Bibliothèque Nationale, Paris, Manuscrits, Fonds français 12104, pièce 68, Toussaint Louverture to Étienne Laveaux, 1 ventôse IV [20 Feb. 1796])

(b) . . . our brothers in the commune of Saint Louis du Nord.

For how much longer will you let your most dangerous enemies lead you like blind men? Oh, you Africans, my brothers, you who have cost me such toil and sweat and work and misery! You, most of whom have sealed your liberty with half of your blood! For how much longer will I have the pain of seeing my wayward children shunning the advice of a father who adores them? Have you forgotten that it was I who was the first to raise the standard of insurrection against tyranny and the despotism that kept us in chains? Are you forgetting that the rights that Nature and God himself bestowed on us have been restored to you and that henceforth you need only to give thanks to him?

What are you hoping to gain from the disorder into which people are trying to lead you? You are free; what more can you want? What will the French people who are ready to arrive here say when they learn that, having been given this gift, you have been so ungrateful as to dip your hands in the blood of their children?

But, brothers and friends, I know that you are, by yourselves, incapable of these atrocities. Crime-laden monsters who no longer dare show themselves have been seeking to lead you with them into the abyss. . . . They have led you astray by telling you that France will return you to slavery! How could you believe such an atrocious slander? Don't you know how much France has sacrificed for universal liberty and the rights of man? Young people of dazzling ability, the most flourishing commerce, the greatest treasures of Europe, the most formidable navy, palaces without number, the richest of industries: that is what France has sacrificed for universal freedom and human happiness! How could you believe, dear friends, that it would want to lose something that had cost it so much? . . . No, citizens, this generous and magnanimous people has too noble a soul to ever plan such a project. Only those who want to achieve such a dreadful outcome can want to spread such rumors.

Note well, my friends, that there are more blacks in the colony than there are whites and men of color combined. If there are disturbances, the Republic will blame us, the blacks, because we are the strongest, and it is up to us to maintain order and peace with our good example.

(Bibliothèque Nationale, Paris, Manuscrits, Fonds français 12104, Proclamation, 6 floréal IV [25 Apr. 1796])

60) A British Soldier's Diary

The huge influx of non-immune soldiers into the Caribbean during the 1790s fueled a yellow fever pandemic that lasted a decade and was carried by refugees to North America. Its effects were worsened by multiple infections, the troops' concentration in towns, and their alcoholic excesses that were both a cause and an effect of their high death rates. Before the mid-nineteenth century, Western medicine was largely ineffectual treating tropical fevers. The hemorrhagic disease described here might have been falciparum malaria or yellow fever. Britain sent roughly 25,000 soldiers to Saint Domingue; more than 60 percent died there.

[July 1796] In about three or four Days after our arrival, the Troops . . . began to feel in the most horrid manner the Plague, for I can call it by no other name. . . . It is impossible for words to express the horror that presented itself at this time to those who were still able to crawl about. 30 Negroes were constantly employed in digging Graves and burying the unhappy wretches that perished; & scarcely could they working the whole of the Day, from sun rise to sun set, again dig Holes enough for the dead, tho' three, four & five were tumbled into the same grave together. . . . Men were taken ill at dinner, who had been in the most apparent Health during the Morn; & and were carried to their long Homes at night. In short, the putridity of the Disorder at last rose to such an hight that hundreds, almost, were absolutely drowned in their own Blood bursting from them at every Pore, some died raving Mad, others forming Plans for attacking, others desponding. . . . [F]rom the 3rd July to the 13th, our Regiment alone had lost eight Officers, three Quartermasters, thirteen Serjeants and Corporals, and one hundred & fifty Hussards. . . . The heat we experienced cannot be expressed by Words: broiling on a gridiron must be fools play. . . .

On a Muster made of our Regt. the 20th of March 1797, not one Year & a month since we left England, we could not produce 200 Men . . . the Regt. was 700 strong when we left Portsmouth, and we had lost but 7 Men in Action, the remainder having all fell a Sacrifice to the Climate. . . .

I was credibly informed the other Day that the Irish Brigades that came-out here about ten Months ago fourteen hundred strong, have not now one hundred Men fit to serve. . . .

(Boston Public Library, Ms. Haiti 6f, Lieutenant Howard's Journal, 1:61–62, 2:40, 3:41 [original spelling])

61) The Fall of Port-au-Prince, May 1798

In 1798, the British gradually withdrew their forces from the western and southern regions where they had sought to maintain slavery for nearly five years. This eyewitness account expresses the reactions of a colonial lawyer in the capital city (renamed Port Républicain) to his first view of the revolutionary army and how former slaveowners had to come to terms with their new masters. Christophe Mornet had been a prominent officer in Toussaint's army since 1794 and had fought many campaigns against the British, but Toussaint would have him shot the following year. A year after the departure of the British, their common enemy, Toussaint and the southerner André Rigaud began fighting each other for supremacy in Saint Domingue. Toussaint suspected Mornet, as an ancien libre *(freeman before the revolution), of secretly favoring Rigaud.*

The evacuation of this town fortunately was achieved without any disorder on the part of the English forces. The vigilance of General Maitland kept in check their desire to steal, which certain French officers in their army called the customary rights of war under such circumstances. What the inhabitants of the city owed him on this occasion has to be compared with what they equally owe to the Brigade Chief Christophe Mornet. Considering the difference between the forces each commanded, their obligation to the latter is perhaps very much greater. His half-naked soldiers wearing just a few rags in the form of loincloths—true *sans-culottes*[12]—were starving and in need of all sorts of things and naturally should have thought only of pillage. But far from that, not only did they not commit the slightest affront, but they went without rations for two days without complaining after their entry into the town evacuated by the enemy. What European troops would have maintained such tight discipline under the same conditions? It must be admitted that such patience as well could hardly have been expected except from the character of the black, who is naturally docile, sober, and accustomed to all sorts of privations. However inclined he might also be to excess and brigandage, in a group, he never loses control, unless manipulated by agitators.

May 27 (Floréal 29): the garrison of Fort Bizoton evacuated the post and the convoy set sail with 4,000 to 5,000 colonial troops, 400 or 500 English troops, and more than a thousand free persons of both sexes and all colors and ages. Perhaps as many black slaves were carried off as well, either by the officers of the black corps and a few lessees of absentees' property or, half willingly and half by force, by their masters. The latter clung to the hope that, on leaving the colony,

---

12. A play on words. The term (meaning "without knee-britches") was applied to working-class radicals in Paris, because they wore trousers, unlike middle- and upper-class Frenchmen.

they would be able to use their slaves' strength to set themselves up in business on the American continent or in one of the Spanish islands. . . .

Before the General in Chief, Toussaint Louverture, had his troops take possession of the various places the English evacuated, he proclaimed an amnesty on 18 Floréal with the permission of the Directory's Agent, T. Hédouville. It generously promised those former inhabitants of the colony living in the evacuated areas who had not emigrated or served with the English forces that the past would be forgotten and guaranteed the security of their persons and property.[13] . . .

The army that had just taken possession of the western region had very considerable needs. Landowners and merchants were approached on the matter, and they clubbed together immediately to provide basic necessities. Port Républicain's merchants and shopkeepers provided nearly 100,000 francs in cash and foodstuffs.

The first orders of the commander, Christophe Mornet, showed his intention to re-establish discipline on the plantations and put an end to the vagabondage that had become generalized among the workers due to the state of war in which they had lived for several years and the proximity of the mountains of Jacmel and Léogane. The habit of idleness and lawless ways had become particularly deep-rooted there, as the local landowners had been forced to entirely abandon them. As of the 22nd, Christophe Mornet issued an order that all the cultivators who had flooded into Port Républicain had to return with twenty-four hours to their respective plantations.

The city was expecting the arrival of the General in Chief, and he made his entrance on the 25th. Anxious to make themselves known to him, a deputation of citizens hurried out to meet him. . . . Lespinasse, senior, planter and commandant of the National Guard . . . complimented the general in the name of the city's inhabitants, who had been told nothing about their plan. The General in Chief seemed to react favorably, and the next day he sent them a reply to the speech they had read out to him in the name of the town's inhabitants. The time of fanaticism was over, he said; anarchy had given way to the rule of law. If, contrary to the national will, some Agents of the French government had early in the revolution brought death and devastation to this beautiful part of the French Republic,[14] there was no longer anything to fear from their destructive politics. Having learned by experience, the executive Directory had recently sent here a single Agent chosen from among its best citizens. Let us all help him in his important mission by offering total obedience.

---

13. Flouting French law, Toussaint in fact went further and welcomed back colonists who had emigrated to enemy countries, which was a capital offense (doc. 64).

14. The allusion is to Sonthonax and Polverel, who had bombarded the capital into submission in April 1793 when it opposed racial equality. Toussaint, who had recently deported Sonthonax, was hinting that he and the white colonists shared common ground in their hostility toward the French commissioner.

The 28th, he gathered the inhabitants in the former parish church, where they were administered the oath of loyalty to the French Republic. After the oath-taking the Catholic priest sang the Te Deum, at the general's request, to give thanks for the victory over the English and he celebrated mass.

(Bibliothèque Nationale, Paris, Manuscrits, Nouv. acq. fr. 14878, f. 323–25)

62) The Expulsion of Sonthonax

The conversations reported in this fascinating text between the Haitian Revolution's two most important figures may be entirely, or only partly, fictitious. The report represents Toussaint Louverture's official explanation of why he suddenly deported Sonthonax in August 1797. A mysterious event, it was apparently linked to the increasingly conservative climate of French politics that threatened a revision of colonial policy. This may have made the radical commissioner anxious to turn his back on France. (He had formed a family with a local woman of color.) Or, more probably, it may have encouraged Toussaint to send the French government a warning. The irony is that, in accusing the Frenchman of seeking to make Saint Domingue independent, the black general eliminated a rival and weakened French control, while claiming for himself the role of loyal colonial servant. Julien Raimond (doc. 7), since May 1796 Sonthonax's fellow commissioner and rival, wrote the text together with the bureaucrat Pascal.

FIRST DISCUSSION, between the commissioner Sonthonax and General Toussaint Louverture regarding the former's plan to declare the colony of Saint Domingue independent of France and to murder all the Europeans:

Toward the end of the month of Frimaire or beginning of Nivôse last [December 1796], when I went to Le Cap, I paid a visit as usual to Commissioner Sonthonax. After the customary pleasantries, he had everyone leave his office and, when we were alone together, he made the following proposals to me. So as to present this interview to my fellow citizens in the most organized and exact manner, and in order to leave out nothing of what was said, I have adopted the form of a dialogue. Because the questions that were put to me have remained deeply engraved in my memory, I hope that by using this method I will not forget anything and will, so to speak, enable my government and my fellow citizens to be present at this meeting. I have endeavored to transmit to them not only the sense of the propositions that were made to me but the exact words and expressions, and the order in which questions and answers were made.

Commissioner Sonthonax. "Do you trust me? Do you like me?"

General Toussaint. "Yes, commissioner, I trust you, like you, and respect you."

Commissioner Sonthonax. "If you like me, if you like yourself and your brothers, there is a very simple means to protect yourself."

General Toussaint. "What is that?"

Commissioner Sonthonax. "Declare us independent of France. What do you think? That is my project."

General Toussaint (astonished and embarrassed). "That's a bit much. . . . But give me some time to think about it, before I give you my reply."

Commissioner Sonthonax. "That's fine, that's fine. I'm sure you'll find it a good idea. I know your principles; I know how committed you are to freedom." (We were sitting down and he said, "Come a bit closer, I can't hear you well. Come closer.") "Are you sure of all your officers and your soldiers; are they committed to you?"

General Toussaint. "I am sure of it. They all like me." . . .

Commissioner Sonthonax. "My friend, have no doubt that I am greatly attached to you and that I look on you as the savior of the colony. Tell me frankly what you think."

General Toussaint. "Commissioner, explain yourself first of all. Do you believe France will change its mind about emancipation? Do you fear it might?"

Commissioner Sonthonax. "Perhaps not for the time being, but I know how the colonists are stirring things up in France. Are you aware that it is I alone who fought against the colonists in France and that without me you would have been destroyed? You must trust me completely. When I tell you something, you should believe me. I am honest and will always tell you the truth."

General Toussaint. "Commissioner, tell me if you have received news about what is happening in France, and if you fear for our freedom. What you are saying is not very clear. . . . Didn't France decree universal liberty? Can it go back on its decrees? Doesn't the constitution assure us our rights?"

Commissioner Sonthonax. "France has indeed decreed them, but the colonists are there, and I'm telling you that you will have nothing more to fear when we are independent."

General Toussaint. "Commissioner, I don't believe that that will be possible."

Commissioner Sonthonax. "You don't want to? It's not for me that I'm talking. It's for you and the blacks."

General Toussaint. "How do you expect me, a black leader who has been favored by France, who has children being raised by the Republic, who was named brigadier general by the Directory and confirmed by it in the rank of division general, how do you expect me to betray my government?"

Commissioner Sonthonax. "It is I who am the architect of emancipation; I who am the sole support of the blacks, who defended them against the colonists.

You must leave it to me. Without me emancipation would never have been proclaimed. I am your true and only friend. You must believe that."

General Toussaint. "There must be something you are not telling me. If our freedom is being threatened, let me know. Then, perhaps, I will change my mind. But you are not telling me anything. . . . Don't you remember what I replied when, after your arrival, you asked me why I didn't join you when I first began to fight for my freedom?[15] I replied then that I didn't have confidence in you, because I didn't know you."

Commissioner Sonthonax. "At that time I had to be cautious in preparing for emancipation; otherwise I would have been killed."

General Toussaint. "If you had proclaimed universal freedom when you arrived here, we would have rallied to you. But do you recall that, on the contrary, you swore in the name of the Supreme Being to maintain slavery forever? After that, we couldn't trust you."[16]

Commissioner Sonthonax. "Do you now?"

General Toussaint. "Yes, commissioner, but it depends on your conduct."

Commissioner Sonthonax. "I promise you that all will go well, as long as we are in agreement. We have to be the supreme leaders of the colony. . . . You will command the army, and I will be your adviser. I will direct you."

General Toussaint. "Commissioner, let us talk no more about independence. Coming from your mouth, that word makes me tremble. . . . "

Commissioner Sonthonax. "France has no navy. You can see that it sends us nothing. It will be forced to act like England did with the United States. France and all other nations will be perfectly happy to come here and trade with Saint Domingue. The country will become more prosperous. . . . "

General Toussaint. "Don't you see that all the European powers want slavery? Only France wants liberty. If we had the misfortune to make ourselves independent, France would perhaps say nothing for the moment, but this is what would happen later. France would make peace with the other powers and then say to itself: The colonists were right to claim that the blacks were not worthy of the freedom and advantages bestowed by France. Then France, in agreement with all the proslavery powers, would join them in taking vengeance, and we would be finished."

Commissioner Sonthonax. "We will fight them. If we are united, we can never be defeated."

General Toussaint. "On the contrary, commissioner, you would be the first to leave us. France would then come and blockade all our ports in concert with the other powers. No foodstuffs or other products would enter the colony, and we

---

15. Toussaint had already been free, of course, but now was trying to cover up his past as a freedman and identify with the cause of slave emancipation.

16. Toussaint's concern here is to excuse his remaining with the proslavery Spanish long after Sonthonax issued his emancipation proclamation.

would die of hunger and poverty. We might well have food crops in our mountains, but what sort of life would we have? We would be like beasts in the forest. Besides, such treachery would fill me with remorse and I would die of sadness."

Commissioner Sonthonax. "I will never leave you, I will eat roots in the mountains with you, I will die with you, I like you too much. I am an enemy of slavery."

General Toussaint. "Commissioner, I don't believe any of that. Besides, it does you no honor. You were sent to maintain liberty and preserve the colony for France, not to betray your country. If you knew how much this conversation hurts me, you would have finished it a long time ago." . . .

Although Commissioner Sonthonax had promised me to no longer talk of independence, he repeated his proposal every time I went to see him. . . . The morning after [I was made commander-in-chief—in May 1797] I went to the commissioner's, so I could leave from there for the parade with all the commissioners. . . .

Commissioner Sonthonax. "We absolutely must carry out our project. It is the most propitious moment. Circumstances were never more favorable, and no one is better suited to act than you, together with me."

General Toussaint. "That means, Commissioner, that you want to destroy me . . . Murder the whites! Make ourselves independent!" . . .

Commissioner Sonthonax. "Not murder the whites but drive them out."

General Toussaint. "Today you say drive them out, but yesterday and just now you said we had to kill them. Yet if there were one white killed here, it is I who would be responsible. (Impatiently) I'm leaving. . . . I'm very angry with you. . . . The last time you came here,[17] you told the men of color to kill all the whites, and the new freedmen to kill the men of color. That's what caused the civil war, which caused French territory to be handed over to the British and Spanish. Then you left, leaving us with trouble." . . .

Commissioner Sonthonax. "But General, haven't you noticed how I defended the men of color in my debates, although they are scoundrels?"

General Toussaint. "There are good and bad, as among people of all colors. And you are all the more wrong to call them all scoundrels, since it is among the biggest scoundrels among the men of color, blacks, and whites that you have chosen your advisers and your spies. . . . Commissioner, this conversation will never likely finish, and to put an end to it, I am informing you that you have to return to France."

Commissioner Sonthonax. "No, General, I am sorry. Let us forget the past."

General Toussaint. "The colony's safety demands that you leave for France. You absolutely must leave."

> (*Extrait du rapport adressé au Directoire exécutif par le citoyen Toussaint Louverture* [Cap Français, 1797], 1–15, 36–37)

---

17. Sonthonax's first residence in the colony, September 1792 to June 1794. He returned at the head of the third civil commission in May 1796.

8. THE GOVERNMENT OF TOUSSAINT LOUVERTURE

As Toussaint Louverture emerged as the major figure in the Haitian Revolution in 1796–1797 and the egalitarian post-slavery regime was consolidated in Saint Domingue, both he and the new regime were threatened by the political reaction in France that followed the demise of Jacobinism. By 1797 the absentee planter Viénot Vaublanc and the former intendant Barbé-Marbois sat in the legislature and headed a royalist pressure group that hoped to remake colonial policy. Toussaint responded with a number of impressive publications that defended the character of blacks and their treatment of whites, the state of the colonial economy, and the success of the forced labor system. While seeking to assuage French suspicions of his intentions, he warned bluntly against trying to reimpose slavery (doc. 63).

In 1798, the French government sent out General Hédouville to replace the compliant commissioners Sonthonax and Raimond and reassert metropolitan control over Saint Domingue in the face of Louverture's growing ascendancy (doc. 64). But they failed to give Hédouville his own military force. His attempts to reorganize the administration, to impose long-term contracts on plantation workers, and to reduce the size of the colonial army as the British threat waned, were outmaneuvered by the black governor. The two men also clashed over Toussaint's promotion of religion and amnesty for colonists who had sided with France's enemies. Matters came to a head after Toussaint negotiated the evacuation of the British without Hédouville's participation and then expelled the Frenchman a month later. He went on to expand a secret trade treaty with the British to include the United States, and to expel French privateers from Saint Domingue, thus putting the colony's needs ahead of those of French merchants and the French state, which was still at war with Britain and the United States. In an ironic clash between the French and Haitian Revolutions, he also covertly betrayed to the British a French plot to organize a slave revolt in Jamaica. Prudence suggested that attempts to export slave emancipation elsewhere might endanger its preservation at home.

Fearful of Toussaint's ambitions, Hédouville encouraged the rivalry between him and André Rigaud that led to the War of the South (June 1799–July 1800). A brutal war of caste and region, it began as a propaganda war (doc. 65). Each leader posed as a loyal Republican and accused the other of seeking to restore slavery. Whereas Louverture accused Rigaud of massacring whites, however, the southern general depicted Toussaint as the tool of reactionary planters and the British. Most historians emphasize the destructiveness of General Dessalines' campaign in the South, but Toussaint's homefront suppression of *anciens libres* and their rebellions against him are less well known. It is not easy to distinguish cause and effect in the waves of arrests, executions, and revolts that shook the North and West departments. Men were shot, bayoneted, and drowned in large groups. Although Toussaint's opponents tended to be men of mixed racial descent, prominent free blacks like Belley, Jean-Pierre Leveillé, and Étienne Mentor, (docs. 51, 60) had already fled with Hédouville, and former slave leaders like Pierre-Michel, Thomas Mondion, and Barthélemy (docs. 36, 49) were also among his victims. In asserting his personal power, Toussaint narrowed his base of support. The war drove into exile hundreds who would return to fight against him in 1802.

His efforts to revive plantation agriculture also cost him support among the mass of former slaves who aspired to become independent smallholders or to move into the towns. The forced labor regime that Sonthonax and then Hédouville had sought to establish took years to elaborate and met with various local obstacles (doc. 66). During the revolution there emerged a generation of adolescents that had never done field labor and earned the black governor's special disapproval. Preaching a gospel of hard work and self-sacrifice, Toussaint's response was to tighten the forced labor laws and essentially militarize plantation work (doc. 67). As Inspector of Agriculture, Dessalines used soldiers to repress protests with beatings and executions. The black generals were now planters themselves, having leased sequestered estates. Beyond their personal interest, however, they knew that, if the forced labor system failed, a French attempt to restore slavery would be more likely. Above all, the black army that was both the source of their personal power and the guarantor of emancipation, was financed by export taxes on coffee and sugar and the leasing of absentee estates. This was Toussaint's predicament. His slogan that freedom required work thus had a very particular meaning.

Contemporary eyewitnesses varied in their assessments of the new colonial regime. Defenders such as Captain Rainsford and Agent Roume (docs. 67, 68) were enthusiastic about its egalitarian ethos and post-racial promise, and downplayed the harshness of military rule. If sexual mores seemed lax, they recognized they were structured by the polygamous patriarchal family that had its own customs. Both observers deserve respect. Since Rainsford was a defender of colonial slavery, his sympathetic account cannot easily be attributed to ulterior motives. Roume Saint-Laurent was a white creole from the south Caribbean who served as a French government representative in Hispaniola for most of the period from 1791 to 1801. After replacing Hédouville as Agent early in 1799, he supported Toussaint in his conflict with Rigaud, but the two men clashed as Toussaint increasingly flouted French government orders.

Colonial whites were generally much more hostile. They depicted Louverture's character as devious and irascible, and his regime as a ramshackle tyranny (doc. 70). Not only did the army officially requisition property, impose corvées and forced levies of cash, but individual officers were a law unto themselves and allowed to amass fortunes. The regime's egalitarianism also had its limits. Power was concentrated in the hands of black ex-slaves, all creoles, at whose center was the familial group of Toussaint, his nephew Moyse and brother Paul, and his daughter's former slave, Dessalines. His mixed-race generals and white chief of staff were all marginal figures. Few senior officers were Africans. Civilian officials and planters were still mainly whites, but historians disagree whether he looked on them as essential partners in the new enterprise. The fact that many whites felt victimized and insecure, whereas many blacks thought whites exercised undue influence over the governor, testifies to the difficulties of Toussaint's situation.

Toussaint governed tirelessly. He traveled constantly, checking up on subordinates, and he issued an impressive stream of regulations. His most important document was the constitution he promulgated in July 1801 after uniting the whole island of Hispaniola (doc. 71). Although unauthorized, Toussaint deftly justified the measure by Napoleon Bonaparte's having removed the colonies from the protection of the French constitution when he seized power in late 1799. Louverture claimed to be merely filling a legal void, while parrying this threatening action. As a warning, Article 3 declared slave emancipation irreversible. It was ironic that the governor used Bonaparte's extension of metropolitan control to assert de facto independence.

Besides harkening back to the radical autonomism of the Saint Marc Assembly of 1790, the constitution reflected Louverture's social and political conservatism. Besides maintaining the forced labor system to which most ex-slaves were condemned, it reopened the slave trade from Africa to replenish the workforce. While affirming some revolutionary principles, such as equality before the law and meritocracy, and making slavery's abolition permanent, it looked back to the old regime in matters of religion, the family, and executive power. Eschewing the liberal democratic values of the Age of Revolution, it maintained the unapologetic authoritarianism that had characterized the black revolution since 1791 and would be continued by Louverture's successors, Dessalines and Christophe, after independence.

Barely three months after publishing the constitution, Toussaint confronted a widespread uprising by plantation workers in the North Province, which further decimated the white population (doc. 72). His thirty-year-old "nephew" Moyse was apparently responsible. Such was Toussaint's reputation for deviousness, that some (like Descourtilz) would claim that he was really behind it, and that he framed his young critic in order to eliminate him. The charge is unconvincing, however; Moyse had long had a turbulent reputation. Exactly what type of populism he represented—anti-forced labor or just anti-European?—is not clear. Toussaint stifled dissent. Moyse was not allowed to testify at his courtmartial, and no interrogation report, was presented to the judges, only denunciations. All other rebels were summarily executed.

In the aftermath of the rebellion, Toussaint issued a long, moralizing proclamation that reads like a bitter critique of the new society (doc. 73). Some think its invocation of religion (Christianity) indicated concern with the spread of Vodou, but nothing in the text confirms this. Like many revolutionaries in world history, the governor wanted to remake society by legislating moral behavior. The dissolute reputation of General Moyse and his laxity as commandant of the North Province was the apparent rationale for linking the suppression of sedition with a plan for moral education. The proclamation testifies to the distance that now separated the general and the masses from whom he had descended.

Struggling to find a middle ground that would conciliate free labor with export agriculture, and colonial status with political autonomy, Toussaint had undermined the position from which he now had to confront a new threat from France.

63) Toussaint Confronts His Critics

This open letter to the Directory, the executive body of the Republic, is one of several artful and eloquent texts Louverture authored in fall 1797 in response to the conservative drift in French national politics and the complaints of disgruntled colonial officials like General Rochambeau. Toussaint defends the functioning of the post-slavery regime that relied on forced labor and the sequestration of absentee estates, and he warns against any attempt to restore slavery. Blaming the slave revolt on white instigators, a theory that had become Republican orthodoxy (docs. 40, 53), he contrasts the treason of the planter class with the former slaves who were now the defenders of French republican rule.

Citizen Directors,

At a time when I was thinking that I had rendered eminent service to the Republic and my fellow citizens, . . . and made myself worthy of the confidence that the government had placed in me, . . . a speech given in the legislature by Viénot Vaublanc on 29 May 1797 has just been sent to me from the United States, and I am pained to see that every page of it slanders my intentions and threatens the political existence of my brothers.

Such a speech, from a man whose fortune the revolution in Saint Domingue has temporarily taken, did not surprise me. He who loses has the right to complain, up to a point. But what profoundly distressed me is that such declamations, which were hardly calculated to restore calm among us and encourage the cultivators to work, but on the contrary embitter them, giving them the impression that the French people's representatives were their enemies, might have been approved and sanctioned by the legislative body itself.

To justify myself . . . I shall refute citizen Vaublanc's assertions . . . and prove that the enemies of our liberty were in this instance motivated solely by a spirit of personal revenge, and that they have constantly trampled on the public interest and respect for the constitution. . . . Citizen Vaublanc wishes to insinuate that the freedom given to the blacks is the cause of [Saint Domingue's] misfortune, but it will be easy for me to show that freedom itself would have caused nothing but good, if those charged with establishing it had not used this sacred word to increase their personal power.[1] . . . If only I had enough time, I could easily demonstrate that it was Europeans who were the first to put torches in the hands of my unfortunate brothers and who took the lead in the burning and killing. . . .

As for the North Province, which truly had suffered a lot, public safety has been as perfectly restored as could be desired. Agriculture makes noticeable

---

1. Toussaint meant Sonthonax, whom he had just deported. He was hoping to find common ground with the legislature, which included many enemies of Sonthonax.

progress every day. All the plantations have been leased out, and all the lessors are delighted by the workers' enthusiasm. . . .

[Vaublanc claims,] "Everyone agrees that the colony is in the worst state of disorder, . . . entrusted to the hands of ignorant, uncouth Negroes that are incapable of distinguishing between unbridled license and austere liberty whose laws they must obey." . . .

When France was threatened with losing the colony, it was the blacks who used their strength and their weapons to preserve it for her. They reconquered most of the districts treasonously surrendered to the Spanish and British, and they stopped the general contagion. It was the blacks who, together with the good citizens of the two other colors, flew to the aid of General [Laveaux]. . . .

Such are the Negroes whom Vaublanc accuses of being ignorant and uncouth. No doubt they are, for without education there is only ignorance and crudity. But should they be criminalized for this lack of education, or should we accuse those who used terrible punishments to prevent them obtaining it? Is it only civilized people who can distinguish right and wrong, and know charity and justice? The men of Saint Domingue have been deprived of education, but thereby have remained closer to nature, and they do not deserve, because they lack the refinement that comes with education, to form a group separate from the rest of humanity and to be confused with the animals. . . .

No doubt, the people of Saint Domingue, including the blacks, can be accused of many failings, even terrible crimes. But in France itself, where the boundaries of social behavior are established, did not its inhabitants, during the struggle between despotism and liberty, commit the same excesses of which the blacks are accused by their enemies?

[General Rochambeau[2] claims] "there is no freedom in this land except for the commanders of the Africans and men of color, who treat the rest of their fellows like beasts of burden. The whites are everywhere harassed and humiliated." . . .

When Europeans were every day treacherously surrendering their districts to their country's enemies, prudence commanded that the government confer their defense on men of color and blacks, whose interests were intimately connected to the triumph of the Republic. . . . As the military government that then ruled the colony gave a lot of power to local commanders, they may have erred in the maze of uncertainty into which the silence of the laws thrust them. . . . Were he less biased, Rochambeau would not have generalized from the intentions of blacks toward a few anti-republican whites; he would not have asserted that all were harassed and humiliated. I won't mention those who, faithful to the principles of the constitution, respected them, even their color that pride

---

2. Donatien de Vimeur, vicomte de Rochambeau (1755–1813). Briefly Governor of Saint Domingue in late 1792, and in 1802–1803, he had returned in May 1796 with the third civil commission, which quickly deported him for insubordination.

and greed had shunned. It was natural that blacks would show them gratitude. But I call on those who had openly declared them their enemies and fought against them until a more or less sincere repentance reconciled them to their country, I call on them to pay tribute to the truth. Let them say if they were not welcomed and protected. . . . If Europeans and colonists who go to Saint Domingue demonstrate respect for the freedom of the black people instead of echoing citizen Vaublanc and trying to spread doubt about it, they will see grow in the hearts of these men the love and attachment that they have always had for whites in general and for their former masters in particular—in spite of all they have attempted to do to restore them to slavery and bring back to Saint Domingue the reign of tyranny. . . .

General Rochambeau continues, . . . "I do not fear even to predict that, having armed [the blacks], we will one day be obliged to make war on them to send them back into the fields."

General Rochambeau's prediction would doubtless come true if he returned at the head of an army to return the blacks to slavery, because then, with the constitution in one hand, they would defend the freedom that it guarantees.[3] But that this army would be necessary to force them to resume agricultural labor is already completely disproved by what has been happening in agriculture for the last year. . . . If there is among them a few men stupid enough not to feel the need for work, their leaders have enough authority to make them understand that, without work, there is no freedom. . . .

However, should it happen that citizen Vaublanc's projects have some influence on the French government, let it remember that in the heart of Jamaica, in the Blue Mountains, there exists a small number of men sufficiently protective of their liberty to have compelled the proud and powerful English right down to today to respect the rights given them by nature and which the French constitution guarantees to us.[4]

(Toussaint Louverture, *Réfutation de quelques assertions d'un discours prononcé au Corps législatif le 10 prairial, an cinq par Viénot Vaublanc* [Paris, 1797], 1–6, 9–12)

---

3. The prediction was realized in 1802, though Rochambeau was initially only second in command of the expeditionary force sent by Napoleon.

4. The Blue Mountain Maroons were descendants of fugitive slaves who won recognition of their freedom from the Jamaican administration after a lengthy war in the 1730s. They became a popular symbol among French intellectuals. Cf. doc. 64.

64) Toussaint and Agent Hédouville

General Kerversau (doc. 54) here gives the view of a nationalistic French officer who lamented the decline of French power that he witnessed in Saint Domingue. He offers a more favorable view of Hédouville than historians usually give and notably omits the way the Agent targeted Moyse's regiment. He emphasizes the final phrase because he blamed the British in particular for encouraging Louverture's ambitions during their final negotiations with him. Hédouville was expelled only a month later. As in the previous document, Toussaint again alludes to the Jamaican Maroons.

When the new Agent[5] passed through Santiago, I spared no effort to inform him, so far as I could, of the state of the colony. I did not cover up the various obstacles and dangers he would have to confront, the complete lack of resources the country would provide, and the impotence to which the national authority had been reduced. The entire power structure had been turned upside down. Military commanders overruled sentences passed by justices of the peace; they gave orders to administrators and helped themselves at will in the government warehouses. General Moyse had forbidden officials in his district to lease out any sequestrated property; he was reserving it, he said, for the officers in his army. Moreover, he had dared to forbid the holding of primary assemblies in his area and had several broken up by his lieutenants. . . .

In a report I gave [Hédouville] in Santiago on the state of Saint Domingue, I wrote, "The forces that you lack, you will find them in a close partnership with General Toussaint Louverture. He is a man of great intelligence whose loyalty to France cannot be doubted, whose religion guarantees moral conduct, whose firmness is equal to his prudence, and who enjoys the confidence of people of all colors. His influence over his own people is a force that cannot be outweighed. With him you can accomplish anything; without him, nothing. You are arriving in a country whose inhabitants are very far from the highest degree of civilization. Fetishism has always been the religion of Africans and it still is. Here more than elsewhere the popularity of a leader is the foundation of authority. Law, to be respected, needs the credit of the man charged with enforcing it. . . .

Hédouville lived up to the expectations of France's friends and offered the colony the new spectacle of an Agent who felt the dignity of his mission. He was firm but not harsh, obliging but not obsequious, imposing but not proud. . . . [F]ar from winning over Toussaint, this greatly worried him. . . . He wanted to

---

5. General Théodore Hédouville (1755–1825). The title "agent" replaced "civil commissioner."

dominate, and Hédouville did not wish to be dominated. The Agent's abilities and the praise he received offended Toussaint's pride and ambition. . . .

The Agent managed to please the three colors, soldiers, landowners, and cultivators. The General in Chief [Toussaint] strove to make him hated by everyone. He denounced him to soldiers as trying to destroy the army, because he had wanted to reorganize it and reduce its size. He told cultivators that Hédouville was the enemy of freedom, because he demanded commitments from them that people told them were a clear form of servitude and the first step toward the restoration of slavery. And he told whites that the Agent was their persecutor, because he ordered the laws against the émigrés to be enforced.[6] . . .

From Port-au-Prince to Le Cap, all public officials were incarcerated along with most whites. All communications to Le Cap were cut, and all the ports were closed. The General in Chief and Moyse traversed the mountains stirring up their savage inhabitants. . . . Toussaint spewed insults and threats intoxicating his people with his fury. He denounced a plot aimed at enslaving or killing people of his caste; he identified Hédouville as the leader and those who supported the national authority as his accomplices. . . . On 22 October [1798], more than 15,000 men took up arms in Le Cap; . . . by two in the morning they had taken over the forts. . . . Blood and pillage were in the air, and it seemed the day would be even more fatal than 20 June [1793],[7] if Hédouville had not avoided such an outcome by boarding a ship. . . .

At dinner at Moyse's house with a few people from his inner circle, the General in Chief said, ". . . Does Hédouville think he can scare me? I've been making war for a long time and if I have to continue, I will. I've had to deal with three different nations, and I've defeated each one, so I have no worries. My soldiers will always stand firm in the defense of their freedom. . . . I don't want war with France. I have preserved the country for her up to now, but if she attacks me, I will defend myself. Doesn't General Hédouville know that in the mountains of Jamaica there are blacks who forced the English government to make treaties with them? Well, I'm black like them, and I know how to make war. *And what is more, I have advantages they didn't have, because I can count on getting help and protection.*"

(Archives Nationales d'Outre-Mer, CC9B/23, "Rapport au Ministre," 22 Mar. 1801)

---

6. Under the Directory, French subjects who emigrated to enemy territory were liable to execution. See section 7, doc. 61, note 13.

7. When Le Cap had been burned in fighting that ranged Sonthonax and the free coloreds on one side and the governor and white conservatives on the other.

65) The War of the South

This chronicle of the opening months of the War of the South comes from an anonymous journal by a white lawyer living in Port-au-Prince (Pélage-Marie Duboys). It includes lengthy citations from publications issued by the protagonists. The author provides one of the most impartial eyewitness accounts of the Haitian Revolution; although no admirer of Toussaint Louverture, he displayed considerable sympathy for free people of color. He suggests that reports of Rigaud's atrocities were propaganda, and that anciens libres *rebelled in reaction to Toussaint's persecution. He is unusual in the blame he assigns to white radicals and royalists, and to foreigners, in fomenting the conflict.*

On [19 May 1799] General Toussaint respond[ed] to the slanders and untruthful publications of Brigadier-General Rigaud, commander of the Southern Department. The reply was a sort of manifesto and declaration of war. . . . To win them over to his side, Rigaud had spread the word everywhere that General Toussaint Louverture hated the men of color so much that the complete extinction of the present generation would hardly satisfy him. To win over the cultivators and make them suspicious of the general in chief, he gave them to understand that his disagreement with Louverture was due to his refusal to be part of the project Louverture had agreed to with the English to force them back into slavery. . . .

"Is it you, who have oppressed them and bathed in their blood, who have deported them and let them die in dungeons, who can declare himself to be their defender against the one who was the first to break their chains, and to whose courage and constancy they owe their freedom? What black would be so stupid as to be fooled by such a crude trick? . . . You have used all sorts of ploys to rally the men of color around you, using public funds . . . to lure soldiers from the North and West so as to disorganize the army I command and of which you are a part." . . .

At dawn on June 17, Rigaud's officers Faubert and Desruisseaux took Petit Goâve by surprise, capturing there part of the forces commanded by General Laplume. . . . Forty or so local inhabitants were killed. . . .

The old hatred and resentment of the free men of color had a lot of bearing on these new troubles. The friends of England could not pardon Rigaud for having always refused to listen to their proposals. . . . The leaders of the Saint Marc faction[8] in Arcahaye did not fail to profit from these events to infuriate the General in Chief with the men of color, whom they represented as all devoted to Rigaud. . . . Awakening the suspicions of a naturally mistrustful black is to make him look for the best way to protect himself. . . .

---

8. The radical supporters of the Saint Marc Assembly of 1790.

The arrests . . . and especially the threatening comments made publicly about the men of color and other *anciens libres*, spread alarm and caused several to flee. Some were caught . . . and shot without any form of trial. . . . The remains of the fatal Saint Marc faction, still friends of England and the eternal enemies of the men of color, . . . worked on the suspicious and domineering nature of the blacks by pretending the men of color wanted their jobs and hated to be subordinate to them. They wanted their complete destruction and soon succeeded in getting agreement they should be exterminated between Léogane and the farthest point of the Northern Department. . . .

At this time [July] the man of color Bellegarde, . . . took over the Môle Saint Nicolas after winning over its garrison by telling them that a clause in the treaty between General Toussaint and General Maitland was to place an English garrison there.[9] . . . The Môle takeover may or may not have been linked to the various movements that took place at this time in the neighboring districts. Perhaps it was itself merely the result of the alarm spread among the men of color by the arrests carried out in Léogane, Arcahaye, and some other places. . . .

Murders of men of color multiplied; they were no longer safe anywhere. The simple order of a military commander, or even a lesser officer, was for them a death sentence without appeal. . . .

In his address of June 2 to his fellow citizens, Rigaud complained of the slanders that the émigrés who had returned to the Western and Northern departments . . . used to discredit him in the mind of the General in Chief, so that the general already treats him as guilty and seeks to dishonor him, without any regard for his conduct since the beginning of the revolution, for his zeal for the defense of freedom and equality, and his defense of the Republic in the Southern Department. He cries out, "I cannot and must not keep silent. My honor has been attacked. But if the blind passion that drives the General in Chief went no further than the personal insults and baseless accusations that fill his writings, I would have remained silent, because I scorn slander and am beyond reproach. However, although the General in Chief has no cause for complaint against the inhabitants of the South, he threatens them and the entire department. . . .

"If I had not recognized in General Toussaint's threats and preparations a desire for personal vengeance pushed to an extreme, and if I thought my absence might inspire in him a more peaceful attitude, I would have resigned my post and gone to France and reported to the Executive Directory on the state of Saint Domingue and the reasons behind it. . . . However, as the troops of the West have taken up a threatening position, I will meet force with force, . . . and I will not abandon this colony to the rage of the English and the émigrés, because I am

---

9. Although untrue, the rumor was spread by the British press, probably to worsen relations between Toussaint and France. The Môle was an important naval base at the tip of the northwest peninsula.

certain that the agents and vessels of that eternal enemy of France are welcomed in the Western and Northern departments."

On 9 September 1799, after the surrender of the Môle, the General in Chief . . . published in reply a long proclamation . . . in which he reproached Rigaud for the means he had used to usurp power. . . . "The agents of his barbarous project traveled through every district to win over the men of color to his party. They told them that the mulattoes were the sole inhabitants of Saint Domingue, and that the country belonged to them by right. It was theirs; France was for white people, and Guinea [Africa] for the blacks. They should help Rigaud, who was fighting to win them possession of the whole country. To the more sensible people who realized the foolishness of such an idea, they said that their color was resented and that I intended to destroy their caste, and that their sole means of salvation was to unite with Rigaud. . . .

"They slandered me among the whites, claiming I had broken the bonds that forever will unite Saint Domingue to the mother country and had sold my country to the English. To the blacks they accused me of receiving immense sums from the English government to force them back into slavery and submit them to foreign domination. . . . Loyal to the principles of Machiavelli, they built up with their treacherous suggestions insurmountable barriers between whites and blacks, representing the former as the implacable enemies of the latter and inspiring mutual suspicion between these two classes of citizens . . . whose unity they feared. . . .

"I will remind you of the 30 Ventôse affair[10] stirred up by Rigaud. . . . Investigations I have since made into this event leave no doubt that Rigaud's intention then was to seize power by destroying legitimate authority. Everything had been prepared. At the same time as Rigaud was to seize supreme power, Villatte was to become commander of the North, and Bauvais[11] commander of the West. . . . Remember all the measures that were taken to win over the troops in the North, and to make the cultivators revolt.

"[Rigaud's] attacks on my authority are merely the necessary result of his hatred of blacks. Believing them inferior to men of color, he felt humiliated, he a mulatto, to obey a Negro. He has therefore sought to overthrow his legitimate leader and to put himself in his place. . . . He has accused me of having sold the colony to the English. . . . What! When there was a chance of real benefit for my country, my reception of the English general has been turned into a crime. . . .

---

10. 20 March 1796. See Introduction, p. xxiv. Only circumstantial evidence links Rigaud to Villatte's plot.

11. Louis-Jacques Bauvais (1756–1800), a light-skinned schoolteacher, promoted to brigadier-general in July 1795, the same time as Toussaint and Rigaud. Much less partisan than Rigaud, he in fact refused to take sides in his conflicts with Sonthonax and Toussaint, and fled Saint Domingue in September 1799.

Because Rigaud dislikes me, because I am black, I alone am supposedly guilty for accepting English envoys in Saint Domingue's ports. . . .

"If the men of color cast their gaze on the North and West, they will lose this idea they have that we are trying to destroy their caste. They will see whole districts and regions entrusted to the command of men of color. If they walk through the ranks of Saint Domingue's loyal army, they will see, from generals to privates, a large number of men of color fighting under the flag of the Republic against the rebellion of their guilty brothers."

(Bibliothèque Nationale, Paris, Manuscrits, Nouv. acq. fr. 14879,
ff. 62–64, 67–68, 72–75, 86–87, 98, 112, 116–120)

66) Plantation Labor in the Southeast

Historians know little about the functioning of the forced labor regime. These reports from two contrasting parts of the southeast coast in August 1798 offer rare glimpses. In both areas, most plantations survive as social units, but the drift toward a peasant lifestyle is already perceptible. Remote and mountainous Cayes-Jacmel was relatively peaceful and productive. In neighboring Bainet, the influence of local insurgent leaders compounded social conflict. Both Rigaud and Toussaint have been suspected of using them to undermine General Bauvais, the regional commander.

(Cayes-Jacmel) About a third of the plantations, particularly the least important, are growing the same amount of crops as before the troubles. On the others a fairly large area is overgrown with weeds, in proportion to the loss of workers they have experienced in the revolution, and even more according to how close they are to the area formerly held by the enemy,[12] because on them it was impossible to use the same means in repressing laziness and vagabondage. . . . A small number have been completely abandoned in the highest part of Fonds Jean Nouel and on La Selle mountain, which are neighboring regions. This could be because of their distance from any market, and because their plantings are still too young to bear fruit. The climate and the nature of their soil, although suitable for coffee cultivation, do not yield much before the trees are six or seven years old, and they are not good for the food crops the cultivators most like. . . . The only food crops found there are the ones grown in the cultivators' own

---

12. The British-occupied zone.

provision grounds, many of which are more extensive than they should be. This is not a problem that can be solved overnight. . . . Draught animals, so important for production and transport, are in very short supply. . . . The only thing that keeps the cultivators working steadily is the punishment meted out for infractions of the police regulations. Even these measures are not enough to deal with the several plantations whose foremen, in complicity with their subordinates, cover up the valuable time lost to agriculture by certain individuals taking off the ninth and first days of the week to go and come back from Jacmel market.[13] They happily flock to private parties given at people's houses but show up to civic festivals without enthusiasm. Out of self-interest, love of a sort of independence, or some dissatisfaction with their work gang, some move to a different district where they think no one will notice them and they rent land. The same self-interest provides people who will rent to them.

(Bainet mountains) On all the plantations of this region, people have gotten into the habit of not working for the last year or more. . . . Although the owners and managers have been forced to share the net revenue with their cultivators, they cannot get them to work after midday. Most of the cultivators are armed and call themselves dragoons of Conflans or of Lafortune, etc. and are not included in any plantation workforce.[14] This does a great deal of harm to local agriculture. . . .

Citizen Versailles, using his dragoons, has already corrupted several plantations. They called a meeting on the Desnoyers plantation, and Jason, who presided over it, told the dragoon-cultivators that nobody had the right to make them stoop to pull up a weed. He told the foreman he could follow the order Versailles had given them to work from morning to midday, and that the rest of the day was for them. They should not follow the laws of the town, because they were not good.

The commune of Bainet is still in an anarchic state of upheaval. Those responsible for this public disaster, emboldened by their immunity, continue to enjoy a sovereign independence, the purpose of which is to perpetuate their catastrophic reign. . . . When Conflans returned to the Bainet mountains . . . he called several meetings and named captains in all the districts who were ordered to form companies of the best armed men. Guards were placed at intervals on all the roads and crossroads. The planters and lessees were continually harassed and driven out of their homes. They had to have passports from either Conflans or some other rebel chief in order to go about their business. . . . All the produce

---

13. As well as the tenth day. The French adopted in 1793 a ten-day week.

14. Conflans and Lafortune were local maroon or rebel leaders in the mountains south of Léogane, where Romaine la Prophétesse briefly rose to power in 1792 (see section 5, doc. 43, note 19).

from the plantations sequestered for the benefit of the Republic has been pillaged and sold for the profit of these leaders. Most of the animals belonging to the state and to individuals on this mountain have been taken by them. Conflans ordered the cultivators to work only three hours per day, just from 8:00 to 11:00 in the morning. And he forced the planters and lessees to share half the revenues with the cultivators. It's only at this price that a few succeed in getting a bit of coffee picked, in a region that two or three years ago was producing several million pounds of produce. . . .

(Boston Public Library, Ms. Haiti 71–20 and 27, letters by Desvallons, Dongé, Berneleau, and Bauvais, 23–27 Thermidor VI)

67) Toussaint's Labor Decree

Conflict between planters and former slaves characterized most post-slavery societies in the Americas. Saint Domingue was unique, however, in that the survival of plantation agriculture was necessary to the new experiment in slave emancipation, which risked reversal in the event of failure. This translation of Toussaint's labor decree of 12 October 1800 was published in neighboring Jamaica, where interest in the post-emancipation experiment was strong, and Louverture's recourse to forced labor comforted the prejudices of slaveowners.

Citizens,

After putting an end to the war in the South, our first duty has been to return thanks to the Almighty. . . . Now, Citizens, it is necessary to consecrate all our moments to the prosperity of St. Domingo, to the public tranquility, and consequently to the welfare of our fellow citizens. . . .

Whereas a soldier cannot leave his company, his battalion, or half-brigade, and enter into another, without the severest punishment, unless provided with a permission provided in due form by his Chief; field-negroes are forbidden to quit their respective plantations without a lawful permission. This is by no means attended to, since they change their place of labour as they please, go to and fro, and pay not the least attention to agriculture, though the only means of furnishing sustenance to the military, their protectors. They even conceal themselves in towns, in villages, and mountains, where, allured by the enemies of good order, they live by plunder, and in a state of open hostility to society.

Whereas, since the revolution, labourers of both sexes, then too young to be employed in the fields, refuse to go there now under pretext of freedom, spend their time in wandering about, and give a bad example to the other cultivators. . . .

Art. 1. All overseers, drivers, and field-negroes are bound to observe, with exactness, submission, and obedience, their duty in the same manner as soldiers.

Art. 2. All overseers, drivers, and field-labourers, who will not perform with assiduity the duties required of them, shall be arrested and punished as severely as soldiers deviating from their duty. . . .

Art. 3. All field-labourers, men and women, now in a state of idleness, living in towns, villages, and on other plantations than those to which they belong, with an intention to evade work, even those of both sexes who have not been employed in field labour since the revolution, are required to return immediately to their respective plantations. . . .

All those who shall be found in contravention hereto, shall be instantly arrested, and if they are found guilty they shall be drafted into one of the regiments of the army. . . . [L]iberty cannot exist without industry.

(*Supplement to the Royal Gazette* [Jamaica], 22:47 [15 Nov. 1800])

68) A British Visitor

Marcus Rainsford was an army captain stationed in Jamaica who visited Saint Domingue shortly before the British occupation ended. Though a defender of slavery, he offered a highly sympathetic portrait of post-emancipation society and its black governor. He was unusual in predicting in 1802 that the French could never reconquer the colony. Here he provides valuable details on its changing demography, social structure, the army, and the rural family where African influences prevailed.

Although the defection [emigration] of the whites was striking in the towns where they had been most numerous, that of the blacks was increased in a proportion so large, as to astonish those who had witnessed their losses, and the decrease which was remarked after the first insurrections of the negroes. This is accounted for in a satisfactory manner, by the greater degree of comforts experienced by the females, and the decrease of general labour. Although, for some time, the change of government appeared to tinge with a melancholy hue, the parts of the island formerly in the possession of the English, yet the rude happiness of those who had now become its possessors, soon suppressed every other effect; and, notwithstanding the despotic rule of martial law, circumstances in general began to wear a promising appearance.

The number of Americans at this port [Cap Français] could not fail to attract particular notice, and every attention seemed to be paid to the accommodation of their commerce, and a striking degree of interest in every occurrence that concerned them. Even the women seemed to renew a fondness long repressed for the whites, in favor of the meanest of the American sailors. . . . [The author] immediately perceived that the usual subordinations of society were entirely disregarded, and that he was to witness, for the first time, a real system of equality.

Here were officer and privates, the colonel and the drummer, at the same table indiscriminately. . . . The appearance of the house and its accommodations were not much inferior to a London coffee-house, and on particular occasions exhibited a superior degree of elegance. Toussaint not unfrequently dined here himself, but he did not sit at the head of the table, from the idea, (as was asserted,) that the hours of refection and relaxation should not be damped by the affected forms of the old regimen, and that no man should assume a real superiority in any other place than the field. . . .

Having been informed of a review which was to take place on the plain of the Cape, the writer availed himself of the opportunity, accompanied by some Americans, and a few of his own countrymen who resided there under that denomination. Of the grandeur of the scene he had not the smallest conception. Two thousand officers were in the field, carrying arms, from the general to the ensign, yet with the utmost attention to rank; without the smallest symptom of the insubordination that existed in the leisure of the hotel. Each general officer had a demi-brigade, which went through the manual exercise with a degree of expertness seldom witnessed, and performed equally well several manoeuvres applicable to their method of fighting. At a whistle a whole brigade ran three or four hundred yards, then separating, threw themselves flat on the ground, changing to their backs or sides, keeping up a strong fire the whole time, till they were recalled; they then formed again, in an instant, into their wonted regularity. This single manoeuvre was executed with such facility and precision, as totally to prevent cavalry from charging them in bushy or hilly countries. Such complete subordination, such promptitude and dexterity, prevailed the whole time, as would have astonished any European soldier who had the smallest idea of their previous situation. . . .

As in all states of human society, particularly in the vortex of a revolution, which effected so complete a change, the able and the cunning had elevated themselves above those who were of the same rank of life. Negroes, recollected in the lowest state of slavery, including Africans, filled situations of trust and responsibility; they were likewise in many instances, occupied by those who had been in superior circumstances under the old regimen, free negroes and mulattoes.

The superior order had attained a sumptuousness of life, with all the enjoyments that dignity could obtain, or rank confer. The interior of their houses was in many instances furnished with a luxe beyond that of the most voluptuous European, while no want of trans-Atlantic elegance appeared; nor, amidst a general fondness for shew, was the chastness of true taste always neglected. . . .

The men were in general sensible and polite, often dignified and impressive; the women frequently elegant and engaging. The intercourse of the sexes was on the most rational footing, and the different degrees of colour which remained had lost most of that natural hostility that formerly existed. . . .

The drama, that source of rational delight, always so prevalent in St. Domingo, existed, in more strength and propriety than it had done before;[15] and that licentiousness that appears inseparable to it, in a higher state, was actually restrained. The representations were chiefly comedies *en vaudeville* and a sort of pantomime; sometimes serious representations allusive to local circumstances, and sometimes merely humourous burlesques. . . . The black performers, who preponderated in number, were not behind in talents; the writer saw a play of Moliere's performed with an accuracy that would not have disgraced the first theatre in Europe. . . . Yet . . . the rich blacks suffered the greater part of the capital to lie in ruins; they appeared to shrink from reinstating it, as if in rebuilding their former residences, they should create new masters.

The situation of those . . . who formed the great bulk of the people, was indeed very greatly changed. Their condition, agreeably to their capacities of enjoyment, approached nearer happiness than many others which are considered its ultimatum. Crimes were by no means frequent. . . .

In one instance, the writer was introduced . . . to the cottage of a black laborer, of whom an account may not be uninteresting. He had a family of thirteen children; eight of them by one woman, and the remainder by two others; the former only lived with him in the same cottage, with his mother who was aged and infirm; the other separately, at a small distance. This man was an epitome of legislature, and his family a well regulated kingdom in miniature. His cottage consisted of three irregular apartments, the first of which was his refectory, where, as often as possible, and always on *jours de fêtes* [holidays], his subjects assembled, including on those occasions his three wives. The furniture of this apartment was entirely of his own making, even to the smallest utensil, and with an ingenuity beyond what might be expected from perfect leisure; notwithstanding the artificer, during the process had been obliged to attend his labor in the fields, and was a considerable time in arms. On a neat shelf, appropriated peculiarly to their use, lay a mass book, and a mutilated volume of *Volney's Travels*, some parts of which he understood more than his visitor. Every thing convenience required was to be found on a small scale, and the whole so compact, and clean . . . as was absolutely attractive. His own bedroom was furnished with an improved bedstead, supported by trussels, with a mattress and bedding of equal quality with the other furniture, but that of his mother and children surpassed the whole. One bedstead contained them, yet separated the male from the female, the young

---

15. The colony had six theaters in 1789. That of Cap Français could seat an audience of 1,500.

from the aged, and was separated or combined in an instant. . . . The wife of this laborer (for he had submitted to the ceremony of marriage with the female who had borne him the most children, as is the general custom with them) was nearly as ingenious as himself, and equally as intelligent. The mode he pursued in the regulation of his domestic economy was excellent; as continence is not a virtue of the blacks, the increase of his family was not confined to his own house; yet, even in his amours he was just; and as the two mothers before mentioned were less protected than his ostensible wife, the primary object of his consideration was to have the whole of his children under his own care. This was reconciled to all parties from the first, in so mild a way, that no distinction was perceivable but in age, while the mothers held a relationship to their domiciliated offspring similar to that of an aunt or cousin, each exerting herself for the purpose of adding to the comforts of her own child. On festive occasions, the two mothers sat alternately on the right or left of the mistress of the house, with as much etiquette as might be perceived in a more elevated station, and with utmost harmony. The master of the family was absolute, but with him it was in theory, not in practice. As soon as the children could contribute their little powers to labor, they were employed. . . . In accordance with that reverence for age so remarkable among blacks of every condition, the grandmother received the attention and affection of all; and though often crabbed, infirm, and discontented, no one seemed to consider her failings as such, but as a duty prescribed to them to bear. . . .

Every individual employed a portion of his time in labor, and received an allotted part of the produce for his reward, while all took [to] the field, from a sense of duty to themselves. A perfect combination appeared in their conduct, and every action came directly from the heart. More than sixty thousand men were frequently exercised together on the plain of the Cape, in excellent discipline, whose united determination against an invading enemy, would be victory or death. Little coercion was necessary, and punishment was chiefly inflicted by a sense of shame produced by slight confinement, or the like. Labor was so much abridged, that no want of leisure was felt; it would be a great gratification to the feeling heart, to see the peasant in other countries with a regulated toil similar to that of the laborer in St. Domingo.

(Marcus Rainsford, An Historical Account of the Black Empire of Hayti
[London: Albion Press, 1805], 213–28)

69) Roume's Praise for the Cultivators

A white creole from the south Caribbean, Agent Philippe Roume was a radical idealist like Sonthonax, at home in revolutionary politics and Caribbean society. This letter from May 1799 makes brief reference to Toussaint's nephew, Moyse, and to Henry Christophe, who, when king of Haiti (1811–1820), would enthusiastically promote education.

Our new brothers the cultivators generally see the need to give their children the education they have been deprived of. . . . The plantations under cultivation are mainly managed by illiterate blacks, who need whites to keep the books and write letters. Some of the latter teach the neighborhood children, who go to them every day except holidays traveling up to three miles. At least this is the case on the Saint-Michel plantation near Le Cap that is leased to General Christophe, who says the same occurs on many other plantations. Fathers and mothers give up to ¾ gourde [75 cents U.S.] to these "teachers." . . . There has been a fortunate change . . . throughout the colony in the morality of the former slaves. . . . I admire the energy of these virtuous republicans. The blacks are naturally polite; it is extraordinarily rare to hear swearing or arguing. Previous experience has made them mistrustful of all those whom they have not yet got to know, but they have an exquisite tact, and are swift judges of sincerity and duplicity. . . .

The power wielded by the military leaders is necessary, and also impartial and firm, including that of Moyse, who is one of the bravest and wisest, and at the same time most gentle men that I have ever seen.

(The National Archives, London, CO 245/2, Roume to
Ministre de la Marine, 28 Germinal VII)

70) A Colonist's Complaints

Descourtilz arrived in Saint Domingue when he was twenty-three years old in early 1799 and stayed four years. Having married into a wealthy planter family in France, he was really an outsider. The following extracts make two contributions. They recount the difficulties of plantation life for whites in the Artibonite plain under the forced labor regime. And they include personal observations of Toussaint Louverture.

Since the Negro anarchists threw off the yoke of slavery, they use poison less often to wreak vengeance on the whites, against whom they will always harbor an envious resentment. . . . They have other means of seeking revenge. . . . They take advantage of their superior numbers to vex the whites and humiliate them at every opportunity, with nasty surprises, thefts, or insults that go unpunished. "You punish me. Me punish you in return!" Such is their unanimous cry. . . .

Titus [the district commander] had the animals of our stud farm stolen . . . and caused our own subjects to harass us. Tormented by slaves[16] who loudly refused to obey us, we who till then still possessed 753 Negroes, were obliged to serve ourselves, whilst this audacious officer habitually used them himself with impunity and against our wishes. . . . Toussaint Louverture also turned against us the administrators of the land office, who, using pretexts that favored the government, kept the revenue of the leases granted to us and, usurping our rights, exploited us with imperious demands. Thus in this region they violated the promises made to the landowners. . . .

The black policemen who were to carry out these favorable orders refused to act against their friends or those of their acquaintances, let alone their relations or *compères*, because of a sacred bond that permanently unites them. That is why, when a crime was committed, the patrol disappeared. Such tolerance allowed a dangerous impunity to flourish. We had to suffer in silence; whites at this time counted for little the sacrifices they were forced to make to avoid putting their lives in danger. Backed up by Titus, the cultivators laughed at our weakness, and made a point of stealing from us without even trying to hide it. . . .

We were masters of our property without being able to use it. The best land was divided up amongst the insolent and ungrateful cultivators, and they refused us the vegetables we had every right to expect. . . . Our persecutors went so far as to frequently break into our home during the night, obliging me to open fire from my very bedroom, and several times burning torches were applied to the house; . . . I was shot at occasionally but unharmed; . . . our carriages were stolen by the authorities; . . . our saddle horses were wounded in the paddock or poisoned at the house; our orchards were pillaged, the trees broken, and the fruit refused to us. . . .

In his private life, Toussaint Louverture was restrained, perhaps out of suspicion. . . . He drank only water, so his mind was never affected by alcohol. That is why he generally chose to eat whole pieces of food that were unlikely to have been poisoned, like fruit, eggs, or unpeeled bananas. It was strange to see him at the center of a formal banquet peeling an orange or an avocado. . . . Toussaint Louverture's court was splendid; he maintained a haughty attitude toward those around him, his generals and adjutants, imposing the silence

---

16. Five years after slavery's complete abolition, this telling slip gives some insight into the causes of Descourtilz's difficulties.

that was due to the importance of his office. . . . At formal dinners he aped the magnificence of the French authorities and attached a lot of importance to having his general officers do the honors, especially when receiving foreigners like Swedes, Americans from New England, Danes, English, and other ship's captains who traded with the colony. His aim was to secretly extract gunpowder from them, with which he stocked to overflowing his backup warehouses in the mountains. . . .

He rarely failed to attend mass and, wherever he was, he busied himself with the smallest details of preparation. He went into the sacristy himself to question all those officiating and to give them a short moral lesson. . . . Often interfering with the role of the priest, he commented on his sermon and harangued the people and his troops. He preached a morality that he was very far from following. He spoke out against bachelors who lived in concubinage, which is the custom in the country; he ordered people to get married, and threatened with punishments those who violated these sacred oaths.

All this, counted for nothing, however, as at the end of each service he gave personal audiences to ladies that he favored, alone and with the doors closed. I knew a husband, Mr. G., whose complacency and amenability extended to his standing guard at the door during his wife's interview, which sometimes lasted a very long time and of whose purpose he was unaware.

(Michel-Étienne Descourtilz, *Voyages d'un naturaliste* [Paris, 1809], 2:453, 3:242–48)

71) Toussaint Louverture's Constitution, July 1801

Officially the work of a small assembly nominated by Toussaint, which included some whites with a radical past, the constitution was probably written by Raimond and Pascal (docs. 7, 62). It was radical in its claiming of colonial autonomy but an otherwise conservative document, of which the provisions paralleled Napoleon Bonaparte's own emerging autocracy in France and re-establishment of the Catholic church and traditional family.

The deputies of the departments of the French colony of Saint Domingue, gathered in a central assembly, have laid down and decreed the constitutional foundations for a government of the French colony of Saint Domingue, as follows. . . .

First article. Saint Domingue in its entire extent . . . and other adjacent islands constitute the territory of a single colony that forms part of the French empire but which is subject to special laws. . . .

3. There can exist no slaves in this territory, where servitude is forever abolished and all men are born, live, and die free and French.

4. Every man, whatever his color, has access to all types of employment.

5. No distinction other than those of virtue and talent exist there, and no superiority other than that which the law bestows on the exercise of a public function. The law is the same for everyone, with regard to both protection and punishment. . . .

Religion

6. The only religion to be publicly practiced is the Catholic, apostolic, and Roman religion.

7. Each parish will provide for the upkeep of the faith and its ministers. . . .

8. The colonial government will prescribe for each priest the extent of his spiritual administration. Priests can never, under any pretext, form an association in the colony.

Customs

9. As the civil and religious institution of marriage encourages uncorrupted behavior, spouses who practice the virtues demanded by their status will always receive special attention from, and be specially protected by, the government.

10. There shall be no divorce in the colony.

11. The status and rights of children born out of wedlock will be defined by laws that help to spread and maintain social virtue and encourage and strengthen family ties.[17]

Agriculture and Trade

14. As the colony is based on agriculture, it cannot permit the slightest interruption in agricultural work.

15. Each plantation is a manufacturing unit that needs both agricultural workers and artisans. It is the peaceful refuge of an active and steadfast family, of which the landowner or his representative necessarily acts as the father.

16. Each agricultural worker and artisan is a member of the family and shares in its revenues. Any change of domicile by an agricultural worker brings about the ruin of agriculture. To put an end to a vice that is as fatal to the colony as it is contrary to public order, the governor will draw up all necessary regulations in conformity with those of 20 vendémiaire year 9 [12 October 1800] and the proclamation of the following 19 pluviôse [8 February 1801] by the general in chief, Toussaint Louverture.[18]

---

17. At its radical height, the French Revolution had given equal inheritance rights to children born in and out of wedlock. Toussaint clearly intended to return to a more conservative position.

18. Tying most ex-slaves to their former plantations, these regulations essentially continued the forced labor regime established by Sonthonax. See doc. 67.

17. Agricultural workers essential to the revival and expansion of agriculture shall be brought to Saint Domingue. The constitution charges the governor with taking suitable measures to encourage this increase in the labor force, to define and balance the different interests involved, and to insure and guarantee that the resultant agreements are carried out.[19]

Legislation and Legislative Authority

19. Life in the colony is governed by laws proposed by the governor and promulgated by an assembly of inhabitants that will meet at stipulated intervals in the colony's center. It will have the title Central Assembly of Saint Domingue....

23. Half the assembly will be changed every two years.... Municipal administrations will each nominate a deputy every two years.... These deputies will form departmental electoral assemblies that each will choose a deputy to the central assembly.... In the case of the death or resignation of one or more deputies, the governor will have them replaced. He will likewise designate the members of the present central assembly....

24. The central assembly votes the adoption or rejection of laws submitted to it by the governor. It gives its opinion regarding existing regulations and on the application of existing laws, on abuses to be corrected, and on improvements to be made in all aspects of public service.... Its meetings are not public....

Government

27. The administrative reins of the colony are bestowed on a governor, who will correspond directly with the metropolitan government regarding everything that concerns the interests of the colony.

28. The constitution designates as governor citizen Toussaint Louverture, general in chief of the army of Saint Domingue. In consideration of the important services this general has rendered to the colony in the critical circumstances of the revolution, and in accordance with the wishes of the grateful inhabitants, the reins are bestowed on him for the rest of his glorious life....

30. To consolidate the peace that the colony owes to the firmness, activity, indefatigable zeal, and rare virtues of General Toussaint Louverture, and as a sign of the unlimited confidence of the inhabitants of Saint Domingue, the constitution attributes exclusively to this general the right to choose the citizen who, in the unhappy event of his death, will have to immediately replace him....

32. A month at the latest before the expiration of the five-year term of each governor's administration, whoever holds the post will convene the central assembly and gather the army generals on active service and the departments' commandants in chief at the central assembly's usual place of meeting, so as to

---

19. The proposal is to purchase Africans from slave ships.

name both the members of this assembly and a new governor, or to continue the service of the old one. . . .

In the event of the death, resignation, or otherwise, of a governor before the end of his term, the government will pass provisionally . . . into the hands of the highest-ranking general, and between those of equal rank the longest serving, who will convoke the members of the central assembly, the army generals on active service, and the departments' commandants in chief, for the same purpose as given above.

34. The governor seals and promulgates the laws, and appoints all civil and military officials. He is the commander-in-chief of the army. . . .

36. He proposes laws to the central assembly as well as any changes to the constitution that experience makes necessary.

37. He directs and oversees the collection, payment, and use of the colony's taxes. . . .

39. He oversees and censures, through his commissioners, all writings intended for publication in the island; he will suppress those coming from abroad that might renew trouble in the colony or corrupt public morals. . . .

40. If the governor is informed of a conspiracy threatening the public peace, he will immediately have arrested the presumed perpetrators and accomplices, and after submitting them to an extra-judicial interrogation, will transfer them if appropriate before a competent tribunal.

41. The governor's salary is fixed for the present time at 300,000 francs.[20] His honor guard will be paid for by the colony.

The Courts

43. No authority can suspend or prevent the execution of judgments rendered by the courts. . . .

46. The judges of these various courts keep their posts for life, unless they are condemned to forfeit them. . . .

47. Crimes committed by soldiers are dealt with by special courts . . . organized by the colonial governor.

Municipal Administration

49. Members of municipal administrations are named for two years and can be continued in post. Their nomination belongs to the governor. . . .

77. The general in chief Toussaint Louverture is and remains charged with sending the present constitution to receive the sanction of the French government. Nevertheless, in view of the absolute absence of laws, the urgency of ending this dangerous situation, the necessity of swiftly reviving agriculture, and the

---

20. This was three times the governor's salary in 1789.

unanimous and clearly stated wish of the inhabitants of Saint Domingue, he is and remains invited *in the interest of the public good* to put it into effect throughout the colony.

(*Constitution de la colonie française de Saint-Domingue* [Paris, 1801], 1–8, 12)

72) Moyse's Rebellion

The bloody revolt of the colony's number-two general darkened and destabilized the final months of Toussaint's governorship. When Toussaint and Dessalines were absent in the West Province celebrating the latter's wedding, Moyse struck. As in 1791, a rural uprising was combined with a still-born rebellion in Cap Français. This white contemporary's account expresses some skepticism as to who was really behind it. The prime beneficiaries were Jean-Jacques Dessalines and Henry Christophe, who brutally repressed the rebellion and replaced Moyse in the military hierarchy. Both later became heads of state committed to plantation export agriculture.

Everything seemed peaceful in the colony when, during the night of 21/22 October [1801], a terrible plot broke out at Le Cap, in Plaine du Nord, Acul, Limbé, Port Margot, Marmelade, Plaisance, and around Dondon. Directed by General Moyse, it appeared to be directed against Toussaint Louverture and against the whites. "General Moyse is on our side," shouted the insurgents. "Death to all whites!"

Moyse had declared a profound hatred for white people. Born, like General Toussaint, on the Bréda plantation, he had been one of the main and most ardent leaders of the first insurrection of the blacks in 1791.[21] . . . What was the aim of this movement? Did Moyse simply want to seize command of the colony? Did he want to secede from France? Who was behind him? Didn't he act alone? The answers to all these questions lie buried with him and all those who were close to him, his aides de camp and secretaries, who were all shot without any form of trial. Or nowadays perhaps the secret belongs to General Toussaint, who refused to allow him a proper trial and wanted him condemned without being heard. . . .

Whatever may be the case, 317 known persons fell victim to this movement. . . . General Moyse had been absent from Le Cap since October 17 when, on the evening of the 22nd, the commandant of the Cap district,

---

21. A slight exaggeration: he was no more than twenty in 1791. See docs. 54, 56, and 68.

Brigadier-General Henry Christophe, was informed there was a gathering of ill-disposed people at the Carénage. He quickly went there and broke up the gathering, and . . . immediately obtained information regarding a plot and the names of its main organizers. . . . More than 30 of their accomplices were arrested that night. General Henry Christophe's vigor saved Le Cap from the disaster that threatened it; only one group of people put up any resistance. . . .

Moyse was no doubt waiting outside the town to learn what the outcome would be. Learning that his plans for the town had failed, he raised a rebellion in the districts of Plaine du Nord, Acul, Limbé, Port Margot, Marmelade, Plaisance, and Dondon[22]—or at least he did not oppose those escaping from Le Cap doing so. . . . Hearing of the massacres being carried out all across this region, Henry Christophe set out on October 24 . . . and ordered the cultivators to return to their plantations. In Port Margot, he had the rebels themselves shoot those whom they pointed out as their leaders. . . . On the 25th, Dessalines reached Plaisance, where he spared no one who appeared to have taken part in the bloodshed. On those plantations where the owner or some other white had been killed, Dessalines had the entire workforce shot. . . .

Toussaint sent Moyse an order to leave his troops and come and see him. Moyse obeyed. "Everything suggests that you are behind this revolt," he told him. "You must justify yourself as a matter of honor. . . . Go back to Dondon. Arrest those who are guilty, but above all don't have them shot. Bring them to me alive under secure guard." . . .

Moyse's conduct spoke against him. If he was not the secret cause of the unrest in Le Cap, it is at least obvious he initially did nothing to oppose the disturbances in the countryside. It is true that, on Toussaint Louverture's orders, he repressed the rebellion in Dondon, but also that he had several participants shot contrary to Toussaint's instructions. His behavior was at least suspicious. On the face of it, everything pointed to him as the organizer of this mayhem. It was therefore decided to arrest him and have him tried. . . .

General Toussaint entered Le Cap on November 4, driving forty prisoners before him. . . . All those connected with General Moyse in this matter, his aides de camp and secretaries and all the officers who were close to him, [were executed]. Thus perished with them anything that might have shed light on these events.

(Bibliothèque Nationale, Paris, Manuscrits, Nouv. acq. fr. 14879, ff. 221–26)

---

22. The western end of the North Plain and adjacent mountains, heartland of the 1791 uprising.

73) **Proclamation, 4 Frimaire X**

The very long proclamation Toussaint issued on 25 November 1801 continued his struggle to impose forced labor on the former slaves in the wake of Moyse's rebellion. Besides reaffirming the forced labor law and introducing a pass system to keep rural folk out of the towns, it espoused a sort of moral crusade while imposing stiff penalties for laxity on officials and military commanders, plantation managers and foremen.

Since the Revolution, I have done everything in my power to bring back happiness to my country and ensure the freedom of my fellow citizens. Forced to fight the interior and exterior enemies of the French Republic, I have made war with courage, honor, and loyalty. . . .

I have always and energetically urged on all our soldiers subordination, discipline, and obedience, without which there can be no army. It is created to protect freedom, the security of persons and of property, and all its members must never lose sight of its honorable purpose. Officers must set a good example as a lesson to their men. . . .

Such is the language I used with General Moyse for ten years in all our conversations; . . . these are the principles and feelings that I put into a thousand of my letters. At every opportunity, I sought to explain to him the holy maxims of our faith, and prove that man is nothing without the power and will of God. . . . Instead of listening to the advice of a father, and obeying the orders of a leader devoted to the well-being of the colony, he wanted only to be ruled by his passions and follow his fatal inclinations: he has met with a wretched end. . . .

In one of my proclamations at the time of the War of the South, I laid out the duties of fathers and mothers toward their children, and their obligation to raise them in the love and fear of God, having always regarded religion as the basis of all virtue and the foundation of happiness in society. . . . And yet with what negligence do fathers and mothers raise their children, especially in the towns! . . . Instead of teaching them to love work, they leave them idle and ignorant of their basic duties. They themselves seem to scorn and to encourage them to scorn agriculture, the first, the most honorable, and most useful of activities. No sooner are they born than these children are to be seen wearing jewelry and earrings, covered in rags, dirty, and shocking decent onlookers with their nudity. They reach twelve years of age without moral principles or training, a taste for luxury, and too lazy to learn. . . . Thus you have bad citizens, vagabonds and thieves; and if they are girls, prostitutes; one and the other all ready to follow the lead of the first conspirator to preach to them disorder, murder, and pillage. . . .

The same reproach applies equally well to a great number of plantation workers. . . . As soon as a child can walk, he should be put to work on the plantations in some useful job suitable to his strength, instead of being sent to the towns where, under the pretext of an education he does not receive, he learns vice and swells the crowd of vagabonds and women of low repute whose existence troubles the repose of good citizens. . . . It is true that Moyse was the driving force behind the recent conspiracy, but he never would have been able to carry out his dastardly enterprise without assistants like these. . . .

The holiest of institutions in human society, that which produces the greatest good, is marriage. A good family man, a good husband entirely devoted to the happiness of his spouse and children, must be for them the living image of God. . . . Military commanders and, especially, public officials whose immoral behavior creates scandal have no excuse. Those who are legitimately married and keep concubines in their houses, and those who are unmarried and live publicly with several women, are unworthy of command; they shall be dismissed. . . .

Any military commander who does not take all necessary measurers to prevent disturbances in his district, . . . any soldier, in the army or national guard, who refuses to obey a legal order will be punished with death, as the law prescribes.

Any individual, man or woman, of whatever color, who is convicted of making comments that seriously provoke sedition, will be tried before a wartime tribunal and punished as the law prescribes.

Any creole, man or woman, convicted of making comments that disturb the public peace, but not judged liable to the death penalty, shall be sent into the fields with a chain on one leg for a period of six months.

(*Vie privée, politique et militaire de Toussaint Louverture* [Paris: Magasin de Librairie, 1801], 58–59, 61–70, 72, 74–75, 80–81)

9. THE WAR OF INDEPENDENCE

Like Saint Domingue, France also acquired a military strongman at the close of the eighteenth century. Napoleon Bonaparte and Toussaint Louverture had much in common. Both were autocrats intolerant of political liberty, but both were regarded as defenders of the basic revolutionary gains of the previous decade, especially the redistribution of land. Both would be destroyed by their own ambition. The emerging contest between the two generals made Saint Domingue an object of international fascination.

Just weeks after Bonaparte seized power in November 1799 he removed France's colonies from the purview of its constitution. This may mean that he was already planning to restore slavery in Saint Domingue, as some scholars believe. Or the measure may have been intended for those French colonies where slavery had never been abolished and whose situation would have to be regularized (doc. 74a). Separate from the slavery issue, was the question of what to do with Toussaint Louverture. At least intermittently, Napoleon seems to have thought he could use him and the black colonial army to extend French power in the Americas. Finding Toussaint too independent, however, he determined "to be rid of these gilded Africans" and reassert metropolitan control over the colony.

Bonaparte initially succeeded, for three reasons. Unlike his predecessors, he managed to get a large army to Saint Domingue during the healthy months of the year. He assured the population that slavery's abolition was permanent (doc. 74b), so that plantation workers already alienated by Toussaint's rule saw little to fight for, nor did black officers who were promised they could keep their jobs. The extent of Bonaparte's duplicity is unclear. He certainly intended to dismantle the black army, but not until mid-June 1802 did government dispatches refer to eventually reimposing slavery in Saint Domingue. General Leclerc, the French commander, appeared surprised to receive them (doc. 75). Historians disagree when Napoleon made up his mind on the issue. Perhaps it was only after Leclerc's successful campaign that ended in May.

After three months of fierce fighting, Toussaint and his top generals surrendered in May 1802. He was deported to France soon after, where he died in prison (doc. 76), but most of his officers were incorporated into the French army of occupation. They were used to disarm the rural population, to whom Sonthonax had distributed guns in the mid-1790s. Popular resistance surged in the summer, when news spread regarding the restoration of slavery, and French losses to yellow fever spiraled (docs. 75, 77, 78). By the time Leclerc himself succumbed in November, the French had lost two-thirds of the 28,000 troops they had sent to the colony. Historians disagree whether the black generals had anticipated this outcome all along, but most now broke with the French. They were joined by their former *anciens libres* opponents, who realized France intended to restore both slavery and racial discrimination. Under the former slave, Jean-Jacques Dessalines, they adopted the name "Armée Indigène," the native-born army, and gradually set their sights on independence.

Extreme cruelty had marred the revolution from its early days, even before slaves were involved, and all sides had used torture, collected severed heads, and slaughtered civilians. In the final phase, the French army's strategy became almost genocidal (doc. 79). Bonaparte had expected the army to live off the land, and that foreign powers would provide loans and commercial assistance while embargoing the black forces. This proved a miscalculation. The insurgents, moreover, now had a decade of military experience and were able to combine conventional warfare with their scorched earth and guerrilla tactics. As soon as Cap Français came within range of their artillery, in November 1803, the French commander capitulated and agreed to evacuate.

Several thousand colonists decided to stay, encouraged by Dessalines and a conciliatory first declaration of independence (November 29). The document that became the official declaration, issued a month later, had a very different tone, however (doc. 80). Much of it was a call for vengeance. Given the violent hostility it expressed to all things French, one might be surprised it was written in the colonizer's language—which, then as now, was understood by only a small minority of Haitians—instead of in the local Créole. Haitian identity, however, would center on race rather than culture until the twentieth century. The declaration justified independence in terms of the physical differences between Haitians and the French, and the latter's cruelty, and stated that secession was necessary to prevent the restoration of slavery. It did not use the word "rights." Like Toussaint, Dessalines was declared governor-general for life with dictatorial powers, and the text ends with a warning about potential dissent.

Far from mere rhetoric, the call for retribution was realized within a few weeks. Between February and May 1804, several thousand of the remaining French were systematically massacred in two waves, men first, women and children afterwards. Haitian leaders were divided on the issue, but after a century of slavery and a dozen years of merciless conflict, it seems to have had a broad degree of support in all social classes. Dessalines' incendiary proclamation of April 28 justified the killing on several grounds (doc. 81). The claim to have "avenged America," echoed an already established trope that depicted the black revolution as retribution for the sixteenth-century genocide of the pre-Columbian Indian population, fellow victims of European imperialism.

At a time when colonial rule was almost unchallenged, and slavery and racial discrimination were normative, the emergence of a black independent state was widely regarded as dangerous. Although the declaration of independence included an assurance that Haiti would not try to export its revolution, the April 28 proclamation's bold defiance of the outside world, its call for revolt in the other French colonies, and its ban on landowning by Europeans, all enhanced the country's inflammatory reputation.

---

74) Bonaparte on Slave Emancipation

Several French colonies had avoided implementation of the 1794 emancipation law, such as Martinique, which was occupied by the British from 1794 to 1802. Historians have argued whether Bonaparte was willing to maintain this legally inconsistent status quo or was determined to restore slavery in all French possessions, as most of the colonial lobby wanted. Certainly, he was quick to end the inclusion of the colonies within the French state, proclaimed in the 1795 constitution. But in this journal entry by one of his ministers (a), we see a cynically pragmatic Bonaparte not yet committed to restoring slavery in Saint Domingue. In all his public statements (b), he appeared to support emancipation.

(a) [16 August 1800, when the Council of State was discussing the colonies] Marbois[1] upheld that there should be no more talk of liberty for the free blacks of Saint Domingue. Bonaparte's position was that their freedom should again be guaranteed to them. He said, "The question is not knowing whether it is good to abolish slavery but whether it is good to abolish freedom in the free part of Saint Domingue. I am convinced that this island would be in English hands, if the blacks were not attached to us by their concern for their freedom. They will perhaps make less sugar than when they were slaves, but they will make it for us and they will provide us with soldiers, if we need them. If we have one less sugar plantation, we have one more citadel occupied by allied troops. My policy is to govern men like most of them want to be governed. That, I think, is how to recognize the sovereignty of the people. It was by becoming Catholic that I ended the war in the Vendée, by becoming Muslim that I established myself in Egypt, by becoming ultramontane that I won people over in Italy. If I governed a nation of Jews, I would restore Solomon's temple. So, I will speak of liberty in the free part of Saint Domingue; I will confirm slavery in Isle de France, and even in unfree Santo Domingo,[2] keeping open the option of limiting slavery and making it less harsh in those places where I maintain it, and of re-establishing order and introducing discipline in those places where I maintain freedom."

(*Journal du comte P.-L. Roederer, ministre et conseiller d'état* [Paris, 1909], 15–16)

(b) Paris, 8 November 1801

Inhabitants of Saint Domingue,

---

1. Barbé-Marbois, former Intendant of Saint Domingue, now finance minister. See doc. 33 and section 8 introduction.

2. The Spanish colony that bordered French Saint Domingue. Early in 1801, Toussaint Louverture would annex the colony and end slavery there. Isle de France is the modern Mauritius in the Indian Ocean.

Whatever your origin or your color, you are all French, you are all free and all equal in the sight of God and of the Republic. . . .

The government is sending you Captain-General Leclerc. He is bringing with him a large force to protect you against your enemies and the enemies of the Republic. If people tell you, "*These troops are intended to take away your freedom,*" you should reply, "*The Republic will never allow it to be taken from you.*"

Rally to the Captain-General, he is bringing you prosperity and peace. All should rally to him. Whoever dares to separate from the Captain-General will be a traitor to the homeland, and the wrath of the Republic will devour him just as fire devours your dried-up sugarcane. . . .

The First Consul (signed) Bonaparte.

> (Lewis Goldsmith, *Recueil de décrets, ordonnances, traités de paix . . .*
> *de Napoléon Bonaparte* [London, 1813], 1: 257–58)

75) General Leclerc and the Restoration of Slavery

Not until 20 May 1802 did First Consul Bonaparte publicly break with the French Revolution's antislavery legacy. He announced that slavery would be maintained in those colonies where it had never been abolished, and that the slave trade was again legal. No mention was made, however, of Saint Domingue or Guadeloupe. Then, in July, explosive news came from Guadeloupe that its military commander was forcing blacks back into slavery. The writing was on the wall. But had Leclerc in Saint Domingue been kept in the loop?

The Navy and Colonial Minister to General Leclerc (14 June 1802)

As regards the return of the former regime of the blacks, the bloody struggle from which you have just emerged a glorious victor indicates that the greatest care is needed. Attempting to smash quickly this idol of liberty, in whose name so much blood has been shed, might mean starting all over again. For a little while longer, it will be necessary that vigilance, order, and a discipline both rural and military replace the positive and official slavery of people of color in your colony . . . [until] the moment has come to force them back into their original condition, whence it has been so fatal to have removed them.

The General in Chief to the First Consul (6 August 1802)

I had asked you, citizen consul, to do nothing that might make [the blacks] fear for their freedom until I was ready, and I was making rapid progress toward that moment. All of a sudden there arrived the decree that legalizes the colonial slave trade along with letters from merchants in Nantes and Le Havre asking whether they can sell blacks here. Worse still, General Richepanse has just issued an order re-establishing slavery in Guadeloupe. . . .

Now that your plans for the colonies are known to everyone, citizen consul, if you want to keep Saint Domingue, send a new army here, and especially send money. I am telling you that, if you abandon us to our own devices as you have done up to now, this colony is lost, and once lost, you will never get it back.

My letter will surprise you, citizen consul, after those I have written to you, but is there a general who could have reckoned with an 80 percent death rate in his army and with the survivors being useless, who has been left without money like me in a country where nothing is bought except with hard cash, and where, with money, I could have eliminated many obstacles?

Could I have expected, in such circumstances, the law on the slave trade and, especially, the orders of General Richepanse that re-establish slavery and deny men of color the status of citizen?

The General in Chief to the First Consul (9 August 1802)

At the time I leave,[3] the colony will be ready for the regime you intend to give it, but it will be for my successor to take the last step, if you believe that to be suitable. I will do nothing contrary to what I have had published here.

The General in Chief to the Navy Minister (25 August 1802)[4]

Do not think of re-establishing slavery here for some time. I think I will be able to do everything so that the person who replaces me will have nothing to do but put into effect the government order, but after the innumerable proclamations that I have issued here assuring the blacks of their freedom, I do not want to have to contradict myself. Assure the First Consul, however, that my successor will find everything in place.

(Paul Roussier, *Lettres du général Leclerc, commandant en chef de l'Armée de Saint-Domingue en 1802* [Paris, 1937], 202–203, 208, 219, 285)

---

3. Leclerc was then intending to return to France around February/March 1803 but died of yellow fever at the beginning of November.

4. This letter, partly written in code, replied to a partly coded dispatch from the Navy Minister that was disguised as an "agricultural plan" but obviously referred to slavery. The dispatch includes the phrases, "This would be a good thing but it cannot be put into print, as it is possible that the soil may prove unsuitable for this type of agriculture, however much care is taken. One cannot pretend, however, our labors will succeed unless this method is more or less established. . . . I want it to be you who achieves this success."

76) Toussaint in Captivity

Seized by trickery in June, Toussaint was deported to France without a change of clothing and jailed in a mountain fortress near the Swiss frontier. From July to November, he sent a stream of written complaints, chiefly to Napoleon. All went unanswered. He sought to justify his actions, accusing General Leclerc of lying and blaming him for his aggression. He recalled his military victories and the seventeen wounds he received in the service of the French Republic. Insisting on his loyalty, he acknowledged his constitution might have been a mistake, but denied responsibility for its content. Most of the letters were in Toussaint's own hand, their pathos increased by his poor spelling and grammar. He died of pneumonia in April 1803.

During the thirty-two day crossing I had to endure not only the greatest fatigues but also such indignities as would be impossible to imagine without having witnessed them. Even my wife and my children endured a treatment that their sex and their rank should have made better. Instead of having us go onshore for respite, they kept us on board for sixty-seven days. After such a treatment, am I not justified in asking: Where are the results of the promises made to me by General Leclerc, who gave me his word of honor, as well as the protection of the French government? . . .

Surely I owe this treatment to my color, but did my color ever prevent me from serving my country with zeal and fidelity? Does the color of my body diminish my honor and my courage? Even if I were a criminal, and there were government orders to arrest me, was it necessary to use a hundred riflemen to snatch my wife and children from their estate without respect or regard for their rank and sex . . . ? Was it necessary . . . to loot and ransack all our property? No, my wife, my children, and my family have no responsibity in the matter and have no account to give to the government. General Leclerc should be honest: Did he fear having a rival? I would compare his conduct to that of the Roman senate, which pursued Hannibal[5] even into his retirement. . . .

Everyone who has known me will do me justice. I have been a slave; I admit it, but I never received even a reproach from my masters. In Saint Domingue I never neglected anything for the island's well-being. . . . If I wanted to list all the services I rendered to the government in all the wars it would take several volumes and would never end. And to repay me for all these services I was arbitrarily arrested in Saint Domingue like a criminal, tied up, and taken on board a ship without regard for my rank and for what I have achieved. . . .

It is from the depths of this prison that I have recourse to the justice and magnanimity of the First Consul. He is too generous and too good a general to

---

5. North African military commander, considered one of the greatest of all generals.

leave an old soldier covered in wounds in the service of his country to die in a dungeon without at least giving him the satisfaction of [a trial]. . . .

First Consul, father of all soldiers, honest judge, defender of the innocent, render judgement on my fate. My wound is very deep. Apply the healing remedy. . . . You are a doctor. I am counting entirely on your justice and equity.

> (Archives Nationales, Paris, AF IV 1213, nd, "Mémoire" of Toussaint Louverture, ff. 20–22, 24–26, 28 [Sept. 1802])

77) U.S. Newspaper Reports

These, entirely erroneous, news reports printed in Philadelphia newspapers (and reprinted in other cities in the United States) show how even literate people lived in a world of rumor and uncertainty. They also show how rumor can foreshadow the future. After surrendering in early May 1802, Toussaint never went into rebellion, and the French army and its casualties were then far smaller than the article stated. Within months, however, the French forces were dwindling fast; Toussaint was deported, accused of conspiracy, and in October Dessalines finally did rebel.

We are informed that Toussaint had revolted, in consequence of which three divisions of Leclerc's troops had been engaged with the blacks and very roughly handled—no quarter given. (*Aurora*)[6]

In corroboration of the above, we have obtained the subjoined extracts of letters, received in this city, from the most respectable authority:

Cape Francois, May 28

In a few days after Toussaint had surrendered, he asked permission to go to one of his plantations, which was granted by the Gen. in Chief. We have just received information by General Christophe, that Toussaint had decamped with a strong body of troops, in opposition to the French.

In the small time of [our source] being here, he discovered the force of the French, which, out of 30,000 soldiers brought into the island, they only remain about 18 or 20,000, and there are dying every day 10 or 12 in this one place. There are in the hospital at the Môle, 2,000 sick men. I feel convinced, if there should not arrive from France, some reinforcements in a very little time, we shall find ourselves in a great deal of trouble, and not unlikely that Toussaint will still be Governor of St. Domingo, which is the fear of every citizen.

---

6. The *Gazette* is citing a report in a rival newspaper, the *Aurora*.

May 29

Toussaint has again taken up arms, but I imagine will not be able to do much, as he is only joined by Dessalines, and a considerable force is every day expected here from France.

(Philadelphia Gazette [15 June 1802])

78) Collaboration and Revolt

The terse and tense letters of thirty-year-old General Leclerc sketch an unfolding military disaster shaped by poor logistical support, catastrophic losses to disease, and an increasingly implacable opponent. Unlike the British and Spanish forces earlier sent to Saint Domingue, his troops were experienced veterans of a triumphant revolutionary army. His orders were first to co-opt, then deport, the principal black officers, but he quickly came to depend on them to suppress rural resistance. Maroons and plantation workers he called "brigands" were joined by more and more units of the colonial army. Whether the co-opted black generals had genuinely cast in their lot with the French or were just biding their time is hard to know.

The General in Chief to the First Consul (6 August 1802)

My position is getting embarrassing and might become difficult. This is it:

The death toll has been so terrible among my troops that, when I wanted to disarm the North, a widespread revolt erupted. Forced to economize, since you leave me without any funds, I had dismantled the colonial army and dismissed three-quarters of its officers. The moment the black troops saw my difficulties, all the officers demanded their back pay. I was forced to pay up, and since I had no cash in my treasury, I had to sell off cheaply the produce I had stored and to commit future customs revenue.

The black troops have gone into action but there is not enough of them, and besides, as all my generals are sick, I have had to use black generals. I'm using Christophe in the northern mountains and Dessalines around Plaisance. I have no worry about Christophe, but I am not so sure of Dessalines. The first attacks have driven the insurgents from the positions they held, but they have redeployed in other districts, and in this insurrection there is a real fanaticism: these men get themselves killed but they won't surrender.

The General in Chief to the Navy Minister (9 August 1802)

I have combined all the colonial and European troops that I have available, and tomorrow I will attack the rebels on all fronts. The black generals lead the columns; they are closely supervised. I have ordered them to make terrible examples; I always use them when I have a lot of dirty work to do. . . .

I've received news of a bloody battle that General Boyer fought at Gros Morne. The rebels have been exterminated; fifty prisoners have been hanged. The men die with an incredible fanaticism; they laugh at death. It's the same with the women. The Moustique rebels have attacked and taken Jean Rabel; it will have to be retaken immediately. This fury is the result of General Richepanse's proclamation and the colonists' indiscreet remarks.

The General in Chief to the First Consul (9 August 1802)

I am pleased with Dessalines, Christophe, and Morpas; these three are the only ones who have any influence. The others are useless. Christophe and Morpas, especially, have been a great help in the current situation. Christophe and Dessalines have asked me not to leave them here when I go. . . .

The General in Chief to the Navy Minister (25 August 1802)

It seems to me you do not have a very clear idea of my position, to judge from the orders you send me. You order me to send the black generals to Europe. It is quite simple to arrest them all the same day, but I am using these generals to stop the revolts that are still breaking out and, in some districts, are taking on an alarming appearance. . . . It is not enough to have deported Toussaint. There are 2,000 leaders here who need deporting.

The General in Chief to the Navy Minister (13 September 1802)

To give you an idea of my losses, the 7th [regiment] arrived here with 1,395 men. It has at present 83 sickly and 107 in the hospital. The rest have perished. The 11th light infantry arrived with 1,900 men. It has 163 men in service and 201 in hospital. The 71st, which received about 1,000 men, has 19 serving the colors and 133 in hospital.

It is the same with the rest of the army. Try and imagine, then, my position in a country that has been in civil war for ten years and where the rebels are convinced that we want to reduce them to slavery.

The General in Chief to the Navy Minister (17 September 1802)

The whole mountain chain from Vallière to Marmelade is in revolt. Fortunately, each district has its own leader, and it is rare that two rebel leaders unite. . . . Since August 30 the sickness has strongly revived and I am losing from 100 to 120 men each day. In order to control the mountains, once I have finally completed the job, I will have to destroy all the food crops and a large proportion of the cultivators; after living as brigands for ten years, they will never be forced back to work.

I will need to wage a war of extermination, and it will cost me many men. A large proportion of my colonial troops has deserted and gone over to the enemy.

(Paul Roussier, *Les Lettres du général Leclerc, commandant en chef de l'Armée de Saint-Domingue en 1802* [Paris, 1937], 201–202, 206, 207, 216–17, 226, 237–38)

79) Atrocities

Bechaud was a French officer who arrived in Saint Domingue in the final months of the fighting. Although the French Revolution and France's military campaigns in Europe gave rise to terrible atrocities, people who witnessed the Haitian Revolution tended to think it exceptionally violent. In this account from the conflict's final months, the French had clearly lost the psychological war of terror.

Drowning is the usual way of putting to death black prisoners. I've been told that, on several occasions, thousands were drowned at the same time, and their bodies were often seen floating . . . on to the shore. Humanity is a casualty here. Those who are caught in the towns secretly plotting against the French are hanged. Those who have done most harm, as leaders or otherwise, are burned, or devoured by dogs. The commander-in-chief has brought many large dogs from Havana for this purpose.

All this suffering is nothing compared to the unspeakable tortures with which the terrible Dessalines puts to death our companions in arms. You can get an idea of the sort of thing this monster is capable of when you know that, so as to trick General Leclerc, when he was commander of the West and Saint Marc, he for a long time hanged—sometimes with his own hands—all the rebel blacks who were captured carrying weapons after the pacification Leclerc had carried out, even though these poor wretches were devoted to him and had been merely carrying out his secret orders. He skillfully played this role of cunning barbarian until October 13, when he suddenly turned the arms of all sorts of blacks against us. This meant that those who had been incorporated into French units began this new revolt by killing their white comrades.

Thus we are no longer surprised to learn that the least of the tortures our prisoners endure is to be grilled or barbecued, sawn between two planks, have their eyes torn out with a bale-hook, and then be slashed with a cutlass and be hauled up under the armpits to expire under the blows of a cudgel, or be given the burning ankles torture, or others, to be made to reveal information: in short, every violence that the most refined cruelty could invent. To be shot is a favor. What a war, good God! The fiercest days of combat in Europe do not expose the soldier to the suffering that the smallest skirmish or ambush here can lead to.

To make things worse, in all their attacks the Negroes carry ropes with slipknots that they use to pull toward them and tie up unlucky soldiers who get too close.

I cannot convey how much this cruel prospect undermines the soldiers' courage. Those who would run impetuously straight at an ordinary enemy have their ardor cooled by the fear of being surrounded; their courage abandons them when they think of the thousand dreadful things that would usually follow their capture.

(John Carter Brown Library, Providence, Codex fr. 32, ff. 119–20, memoir by Jean-Pierre Bechaud)

80) The Declaration of Independence, 1 January 1804

Whereas most early declarations of independence copied that of the United States, Haiti's was unique in several respects. Written by Dessalines' secretary, Louis Boisrond Tonnerre, it employs an heroic rhetoric rather than a rights-based discourse. Its passionate language reflects the recent trauma of the war of independence and targets remaining colonists as a potential fifth column. While guaranteeing the abolition of slavery, the text seeks to assuage Haiti's colonial neighbors by denying any intention to export the revolution. The document established the "State of Haiti," not a republic, as often thought.

To The People of Haiti

Citizens, it is not enough to have driven out of your country the barbarians who have bloodied it for two centuries. It is not enough to have put an end to the persistent factions that, one after the other, made sport with the figment of freedom that France dangled before your eyes. With one final act of national authority, we must ensure forever the reign of liberty in the land where it was born. We must deny the inhuman government that for long has held our minds in humiliating thralldom any hope of reenslaving us. In short, we must live independent or die. . . .

The French name still haunts our country. Everything here is a reminder of the cruelty of that barbarous people: our laws, our customs, our towns, all still bear a French imprint. More than this, there still exists French people on our island, and you believe that you are free and independent of that republic. . . .

For fourteen years we have been the victims of our own gullibility and tolerance, defeated not by French arms but by the pitiful eloquence of their official proclamations. When, therefore, shall we tire of breathing the same air as they do? What do we have in common with this murderous nation? Its cruelty compared to our evident moderation, its color unlike our own, the wide seas that separate us, our avenging climate, all tell us that they are not our brothers and never will be. If they find refuge among us, they will again seek to cause trouble and to divide us.

Citizens of this land, men, women, and children, look all around you on this island: Are you searching for your wives, your husbands, your brothers, your sisters? Are you looking for your children, your babies? What has become of them? I shudder to say it: they became the prey of these vultures.

Instead of finding those victims who were dear to you, your harrowed gaze meets only their murderers. The frightful presence of these tigers still covered in their victims' blood condemns you as unfeeling and slow to avenge them. What are you waiting for to bring peace to their souls? . . .

Know that you have achieved nothing until you have set a terrible but just example to other nations of the vengeance that a people must take when it is proud to have regained its freedom and is determined to maintain it. Let us strike fear into all those who would dare to try and snatch it away from us. Let us begin with the French. May they tremble in approaching our coasts, if not from the memory of the cruelty they have committed here, then because of the terrible oath we will take to put to death whoever is born French and defiles this land of liberty by sacrilegiously setting foot here. . .

We must not let, however, a spirit of proselytism destroy our creation. Let us leave our neighbors in peace to live tranquilly under the laws they have made for themselves. We should not set ourselves up as lawmakers for the Caribbean and, like headstrong revolutionaries, take pride in disturbing the calm of the islands that surround us. They have not been drenched in the innocent blood of their inhabitants like ours has been; they have no need to seek vengeance against the power that protects them. . . .

And you, long unhappy people, who are witness to the oath we are taking, remember that . . . if ever you rejected, or accepted with complaint, the laws that the spirit watching over your destiny will dictate to me for your happiness, you would merit the fate of an ungrateful people. But banish this frightful thought; you shall be the defender of the freedom that you cherish and the support of the leader who commands you. Take therefore from my hands the oath to live free and independent, and to prefer death to anything that might tend to reenslave you. Swear to hunt down forever traitors and enemies of your independence.

(Louis Boisrond Tonnerre, *Liberté ou la mort: Armée indigène*
[Port-au-Prince, 1804], 3–7)

81) Dessalines' Proclamation, 28 April 1804

Written by Paris-educated Juste Chanlatte (doc. 32), this dramatic proclamation justifies the massacres that the Declaration of Independence had demanded

*and declares Dessalines' determination to defend the gains of the revolution. It
was reprinted in Haitian almanacs for many years afterwards. Like the declaration, the seething and truculent text combines vituperation of the French with
an attempt to reassure foreign powers. It compares Haiti's fate to that of Guadeloupe, where France had succeeded in restoring slavery.*

Finally the hour of vengeance has struck, and the implacable enemies of the
rights of man have received the punishment their crimes deserved. I raised over
their guilty heads my arm that for too long had been restrained. At this signal
ordained by a just god, your hands divinely armed set the ax to the ancient tree of
slavery and prejudice. In vain had time and, still more, the diabolical politics of
the Europeans encased it in triple armor. You stripped away this armor and
placed it on your own breasts, becoming, like your natural enemies, cruel and
pitiless. Like an overflowing torrent that roars, uproots, and carries all before it,
your avenging passion has swept away everything in its impetuous path. May
thus perish all who tyrannize the innocent, all oppressors of the human race. . . .

Yes, we have rendered unto these true cannibals war for war, crime for crime,
outrage for outrage. Yes, I have saved my country; I have avenged America. It
is my pride and my glory that I admit to it in the face of both mortals and the
gods. It matters not how the peoples of today and of the future will judge me. I
have done my duty; I have kept my self esteem; that is enough for me. . . . It is
not my only reward. I have seen two classes of men, born to love and help one
another, at last mixed together as one, rushing to vengeance and disputing the
honor of striking the first blows. Blacks and coloreds, you whom the refined
duplicity of the Europeans sought so long to divide, who today make up . . . but
one family, have no doubt that your perfect reconciliation needed to be sealed
with the blood of our executioners. . . . The same ardor to strike your enemies
has distinguished you both, and you are facing the same fate. The same interests
must therefore make you forever united, indivisible, and inseparable. Maintain
this precious concord; this happy harmony among you is the guarantee of your
well-being, your salvation, and your success. It is the secret of being invincible.

To tighten these bonds, do I need to retrace for you the atrocities committed
against our people? The massacre of the entire population of this isle, plotted calmly
in silent council; the execution of this frightful project proposed to me without
shame, and already undertaken with untroubled mien by Frenchmen accustomed
to such crimes! The pillage and destruction of Guadeloupe, its ruins still rank with
the blood of the children, women, and old men put to the sword! Pélage[7] himself,
victim of their trickery after basely betraying his country and his brothers! The

---

7. Ex-slave and chief officer in the army of republican Guadeloupe, Magloire Pélage
collaborated with the French forces Napoleon sent in 1802 to restore slavery, but he was
deported to France.

brave and immortal Delgresse,[8] blown into the air with the debris of his fort rather than accept being chained: magnanimous warrior, your noble fate, far from shaking our courage has only increased our desire to avenge you and follow you! . . . Unfortunate people of Martinique:[9] if only I could fly to your aid and break your chains! Alas, an uncrossable barrier separates us! . . . But perhaps a spark from the fire than burns within us will flame up in your heart . . . and, awoken from your lethargy, you will demand, arms in hand, your sacred and imprescriptible rights!

. . . Tremble tyrants, usurpers, scourges of the New World! Our daggers are sharpened, ready for your torture. Sixty thousand armed men, battle-hardened and obedient to my orders, are burning to offer up a new holocaust to the shades of their murdered brothers. . . . Let them come, then, these murderous cohorts; I await them with a steady eye and abandon to them without regret the coast and the places where towns have once stood. But woe be to him who approaches too close to the mountains! . . .

Generals, officers, soldiers, unlike my predecessor, the ex-governor Toussaint, I have kept the promise I made to you when I took up arms against the tyrants. As long as there is a breath in my body, I will keep this oath:

"Never will any colonist or European set foot on this land as a master or proprietor. This resolution will henceforth be the foundation of our constitution."[10] . . .

As punishing a few innocents for the deeds of their fellows would be repugnant to my honor and character, I have shown mercy to a handful of whites distinguished by the opinions they have always held and who, besides, have taken the oath to live with us obedient to the law. I order that they receive no punishment and that their activities and persons remain unharmed. Once again I recommend and order all departmental generals, district and town commanders to offer help, encouragement, and protection to neutral and friendly nations that will establish commercial relations with this island.

Le Cap headquarters, 28 April 1804, year 1 of Independence

The Governor-General[11]—Dessalines

(Archives Nationales d'Outre-Mer, Aix-en-Provence, CC9B/23)

---

8. Louis Delgrès was a subordinate of Pélage who resisted the French invasion of 1802 and blew himself up rather than surrender.

9. Slavery had not been abolished in Martinique, as it was captured by the British in 1794 before the emancipation act could be enforced. It was returned to France in 1802 with the old regime intact.

10. This clause would reappear in Dessalines' constitution of May 1805 with the phrase "whites of whatever nation" replacing "European." Although later criticized by Haitian liberals, it was retained in all Haitian constitutions, except those of Henri Christophe, down to 1918.

11. Dessalines soon abandoned this incongruously colonial title and, following Napoleon, had himself crowned emperor in October.

10. OVERSEAS REACTIONS

The international repercussions of the Haitian Revolution were richly diverse. Great power politics and world commodity markets, antislavery and slave resistance, migration movements and imaginative literature, attitudes to race and decolonization—all felt its impact. It alarmed and excited public opinion all around the Atlantic world. The first histories, stage plays, and novels about the revolution all appeared while it was still in progress.

Across the Americas, slaves showed their awareness of events in Saint Domingue by singing about them (docs. 82, 85, 86) and by other displays of racial pride (docs. 83, 87). Slaveowners and officials often complained of a new "insolence." Sometimes this meant a neglect of traditional deference, answering back, or even suing in court (doc. 84). Foreigners feared both the influence of Saint Domingue's example and that it would become a source of subversion or invasions. The French Republic indeed planned to use local forces to foment a slave revolt in Jamaica, but Toussaint Louverture and later Haitian rulers blocked such attempts in the knowledge that they would cause a retaliatory maritime embargo. Individuals from Saint Domingue or Haiti nonetheless show up in several slave rebellions and conspiracies, notably in Maracaibo (1799), Louisiana and Martinique (1811), and several cases in Cuba between 1795 and 1843. In other instances plotters discussed Saint Domingue as an object lesson, and the leader of the large Curaçao uprising of 1795 adopted the name of André Rigaud. In Charleston in 1822, Denmark Vesey supposedly promised fellow conspirators Haitian military assistance, as had José Aponte in Havana ten years earlier (doc. 88).

In slavery's 350-year history in the Americas, the 1790s witnessed the highest number of revolts and conspiracies, but there were other causal factors at work besides the Haitian Revolution. Proslavery commentators frequently blamed the emergent abolitionist movement for misleading slaves. Abolitionists were damaged by such charges, but in turn they were able to strengthen their arguments by claiming that a preemptive abolition of the slave trade would lessen the likelihood of rebellions. However, during the course of the Haitian Revolution most parts of the Americas imported far more slaves than ever before. Although the revolution was a terrible warning to slaveowners, it also encouraged them to expand production because it drove up the price of sugar and coffee and sent out waves of refugee planters eager to remake their fortunes. Invariably, ambitions outweighed prudence (docs. 89, 90). The burgeoning of Blue Mountain coffee in Jamaica, Cuba's transformation into a major slave society, and the Frenchness of nineteenth-century Louisiana all owed a great deal to an influx of migrants from Saint Domingue and the lure of high prices.

Slave rebellion was a difficult issue for the antislavery movement; only a few marginal figures whose spirit of Christian universalism subsumed their sense of racial difference were prepared to justify it (docs. 91, 92). Thomas Jefferson continued in private to profess antislavery ideals through much of the Haitian Revolution, but although the conflict alarmed him greatly, he took no action. He wavered a good deal in reaction to Bonaparte's aggressive stance, yet continued his predecessors' policy of trading with the black forces in Saint Domingue (doc. 93). Only two years after Haiti achieved independence did he impose an embargo (1806–1810). This was a favor to Bonaparte, from whom he then wanted help in acquiring Florida. Jefferson's acquisition of Louisiana three years before, which hugely expanded the scope of U.S. slavery, was partially due to Bonaparte's failure in Saint Domingue.

Although fear of slave insurrection did little to help the antislavery movement, the Haitian Revolution indirectly contributed to two major successes. In 1807, it facilitated passage of slave trade abolition through the British parliament by removing worries that France might profit from Britain's sacrifice. And the assistance the Haitian Republic gave to Simón Bolívar in 1816 during the struggle for Spanish American independence, contributed to ending both Spanish rule and slavery in South America. Haiti's violent birth, however, and its unstable development, greatly alarmed colonial liberals like Bolívar (doc. 94), and its example was a major influence in keeping Cuba a colony for most of the nineteenth century. Moreover, when neighboring Santo Domingo declared its independence in 1821, it was quickly snuffed out by a Haitian invasion and takeover.

The revolution's legacy is similarly complex as regards attitudes to race. The violence of the revolution, always selectively reported, discouraged white public opinion from empathizing with the insurgents and helped cast savagery in racial terms. Some ascribed black military victories to endurance, cunning, blind obedience, and familiarity with the climate, the characteristics that made "good slaves." On the other hand, diverse writers were profoundly impressed by the Haitian epic and hailed it as an epoch-making challenge to ideas about racial inequality (docs. 95, 96, 97). Not all were abolitionists; Marcus Rainsford opposed abolition of the slave trade and claimed that emancipation would be cruel to slaves. Yet his meditations on the meaning of the Haitian Revolution foreshadow modern writers who argue that it was an "unthinkable" event that has been unjustly silenced and "banalized" (doc. 97). Imaginative literature in several languages enlisted the revolution as an exotic backdrop to trivial tales and celebrations of "savagery," but in some instances produced works of power and artistry (doc. 98).

Toward the close of the nineteenth century, veteran black abolitionist Frederick Douglass had to struggle with some of these conflicting images in a speech given at the Chicago World's Fair. Although the ex-slaves who won the revolution almost certainly lived better lives than their still-enslaved counterparts in the rest of the Americas, by the 1890s Haiti had become a byword for poverty and political instability. Condemning the country's elite as idle and factious, Douglass praised the peasantry, but was defensive about popular culture and compelled to respond to rumors about human sacrifice and cannibalism that had gained international attention. To redress the balance, he layed out a case for the historical significance of the Haitian Revolution, which, he noted, had remained a subject of intense public scrutiny throughout the century (doc. 99).

---

82) Jamaican Slaves, 1791

*Jamaica had the Caribbean's largest concentration of slaves outside Saint
Domingue and could be reached from it in a day or two by small boat. Jamaica
also had an exceptional record of slave revolt exceeded nowhere else in the Americas.
It is therefore surprising the colony experienced no slave rebellion during the
years of the Haitian Revolution. The strength of its military garrison during this
period is a possible explanation. The following extracts were written by the garrison commander and an anonymous colonist.*

(18 September 1791) Many slaves here are very inquisitive and intelligent,
and are immediately informed of every kind of news that arrives. I do not hear
of their having shewn any signs of revolt, though they have composed songs of
the negroes having made a rebellion at Hispaniola with their usual chorus to it;
and I have not a doubt but there are numbers who are ripe for any mischief and
whenever any insurrection begins it will be . . . on the North side of the island.

(18 November 1791) [The slaves are] so different a people from what they
once were . . . I am convinced the Ideas of Liberty have sunk so deep in the minds
of *all* Negroes that whenever the greatest precautions are not taken they will rise.

(The National Archives, London, CO 137/89)

83) Popular Heroes in Cuba, 1795

*When Spain surrendered Santo Domingo to France in 1795, it faced a
dilemma. What should it do with Jean-François' black insurgents it had
recruited as "auxiliary troops" two years before, when Spain tried to seize Saint
Domingue? Neither the black troops nor the French thought they should stay on
the island. When the governor of Santo Domingo informed his counterpart in
Cuba that he was sending them to him, Governor Las Casas sent this panicked
response to Spain's chief minister, Manuel Godoy.*

General (as he calls himself) Jean-François has filled the inhabitants of the city
and the island with terror. Every colonist imagines his slaves will rebel and the
colony will be totally destroyed the moment these individuals arrive. Wretched
slaves yesterday, they are today the heroes of a revolution, triumphant, wealthy,
and decorated. Such things should not be seen by a population composed

primarily of people of color oppressed by a smaller number of whites. Nothing has such a vivid effect on most men as the perceptions they receive through the sense of sight. It is not easy to foresee how the lower orders and people of color would react and how excited they might get in the presence of Jean-François, decked out in the sash of a general officer of the king's army and navy, with a large following of his subordinate generals and brigadiers wearing the insignia of the ranks he awarded them, dazzling with astonishing pomp in a magnificent coach with six horses, an elaborate household, etc., much superior to that ever seen by the public in the head and principal officer of this island . . . [Jean-François'] name resounds in the ears of the populace like an unconquerable hero, a redeemer of the slaves . . . at a time when the voice of freedom resounds everywhere and the seeds of rebellion are sprouting.

(Archivo General de Indias, Seville, Estado 5, Luis de Las
Casas to Príncipe de la Paz, 16 Dec. 1795)

84) Troublesome Migrants in Puerto Rico, 1796

Undeveloped Puerto Rico proved hospitable to French refugees and their slaves who could contribute to expanding the plantation economy. However, blacks who had witnessed the abolition of slavery in Saint Domingue proved to be troublesome migrants. Administrators therefore had to weigh economic benefits against political dangers. Widespread complaints of blacks' "insolence" in these years covered a variety of self-assertive behaviors. In this document it meant invoking the French emancipation decree to sue for freedom in court. Several dozen slaves taken to the United States did this in the next few decades.

It is most terrible that they [the slaves of certain Dominguan refugees] might be imbued with the pernicious principle of their being free. To our great alarm, we are already experiencing this in this island because of the corruption of some French slaves who have been brought here. Not satisfied with complaining to the courts with daily demands for their imaginary freedom, they lead astray the Spanish slaves, getting them to do the same and to escape by whatever means possible from the control and ownership of their legitimate masters. This insolence . . . has regrettably increased so much on the island that, without stringent measures, it will grow steadily until the island is totally ruined.

(Archivo General de Indias, Seville, Estado 10, Governor
Ramón de Castro to Príncipe de la Paz, 15 June 1796)

85) Jamaican Song, 1799

We cannot say that this song would not have been sung at an earlier point in Caribbean history, but its flagrant rejection of the racialist ideology underpinning all American slave societies seems to capture the moment when, under the rule of a former slave, a new, ostensibly race-blind society was being created in what had been the region's most important colony.

The following was, in the year 1799, frequently sung in the streets of Kingston:
One, two, tree,
All de same;
Black, white, brown,
All de same:
All de same.

(Robert Renny, *A History of Jamaica* [London, 1807], 241)

86) Venezuelan Song, 1801

Scholars dispute whether the bloody insurrection that occurred in 1795 in the hills above Coro in western Venezuela was influenced by the Haitian Revolution. This extract shows how quickly news from Saint Domingue reached the region and, once again, how blacks used song (and puns) as a mode of passive resistance (cf. doc. 8). The document dates from a few weeks after Toussaint Louverture took over the formerly Spanish colony of Santo Domingo, thus making himself master of the whole island of Hispaniola.

There is going around quite openly among the freemen and slaves of the hill country news of the capture of the Spanish island of Santo Domingo by the Negro Toussaint, and . . . they display great rejoicing and merriment at the news, using the chorus "Look to the firebrand (*tisón*[1])," as a response to the words "They'd better watch out!"

(Academia Nacional de la Historia, Caracas, Sección Civiles,
Signatura A13–5159–2, report of 24 Feb. 1801)

---

1. *Tisón* can mean "firebrand," "kindling," and "ember," something both black and incendiary.

87) Brazilian Militiamen, 1805

As maritime links between Brazil and the Caribbean were very limited, it is remarkable that blacks in the colony's capital, 3,000 miles from Haiti, were informed within just a few months when the former slave Jean-Jacques Dessalines was crowned emperor (in October 1804). This tantalizing extract from government correspondence is an enigma. Whether it concerns painted medallions or cameo brooches, where the objects were made and how they got to Rio—nothing more about the incident is known.

In the year 1805, when I arrived in the city of Rio de Janeiro, I was informed by respectable people that, just a few days before, the Criminal judge of that city had ordered that there be torn from the chests of some mulatto and creole freedmen the portrait of Dessalines, emperor of the blacks of the island of São Domingos. Even more extraordinary is that these same men were employed in the city's militia, where I saw them skillfully handling the artillery.

(Arquivo Histórico Ultramarino, Lisbon, Seção Brasil-Diversos [1749–1824], caixa 2, "A escravatura" [1808?], reproduced in Luiz Mott, "A escravatura: o propósito de uma representação a El-rei sobre a escravatura no Brasil," *Revista do Instituto de Estudos Brasileiros* 14 [1973], 133)

88) Aponte's Rebellion, Cuba, 1812

Of all the revolts and conspiracies influenced in some way by events in Saint Domingue, perhaps the most interesting and complex was that of the free black woodworker José Antonio Aponte. A unique feature of the conspiracy's organization was a book of inspirational pictures Aponte made and other pictures or engravings that he acquired and shared with his followers. These included portraits of heroes of the Haitian Revolution. The coronation of Henry Christophe the previous year and the fortuitous arrival of some of Jean-François' former officers were also sources of inspiration; one conspirator actually pretended to be Jean-François. This extract comes from reports of interrogations conducted in March 1812. The conspirators were hanged the following month.

[Clemente Chacón, a free black, was] asked if Aponte explained for what reason he had drawn in the book the fortresses with their entrances and exits. He replied: no. At this point, the pictures were shown to him one by one, from the beginning up to the first one where there are two armies engaged in battle firing at each other, with the one on the right containing various blacks. Similarly, on the following page there are in the same hand white and black soldiers. One of the latter, who is on horseback, has a white soldier's head on the end of a lance; another black also holds a severed head that is dripping blood. The whites have been defeated. Asked what he has to say about the meaning of these pictures, and if Aponte explained it to them, he replied that, although Aponte showed them the book, as he mentioned before, he did not instruct them as to the paintings' significance, and nor did he, the deponent, understand them. . .

[Clemente Chacón was] asked if he understands the picture that contains a view of the sea with two ships, several blacks in religious and secular costumes, a monk of the Preaching Order, a priest, another who is apparently an archbishop, and a Negro with insignia of high rank, a baton, and crossed sashes. He replied he does not understand it, although he does recall that in the picture Cristóval Henriquez [Henry Christophe] was pointing with his left hand and had a saber in his right hand. At his feet was a sign that said, "Carry out my orders."

[Aponte, was] asked if it is true that he showed Clemente Chacón three small pictures, one of Cristóbal Enrriques [Henry Christophe], another of General Salinas [Dessalines], and the other of a general whose name Chacón didn't remember, which had captions in printed letters, as Chacón stated himself in one of his responses about the content of the book; and also if it was true that he, the deponent, told Chacón he'd had them sent to him from Saint Domingue. He replied: It is true that he showed Chacón the portraits of Cristóbal, Laubertú [Louverture], Salinas, and of Juan Francisco [Jean-François] who went to Spain, all of them French blacks. But none of them had a caption in printed letters. And it was false that he had said he'd had them sent to him from Saint Domingue, since the ones of Cristóbal and Juan Francisco were copied by hand from others he had seen, and that the other two were engravings he had acquired at the time of the Ballajá campaign[2] among many others that were brought to Havana. . . .

Asked where are the pictures that he showed to Chacón of Salinas, Juan Francisco, Lauvertú, Cristóbal: He replied that he burned them because he had heard in a general way (and without naming anyone in particular) that they were prohibited engravings. . . .

[Melchor Chirinos was] asked if he saw in master Aponte's house a picture made of green painted paper bearing the image of Our Lady of the Remedies: He replied that he never saw any saint in that house, and that on just one occasion the aforesaid master showed him a picture of a black king of Haiti with others of Generals Lauvertú, Juan Fransuá, and Tusen [Toussaint] that Aponte

---

2. Aponte was probably confusing Bayajá (Fort Liberté) with Guarico (Cap Français) and referring to the French expedition of 1802–1803, when the first engravings of the black leaders were made.

also showed to Ternero. On another occasion, he saw various blacks visiting his house, who Aponte told him were black French officers staying in Casa Blanca.[3]

> (José Luciano Franco, *La conspiración de Aponte* [Havana: Archivo Nacional, 1963], 63, 64, 95–96, 99)

89) Danger and Opportunity: The British Press, 1791

The first reports of the 1791 slave uprising took two months to reach Europe. They suggested danger to some, opportunity to others. The revolt's threat to nearby Jamaica, Britain's most important colony, caused a brief stockmarket swoon in London and a defensive response on the island. But the damage done to a commercial rival also sent the value of Jamaica's crops soaring. Balancing various interests, Jamaica's governor sent Saint Domingue guns but not troops. Proslavery forces like The Times *of London blamed the revolt on the influence of French reformism. Abolitionists blamed the cruelties of slavery and used it as an argument to end the slave trade. The newspaper apparently already knew that alienated French colonists were hoping to hand the colony over to Britain.*

The dreadful slaughter committed between the inhabitants of this unfortunate island is confirmed in every respect by the letters received yesterday from France. . . . The damage done to the plantations is infinitely greater than what was reported in our paper of yesterday. . . .

Commodore Affleck at Jamaica . . . states that, upon the information of a serious insurrection having broken out among the negroes and people of colour at ST. DOMINGO, Admiral Affleck went down with two frigates . . . with the hopes of affording some assistance to the inhabitants; but finding this impractical in an effectual manner, he returned to Jamaica, and dispatched the *Daphne* to England with the information. . . . On the news of the insurrection being received at Jamaica, Lord Effingham [the governor] gathered all the troops together, to be ready on the first alarm, and it was expected that martial law would be proclaimed. . . .

The event that has happened at ST. DOMINGO was apprehended by all well-informed Frenchmen. The decree of the last French Legislature, placing the people of colour on an equality with the whites has been the principal cause of

---

3. After a fifteen-year exile in Central America, a small group of Jean-François' former officers had arrived in Havana in December 1811, en route to Santo Domingo. The Cuban governor lodged them at Casa Blanca on the far side of Havana's harbor hoping to prevent their mixing with the local black population.

the mischief that ensued. M. de Barnave . . . repeatedly warned the [National Assembly] of the consequences that would result, and his ideas are now verified. It is needless to comment further upon the event, which is not the only misery that has attended this boasted Revolution in France.

If the rebellion should grow more serious at ST. DOMINGO, it is most certain that the inhabitants will invite some foreign power to come and take possession of them; for as the National Assembly of France have thought proper to pass a decree, that has occasioned every misery that mankind can experience, the inhabitants would act very proper in putting themselves under the protection of any other power. From the calamities we have suffered from French intrigues, there is no tie upon us for not availing ourselves of a good offer. In consequence of the unsettled state of affairs in the French West Indies, and the apprehensions which timid minds are apt to entertain where there is only the appearance of danger, stocks fell yesterday 1 per cent: though at the close of the market they recovered a little. The rumour was that five men of war were to be immediately commissioned and sent to the West Indies.

(*The Times* [London], 28 Oct. 1791)

90) Greed and Fear in Cuba

Despite considerable expansion since 1760, Cuba was in 1790 only a minor producer of sugar, and whites made up the majority of its population. By 1830, it had become the world's main exporter of sugar and a major source of slave-grown coffee. Francisco Arango y Parreño was Cuba's leading intellectual, who lobbied the Spanish government on behalf of the planter class for reforms that would liberalize the economy. These reports, written during the slave insurrection in Saint Domingue, show the island poised on the brink of dramatic changes. The supposedly more humane form of slavery Arango boasts of here soon became a thing of the past.

(20 November 1791) It cannot be ignored that the French part of the island is almost joined to that of Cuba by Point Maisí and that, even if the insurgents do not cross over and the doctrine of rebellion is not spread by those infernal apostles, we might suffer from the influence of their example. Cubans fear this and are being extremely cautious. However, to allay in some measure Your Majesty's concern, your supplicant proposes that there are three important differences between the two colonies.

The first is that all the free people of Cuba are animated by the same spirit of subordination and blind obedience to their sovereign. The second is that the city of Havana has a larger garrison than does Cap Français. The third and most important concerns the treatment of slaves. The French regard them as beasts; the Spanish, as men. French slaveowners and even their slave laws have always been marked by excessive rigor, so as to inspire the greatest possible fear in the slaves. They believed this was the only way a single white man could govern a hundred blacks engaged in heavy, unending labor in the middle of a forest. . . .

Thus far I have dealt with the well-founded concerns of the Cubans. Now let us turn to their interests and the well-founded advantages that they can extract from the same disaster. Your Majesty should not be surprised, nor think such ideas inappropriate. Nobody sympathizes with the French more than does your supplicant. He would shed his blood to free them from this disaster, but as this is impossible, and as they are swallowed up in a calamity that, even if it does not totally ruin the colony, will set it back infinitely, it is essential to look at it through political eyes and not just with compassion. As a good patriot and a good subject, I am obliged to inform the best of kings that there is an opportunity here to give to the agriculture of our islands advantage and preponderance over that of the French and inform him how this can be achieved. . . .

In order to achieve this, my lord, it will require a lot of effort and that we take full advantage of the time our neighbor is out of action.

(17 January 1793) The events of Cap Français have had contradictory effects on the thinking of wise and sensible politicians. . . . Take advantage of the moment to transfer to our soil the riches that the small region of Le Cap gave to the French nation. To many this will seem an impracticable and ridiculous idea, but only to those who know nothing of agriculture in the Americas. . . . He who knows something about this type of plantation will say with me that, if there was the money to buy and the possibility of importing into Cuba's ports in one year all the slaves needed for the cultivation of its lands, its output in three years would be double . . . that of French Saint Domingue. There is no doubt about it: the era of our good fortune has begun.

(*Obras de D. Francisco de Arango y Parreño* [Havana, 1952], 1:110–12, 133–34)

91) "Rights of Black Men": Abraham Bishop, 1791

A graduate of Yale University and an obscure Connecticut abolitionist, Bishop was unusual among antislavery activists in calling for a race-blind assessment of the 1791 slave revolt. Most whites in the United States sympathized with their counterparts in Saint Domingue and were not ready to accept Bishop's parallel between the black uprising and the American Revolution, or accept that it was divinely ordained.

We believe that Freedom is the natural right of all rational beings, and we know that the Blacks have never voluntarily resigned that freedom. Then is not their cause as just as ours? We fought with bravery and prayed earnestly for success upon our righteous cause, when we drew the sword and shed the blood of Englishmen—and for what!—Not to gain Freedom; for we were never slaves; but to rid ourselves of taxes, imposed without our consent, and from the growing evils of usurpation. Believing our cause to have been just, firmly believe that the cause of the Blacks is just. They are asserting those rights by the sword which it was impossible to secure by mild measures. Stripes, imprisonment, hunger, nakedness, cruel tortures and death, were the portion of those Blacks who even talked of liberty. . . . Did we act coolly when our officers and soldiers were loaded with irons in loathsome dungeons, and dying by hundreds in prison ships?—We did not—Then shall we preach lessons of coolness and moderation to the Blacks? . . .

We talked in the late war about the hand of Providence. . . . I have a firm confidence that we shall now see the hand of Providence more visibly than ever. *The Universal Father seems now demonstrating that of one blood, he has created all nations of men, that dwell on the face of the earth.*

(*The Argus* [Boston], 22 Nov. 1791)

92) Samuel Whitchurch, *Hispaniola, a Poem* (1804)

British industrialist Samuel Whitchurch was a radical Congregationalist who, like Abraham Bishop (doc. 89), was a fringe figure. Written in response to the post-independence massacres, his epic poem of seventy-eight stanzas was a bloodthirsty celebration of "retribution's holy day." It offers an unsentimental view of slavery, and mixes millenarian Christianity with anti-French patriotism. Bonaparte appears as the "enslaver of nations," whose bed is haunted by Toussaint's ghost. It deploys the popular trope of black vengeance for the Taíno genocide of the sixteenth century.

Brought forth on slavery's iron bed,
'Midst savage wilds of ignorance bred,
Where mercy's smiling angel seldom came;
Spurned—outcast of the human race—

Of untaught mind—in manners base—
The negro panteth not for virtuous fame.

Unmoved he hears the sufferer's moan;
Untouched by sorrow's mournful groan,
His callous heart no soft compunction knows;
But burning with revengeful rage,
He spareth not sex nor age;
The white skin only designates his foes.[4]

Proud European blame him not—
Would'st thou act better, if, hard lot!
Thou like the African wert bought and sold?
. . . .

When by the voice of freedom hail'd
If by the tyrant's sword assail'd
Would'st thou not march thro' blood to liberty?
. . . .

Fierce burns the fire of martial strife,
Fast flow the crimson streams of life;
Grim horror strides across th'ensanguined plain;
Lift, son of Ham, thy wrath-red eye,
Behold thy prostrate enemy
Where victory stalks o'er mountain heaps of slain!

(Samuel Whitchurch, *Hispaniola, a poem* [Bath: W. Meyler, 1804])

93) An Anguished Thomas Jefferson

The dramatic predictions of the first two letters suggests how deeply events in Saint Domingue affected Jefferson. Written to fellow Virginian slaveowners, they at least give lip service to his interest in an eventual abolition of slavery. The first followed the burning of Cap Français and the arrival of thousands of French refugees. The

---

4. Although this may not be an unjust description of the long insulted and enslaved African, who has been goaded to madness by ill treatment, and made furious by oppression, yet it is not the true character of the negro in his own country, if the accounts of travellers may be relied on. (*Author's note*)

second alludes to removing freed U.S. slaves to the Caribbean. The last two letters show him maneuvering, or flip-flopping, in reaction to Bonaparte's unfolding policy. Pro-French, and a slaveowner, Jefferson at first encourages the Leclerc expedition. Later he makes a quixotic suggestion to recognize Saint Domingue's independence. This was perhaps to pressure France over the then-simmering Louisiana question.

To James Monroe, 14 July 1793

The situation of the St. Domingo fugitives (aristocrats as they are) calls aloud for pity & charity. Never was so deep a tragedy presented to the feelings of man. I deny the power of the general government to apply money to such a purpose, but I deny it with a bleeding heart. . . . I become daily more & more convinced that all the West India Islands will remain in the hands of the people of colour, & a total expulsion of the whites sooner or later take place, it is high time we should foresee the bloody scenes which our children certainly, and possibly ourselves (south of Potommac,) have to wade through, & try to avert them.

(Library of Congress, Manuscript Division, Washington, DC. Thomas
Jefferson Papers, Jefferson to James Monroe, 14 July 1793)

To St. George Tucker, 28 August 1797

I have to acknowledge receipt of your [Dissertation on Slavery]. . . . You know my subscription to it's [sic] doctrines; and to the mode of emancipation, I am satisfied that that must be a matter of compromise between the passions, the prejudices, & the real difficulties which will each have their weight in that operation. Perhaps the first chapter of this history, which has begun in St. Domingo, & the next succeeding ones, which will recount how all the whites were driven from all the other islands, may prepare our minds for a peaceable accomodation between justice, policy & necessity; and furnish an answer to the difficult question, whither shall the colored emigrants go? . . . But if something is not done, & soon done, we shall be the murderers of our own children. . . . From the present state of things in Europe & America, the day which begins our combustion must be near at hand; and only a single spark is wanting to make that day to-morrow. If we had begun sooner, we might probably have been allowed a lengthier operation to clear ourselves, but every day's delay lessens the time we may take for emancipation.

(P. Ford, ed., *The Writings of Thomas Jefferson* [New York, 1892–1899], 7:167–68)

To French representative Pichon, 19 July 1801

[I]n order that this concert may be complete and effective you must make peace with England, then nothing will be easier than to furnish your army and fleet with everything and reduce Toussaint to starvation. . . . [England] would doubtless participate in a concert to repress this rebellion, and independently of her fears for her own colonies, I am sure she is observing like us how St. Domingo is becoming another Algiers[5] in the seas of America.

> (Carl L. Lokke, "Jefferson and the Leclerc Expedition," *American Historical Review* 33 [1928]: 324–25, citing Pichon's July 22 report)

To French representative Pichon, 31 October 1801

But in fact does France believe that she should attempt by force the reduction of the island? The inclinations and the habits of the Americans will always be in favor of it. Why will France not declare it independent under her protection and that of the United States and England? Perhaps that would be wisest. That island needs an oriental government. After General Toussaint another despot will be necessary. Why should not the three powers unite to confine the pest in the island? Provided that the Negroes are not permitted to possess a navy, we can allow them without danger to exist and we can moreover continue with them very lucrative commercial relations.

> (Rayford W. Logan, *The Diplomatic Relations of the United States with Haiti, 1776–1891* [Chapel Hill: University of North Carolina Press, 1941], 125–26, citing Pichon's report of 31 Oct. 1801)

94) Simón Bolívar: The Disillusioned Idealist

Although Bolívar owed a great deal to Haiti's help, he generally viewed the country as an example that Spanish America should not follow. His correspondence emphasizes its political instability and occasionally presents it as a threat. However, as he grew increasingly cynical and authoritarian, he came to regard the life-presidency system the Haitian Republic adopted as a positive feature. As with Jefferson, the Haitian Revolution appears to have deepened his pessimism about the future aftermath of slavery.

(19 June 1817) Believe me, Briceño, you have nothing to fear. You are neither in Constantinople nor in Haiti. As long as I can breathe and hold a sword, there is no tyranny nor anarchy here.

(23 December 1822) I then cast my gaze over the endless coastline of Colombia, threatened by the ships of every nation, by all the Europeans whose colonies surround us, and by the Africans of Haiti, whose power is stronger than primeval fire. . . . We have two and a half million inhabitants scattered over a wide desert.

---

5. Jefferson's allusion was to the privateers based in Saint Domingue and the North African city-state that preyed on international trade.

One part is savage, another is slave, and most are enemies of one another; all have been corrupted by superstition and despotism. What a fine contrast to display to all the nations of the world! . . . The problem of Peru, as de Pradt says of the blacks of Haiti, is so complicated and terrifying that, no matter how it is viewed, it presents nothing but horror, misfortune, and despair.

(20 May 1825) Do not attempt to liberate Havana. . . . I believe our league can maintain itself perfectly well . . . without creating another Republic of Haiti.

(25 May 1826) The island of Haiti, if you will pardon the digression, was in a state of perpetual insurrection. After experimenting with an empire, a kingdom, and a republic, in fact every known type of government and more besides, the people were obliged to call upon the illustrious Pétion to save them. After they had put their trust in him, Haiti's destiny followed a steady course. Pétion was made president for life with the right to choose his successor. Thus, neither the death of that great man nor the arrival of a new president endangered the state in the slightest. Under the worthy Boyer,[6] everything has proceeded as peacefully as in a legitimate monarchy. Here you have conclusive proof that a *president for life with the power to choose his successor* is the most sublime inspiration among republican regimes. The president of Bolivia will be less dangerous than the president of Haiti, as the succession is provided for in a way that better serves the state's interest. Moreover, the president of Bolivia is deprived of all patronage. . . . Should any ambitious soul aspire to make himself emperor, there are Dessalines, Christophe, and Iturbide to warn him of what he may expect.[7]

(8 July 1826) I am convinced to the very marrow of my bones that only an adroit despotism can rule America. . . . We must not compare ourselves in any way to anything European. . . . We are the abominable offspring of those raging tigers that came to America to shed her blood and to breed with their victims before sacrificing them. Later, the illegitimate offspring of these unions mixed with the offspring of slaves snatched from Africa. With such racial mixtures and such a moral history, can we place laws above heroes and principles above men? . . . [If we tried] we would again witness the beautiful ideal of a Haiti and see a new breed of Robespierres[8] become the worthy magistrates of this frightful liberty. . . . We shall have more and more of Africa. I do not say this lightly, for anyone with a white skin who escapes will be fortunate.

(Simón Bolívar, *Obras completas* [Caracas, nd], 1:241,
1:708–709, 2:135, 3:765–66, 2:428–29)

---

6. Jean-Pierre Boyer (1776–1850) was a free-born, *mulâtre* tailor, who became Pétion's aide de camp during the revolution. His long presidency (1818–1843) was a rare period of stability for Haiti.

7. General Agustín Iturbide was briefly emperor of Mexico. All three monarchs met violent deaths.

8. See section 3, doc. 25, note 21.

95) The Impact of Independence

Besides providing propaganda to both pro- and antislavery forces, Haiti became in the minds of many commentators a test case in the emergent debate about racial difference. Within each camp pundits disagreed whether the new state would seek to liberate slaves in nearby islands and how such slaves would react to its incendiary example. These musings are by an English naval officer opposed to slavery, who professed to keep an open mind on these questions. Like his countryman Marcus Rainsford (doc. 97), he stressed that the French were as guilty of atrocities as the black insurgents.

It has frequently been contended that the mind of the negro is neither as susceptible nor as retentive of impressions as that of Europeans; and that we ought not, therefore, to measure their feelings by our own. The validity of such an opinion may very fairly be called in question, and the point considered as yet undecided. . . . The sudden emancipation of near half a million in St. Domingo forms a new aera in the history of man, which, in the course of a few years, will throw more light on the true character of the blacks than as many centuries have hitherto done. The enormities committed by Dessalines are not to be considered as a criterion by which that character is to be estimated. If that Black power . . . should have been fortunate enough to avoid those horrors which stained the French . . . revolution, how much superior would they have risen in wisdom and humanity to their late masters, whom they have certainly not exceeded in either atrocity or in folly! . . .

The new character, which the blacks have lately assumed in St. Domingo cannot fail of being contemplated with a lively interest by their brethren in the West India islands, and of greatly influencing their future conduct. What the event of it may turnout is at present beyond all human calculation. The danger, however, which threatens to disturb the peace of our colonies is not less certain, whether they assume a regular government, or fall into a state of general anarchy. In the former case they will use every endeavour to set the rest of their brethren free; and, in the latter, the thirst of plunder, and aversion for labour, will drive them to predatory excursions on the neighbouring islands, where the slaves will be but too ready to join them.

(John Barrow, *Voyage to Cochin China* [London, 1806], ch. 4)

96) Charles Brockden Brown: The Haitian Peril, Abolition, and Race

American novelist, editor, and intellectual, Brown was writing following the revival in 1804 of the British campaign to abolish the slave trade. The campaign had seized on Haitian independence as strengthening the prudential argument for abolition, which assumed that African slaves were more likely to rebel than creoles. Like John Barrow (doc. 95), he considered the new state a direct threat to surrounding colonies and also an important argument against ideas of racial inferiority.

What form will the colonial society assume during the continuance of the slave trade? In all human probability, one of two events will speedily happen; either the fate of St. Domingo will suddenly become the fate of all the negro settlements, or the West Indian system will remain a little longer on its present footing. The impending blow may possibly be warded off for a season: negroes will continue to be driven, tortured and wasted in proportion as new recruits can always be obtained from Africa. A scanty portion of the dregs of Europe will still reside in the islands, and compose the whole of that colonial body on whom the preservation of the system depends. Each attempt of the enemy in St. Domingo, or each effort of the slaves themselves to imitate the example of that settlement, will shake to its base the whole western wing of the European community, till, in the course of a few years, the frail tenure will give way, on which are held those fine possessions; and all the monuments of Europe, in the insular part of the new world, will vanish before the tempest which a short-sighted and wicked policy has for ages been raising.

With emancipated Africans, there can be no faith, no treaties, no fixed connections of neutrality, not even the honourable and settled relations of modern warfare. The suppression of such a monster in policy is a duty incumbent on every civilized state connected with the West Indian system. The efforts of France and Spain may possibly be successful in St. Domingo, but what will be the effects of a contrary event on the colonies that remain tranquil? The negroes in St. Domingo are already acquiring something like a navy; they have proposed to Great Britain conditions of alliance, which no civilized government can listen to. These two facts speak loudly of the dangers necessarily inherent in such a neighbourhood. What has England to expect? Or what can she do to brighten her prospects? Till the slave trade is at once boldly and totally abolished (for in the present circumstances delay is not prudence; it is rashness, in fact, though it may result, like many other kinds of temerity, from real cowardice); till the root of all the evil is hardily struck at, and the main, universal cause of all the danger destroyed, an hour's quiet cannot be expected in the slave colonies, nor any sensible alleviation of the manifold evils which crowd the picture of West Indian society. . . .

And what are all the fears of banishment to Siberia, or of French conscription, compared with the risks to which every white inhabitant of Jamaica is exposed, so long as Dessalines is emperor of Hayti, and has a troop of allies in the slaves of every British plantation? In proportion as the number and attachment of those allies is diminished . . . as the British plantations are peopled by home-bred negroes, whom their masters are forced to treat well by the impossibility of filling their places; the danger of the planter is diminished, and the just obstacles to choosing the colonies for a place of residence is removed. . . .

The war of St. Domingo reads us a memorable lesson; negroes organizing immense armies; laying plans of campaigns and sieges, which, if not scientific, have at least been successful against the finest European troops; arranging forms of government, and even proceeding some length in executing the most difficult of human enterprises; entering into commercial relations with foreigners, and conceiving the idea of alliances; acquiring something like a maritime force, and, at any rate, navigating vessels in the tropical seas, with as much skill and foresight as that complicated operation requires.

This spectacle ought to teach us the effects of circumstances upon the human faculties, and prescribe bounds to that arrogance, which would confine to one race, the characteristics of the species. We have torn those men from their country, on the vain pretence that their nature is radically inferior to our own. We have treated them so as to stunt the natural growth of their virtues and their reason. Our efforts have partly succeeded; for the West Indian, like all other slaves, has copied some of the tyrant's vices. But their ingenuity has advanced apace, under all disadvantages; and the negroes are already so much improved, that, while we madly continue to despise them, and to justify the crimes which have transplanted them, it has really become doubtful how long they will suffer us to exist in the islands.

(Charles Brockden Brown, "On the Consequences of Abolishing the Slave Trade to the West Indian Colonies," *The Literary Magazine, and American Register*, 4:26 [Nov. 1805]: 376–79)

97) Race and Barbarism: An Early Historian

Marcus Rainsford was a British army captain who briefly visited Saint Domingue in 1798 (doc. 68). He had already published several pamphlets on the colony, when his Historical Account *appeared in 1805. It was one of the first complete histories of the revolution. Although not an opponent of slavery,*

Rainsford was sympathetic to the revolution's black protagonists and concerned to stress the savage nature of the war that called into question eighteenth-century ideas of progress. Unlike Barrow and Brown (docs. 95, 96), he denied that Haiti would be a threat to other slave societies.

It has frequently been the fate of striking events, and particularly those which have altered the condition of mankind, to be denied that consideration by their cotemporaries, [sic] which they obtain from the veneration of posterity. . . . [D]istant society recedes from the contemplation of objects that threaten a violation of their system or wound a favourite prejudice. The rise of the Haytian empire is an event which may powerfully affect the condition of the human race; yet it is viewed as an ordinary succession of triumphs and defeats, interrupted only by the horrors of new and terrible inflictions, the fury of the contending elements, and destructive disease, more tremendous than all. . . .

It is on ancient record, that negroes were capable of repelling their enemies, with vigour, in their own country; and a writer of modern date has assured us of the talents and virtues of these people; but it remained for the close of the eighteenth century to realize the scene, from a state of abject degeneracy:—to exhibit, a horde of negroes emancipating themselves from the vilest slavery, and at once filling the relations of society, enacting laws, and commanding armies, in the colonies of Europe.

The same period has witnessed a great and polished nation, not merely returning to the barbarism of the earliest periods, but descending to the characters of assassins and executioners; and, removing the boundaries which civilization had prescribed even to war, rendering it a wild conflict of brutes and a midnight massacre. To attract a serious attention to cicumstances, which constitute an aera in the history of human nature and of martial affairs, is the purpose of the present disquisition; which, it is hoped, will tend to furnish an awful yet practical lesson.

(Marcus Rainsford, *An Historical Account of the Black Empire of Hayti* [London: Albion Press, 1805], ix–xi)

98) William Wordsworth, "To Toussaint L'Ouverture"

Wordwsorth wrote this poem in the summer of 1802 after Louverture had been kidnapped and sent to France, where he was jailed in a mountain fortress near the Swiss frontier. It was published in a British radical newspaper two months before Louverture died, as relations between Britain and France deteriorated. Wordsworth, a Romantic poet, who as a young man had been excited by the beginnings of the French Revolution, correctly surmises that the Haitian Revolution would continue in Toussaint's absence.

Toussaint, the most unhappy man of men!
Whether the whistling Rustic tend his plough
Within thy hearing, or thy head be now
Pillowed in some deep dungeon's earless den;—
O miserable Chieftain! where and when
Wilt thou find patience? Yet die not; do thou
Wear rather in thy bonds a cheerful brow:
Though fallen thyself, never to rise again,
Live, and take comfort. Thou hast left behind
Powers that will work for thee; air, earth, and skies;
There's not a breathing of the common wind
That will forget thee; thy hast great allies;
Thy friends are exultations, agonies,
And love, and man's unconquerable mind.

(William Wordsworth, "To Toussaint L'Ouverture,"
Morning Post [London], 2 Feb. 1803)

99) Frederick Douglass, *Lecture on Haiti* (1893)

This talk was given to 1,500 people at the Chicago World's Fair of 1893, to mark the opening of the Haitian pavilion. The veteran black abolitionist and former U.S. minister to Haiti faced a difficult task. Haiti, a symbol of black achievement, had not made the progress its supporters had hoped for, and with anti-black racism at its height, it was the object of lurid rumors. Douglass deployed his prodigious oratorical skills in a performance that combined a defensive appraisal of contemporary conditions in the country with a ringing evocation of Haiti's historical significance.

From the beginning of our century until now, Haiti and its inhabitants, under one aspect or another, have for various reasons been very much in the thoughts of the American people. While slavery existed amongst us, her example was a sharp thorn in our side and a source of alarm and terror. She came into the sisterhood of nations through blood. She was described at the time of her advent as a very hell of horrors. Her very name was pronounced with a shudder. . . .

More thought, more ink and paper, have been devoted to her than to all the other West India Islands put together. . . . There is perhaps no equal number of people anywhere on the globe, in whose history, character and destiny there is more to awaken sentiment, thought and inquiry. . . . She was the first of the New World in which the black man asserted his right to be free and was brave enough to fight for his freedom and fortunate enough to gain it. . . .

The argument as stated against Haiti, is, that since her freedom, she has become lazy; that she is given to gross idolatry, and that these evils are on the increase. That voodooism, fetichism, serpent worship and cannibalism are prevalent there; that little children are fatted for slaughter and offered as sacrifices to their voodoo deities; that large boys and girls run naked through the streets of the towns and cities, and that things are generally going from bad to worse.

In reply to these dark and damning allegations, it will be sufficient only to make a general statement. I admit at once that there is much ignorance and much superstition in Haiti. The common people there believe much in divination, charms, witchcraft, putting spells on each other, and in the supernatural and miracle working power of their voodoo priests generally. Owing to this, there is a feeling of superstition and dread of each other, the destructive tendency of which cannot be exaggerated. . . .

But it is said that the people of Haiti are lazy. Well, with the conditions of existence so easy and the performance of work so uninviting, the wonder is not that the men of Haiti are lazy, but that they work at all. But it is not true that the people of Haiti are as lazy as they are usually represented to be. . . . No one can see the ships afloat in the splendid harbors of Haiti, and see the large imports and exports of the country, without seeing also that somebody there has been at work. . . . There are ebbs and flows in the tide of human affairs, and Haiti is no exception to this rule. There have been times in her history when she gave promise of great progress, and others, when she seemed to *retrograde*. . . .

In just vindication of Haiti, I can go one step further. I can speak of her, not only words of admiration, but words of gratitude as well. She has grandly served the cause of universal human liberty. We should not forget that the freedom you and I enjoy to-day; that the freedom that eight hundred thousand colored people enjoy in the British West Indies; the freedom that has come to the colored race the world over, is largely due to the brave stand taken by the black sons, of Haiti ninety years ago. When they struck for freedom, they builded better than they knew. Their swords were not drawn and could not be drawn simply for themselves alone. They were linked and interlinked with their race, and striking for their freedom, they struck for the freedom of every black man in the world. [Prolonged applause.] . . .

Speaking for the Negro, I can say, we owe much to Walker for his appeal;[9] to John Brown [applause] for the blow struck at Harper's Ferry, to Lundy and Garrison for their advocacy [applause], We owe much especially to Thomas

---

9. David Walker (1785–1830) was a black abolitionist who published in 1829 *Walker's Appeal . . . to the Coloured Citizens of the World.* The others invoked in this sentence were white U.S. and British abolitionists.

Clarkson, [applause], to William Wilberforce, to Thomas Fowell Buxton, and to the anti-slavery societies at home and abroad; but we owe incomparably more to Haiti than to them all. [Prolonged applause.] I regard her as the original pioneer emancipator of the nineteenth century. [Applause.] It was her one brave example that first of all started the Christian world into a sense of the Negro's manhood. It was she who first awoke the Christian world to a sense of "the danger of goading too far the energy that slumbers in a black man's arm." [Applause.] Until Haiti struck for freedom, the conscience of the Christian world slept profoundly over slavery. It was scarcely troubled even by a dream of this crime against justice and liberty. The Negro was in its estimation a sheep like creature, having no rights which white men were bound to respect, a docile animal, a kind of ass, capable of bearing burdens, and receiving strips from a white master without resentment, and without resistance. The mission of Haiti was to dispel this degradation and dangerous delusion, and to give to the world a new and true revelation of the black man's character. This mission she has performed and performed it well. [Applause.]

Until she spoke no Christian nation had abolished negro slavery. Until she spoke no Christian nation had given to the world an organized effort to abolish slavery. Until she spoke the slave ship, followed by hungry sharks, greedy to devour the dead and dying slaves flung overboard to feed them, plouged [sic] in peace the South Atlantic painting the sea with the Negro's blood. Until she spoke, the slave trade was sanctioned by all the Christian nations of the world, and our land of liberty and light included. . . .

To have any just conception or measurement of the intelligence, solidarity and manly courage of the people of Haiti when under the lead of Toussaint L'Ouverture, [prolonged applause] and the dauntless Dessalines, you must remember what the conditions were by which they were surrounded; that all the neighboring islands were slaveholding, and that to no one of all these islands could she look for sympathy, support and co-operation. She trod the wine press alone. . . .

To re-enslave her brave self-emancipated sons of liberty, France sent in round number's, to Haiti during the years 1802–1803, 50,000 of her veteran troops, commanded by her most experienced and skillful generals. History tells us what became of these brave and skillful warriors from France. It shows that they shared the fate of Pharaoh and his hosts. Negro manhood, Negro bravery, Negro military genius and skill, assisted by yellow fever and pestilence made short work of them. . . . Since 1804 Haiti has maintained national independence. [Applause.] I fling these facts at the feet of the detractors of the Negro and of Haiti. They may help them to solve the problem of her future. They not only indicate the Negro's courage, but demonstrate his intelligence as well. [Applause.]

(Frederick Douglass, *Lecture on Haiti* [Chicago, 1893], 23–38)

Bibliography

Introduction

Dubois, Laurent. *Avengers of the New World.* Cambridge, MA: Belknap, 2004.

Dubois, Laurent, and John D. Garrigus. *Slave Revolution in the Caribbean, 1789–1804: A Brief History with Documents.* Boston/New York: Bedford/St. Martin's, 2006.

Geggus, David, and Norman Fiering, eds. *The World of the Haitian Revolution.* Bloomington, IN: Indiana University Press, 2009.

James, C. L. R. *The Black Jacobins: Toussaint L'Ouverture and the San Domingo Revolution.* New York: Vintage Books, 1963.

Popkin, Jeremy. *Concise History of the Haitian Revolution.* Malden, MA: Wiley-Blackwell, 2012.

1. Saint Domingue on the Eve of Revolution

Garraway, Doris. *The Libertine Colony: Creolization in the Early French Caribbean.* Chapters 4 and 5. Durham, NC: Duke University Press, 2005.

Garrigus, John. *Before Haiti: Race and Citizenship in French Saint-Domingue.* New York: Palgrave, 2006.

Geggus, David. "Saint Domingue on the Eve of Revolution." In *The World of the Haitian Revolution*, edited by D. Geggus and N. Fiering. Bloomington, IN: Indiana University Press, 2009.

Ghachem, Malick W. *The Old Regime and the Haitian Revolution.* Cambridge: Cambridge University Press, 2012.

2. Slave Resistance

Fouchard, Jean. *The Haitian Maroons: Liberty or Death.* New York: Blyden, 1981.

Geggus, David. *Haitian Revolutionary Studies.* Chapters 4–6. Bloomington, IN: Indiana University Press, 2002.

———. "Haitian Voodoo in the Eighteenth Century." *Jahrbuch für Geschichte von Staat, Wirtschaft und Gesellschaft Lateinamerikas* 28 (1991): 21–51.

3. The Race and Slavery Questions in the French National Assembly

Blackburn, Robin. *The Overthrow of Colonial Slavery.* London: Verso, 1988.

Garrigus, John. "Opportunist or Patriot: Julien Raimond (1744–1801) and the Haitian Revolution." *Slavery and Abolition* 28 (2007): 1–21.

Geggus, David. "Racial Equality, Slavery, and Colonial Secession, During the Constituent Assembly." *American Historical Review* 94 (1989): 1290–1308.

Sepinwall, Alyssa. *The Abbé Grégoire and the French Revolution: The Making of Modern Universalism.* Berkeley: University of California Press, 2005.

4. The Fight for Racial Equality in Saint Domingue

Garrigus, John. *Before Haiti: Race and Citizenship in French Saint-Domingue.* Chapter 8. New York: Palgrave, 2006.

———. "Vincent Ogé jeune (1757–1791): Social Class and Free Colored Mobilization on the Eve of the Haitian Revolution." *The Americas* 68:1 (2011): 33–62.

Geggus, David. *Haitian Revolutionary Studies.* Chapter 7. Bloomington, IN: Indiana University Press, 2002.

5. The Slave Insurrection

Fick, Carolyn. *The Making of Haiti: The Saint Domingue Revolution from Below.* Knoxville, TN: University of Tennessee Press, 1990.

Geggus, David. "Print Culture and the Haitian Revolution: The Written and the Spoken Word." In *Liberty! Égalité! Independencia!: Print Culture, Enlightenment, and Revolution in the Americas, 1776–1838,* edited by David Shields et al., 79–96. Worcester, MA: Oak Knoll, 2007.

Popkin, Jeremy. *Facing Racial Revolution: Eyewitness Accounts of the Haitian Insurrection.* Chicago: University of Chicago Press, 2007.

Thornton, John. "'I am the subject of the King of Congo': African Political Ideology and the Haitian Revolution." *Journal of World History* 4 (1993): 181–214.

6. Slave Emancipation

Brown, Christopher, and Philip Morgan, eds. *Arming Slaves: From Classical Times to the Modern Age.* Chapters 8 and 9. New Haven, CT: Yale University Press, 2006.

Dubois, Laurent. "'Our Three Colors': The King, the Republic, and the Political Culture of the Slave Revolution in Saint-Domingue." *Historical Reflections* 29 (2003): 83–102.

Popkin, Jeremy. *"You Are All Free": The Haitian Revolution and the Abolition of Slavery.* Cambridge: Cambridge University Press, 2010.

Stein, Robert. *Léger-Félicité Sonthonax: The Lost Sentinel of the Republic.* Rutherford, NJ: Fairleigh Dickinson, 1985.

7. The Rise of Toussaint Louverture

Donnadieu, Jean-Louis, and Philippe R. Girard. "Toussaint before Louverture: New Archival Findings on the Early Life of Toussaint Louverture." *William and Mary Quarterly* 70:1 (2013): 41–78.

Geggus, David. "Toussaint Louverture and the Haitian Revolution." In *Profiles of Revolutionaries in Atlantic History, 1750-1850*, edited by R. William Weisberger et al. New York: Columbia University Press, 2007.

Tyson, George, Jr., ed. *Toussaint Louverture*. Englewood Cliffs, NJ: Prentice Hall, 1973.

8. The Government of Toussaint Louverture

Geggus, David. *The Changing Faces of Toussaint Louverture: Literary and Pictorial Depictions*. Online: http://www.brown.edu/Facilities/John_Carter_Brown_Library/toussaint/index.html.

Girard, Philippe R. *The Slaves Who Defeated Napoleon: Toussaint L'Ouverture and the Haitian War of Independence, 1801–1804*. Chapters 1–4. Tuscaloosa, AL: University of Alabama Press, 2011.

Scott, David. *Conscripts of Modernity: The Tragedy of Colonial Enlightenment*. Durham, NC: Duke University Press, 2004.

9. The War of Independence

Armitage, David, and Julia Gaffield, eds. *The Haitian Declaration of Independence in an Atlantic Context*. Charlottesville, VA: University of Virginia Press, 2014.

Girard, Philippe R. *The Slaves Who Defeated Napoleon: Toussaint L'Ouverture and the Haitian War of Independence, 1801–1804*. Chapters 5–19. Tuscaloosa, AL: University of Alabama Press, 2011.

Jenson, Deborah. *Beyond the Slave Narrative: Politics, Sex, and Manuscripts in the Haitian Revolution*. Liverpool: Liverpool University Press, 2011.

10. Overseas Reactions

Blackburn, Robin. *The American Crucible: Slavery, Emancipation, and Human Rights*. London: Verso, 2011.

Drescher, Seymour, and Pieter Emmer, eds. *Who Abolished Slavery? Slave Revolts and Abolitionism*. New York: Palgrave, 2010.

Gaspar, D. B., and D. P. Geggus, eds. *A Turbulent Time: The French Revolution and the Greater Caribbean*. Bloomington, IN: Indiana University Press, 1997.

Geggus, David, ed. *The Impact of the Haitian Revolution in the Atlantic World*. Columbia, SC: University of South Carolina Press, 2001.

Klooster, Wim, and Gerd Oostindie, eds. *Curaçao in the Age of Revolutions, 1795–1800*. Leiden: KITLV, 2011.

White, Ashli. *Encountering Revolution: Haiti and the Making of the Early Republic*. Baltimore: Johns Hopkins, 2010.

Index